STIRLING SILLIPHANT:
The Fingers of God

STIRLING SILLIPHANT:
The Fingers of God

The Story of Hollywood's Hottest Writer
Who Rode *Route 66*, Mastered Disaster
Films, and Lived His Life Like It Was a Movie

by

NAT SEGALOFF

Author of *Final Cuts: The Last Films of 50 Great
Directors* and *Arthur Penn: American Director*

BearManor Media

2013

Typesetting, layout, and cover by John Teehan
Copy Editors: Michelle Morgan and Wendy Finn

Published in the USA by BearManor Media
Member of the Independent Book Publishers Association

Library of Congress Cataloging-in-Publication Data (TBA)
Segaloff, Nat, 1948 -
    Stirling Silliphant: The Fingers of God /

ISBN — 1-62933-067-1
978-1-62933-067-9

To the memory and mentorship of

Gregory Mcdonald

"There are no wrong questions."

Table of Contents

Introduction and Acknowledgements

STIRLING SILLIPHANT LOVED being Stirling Silliphant. He worked hard at it. At a time when the public only knew a screenwriter's name if he got arrested, blacklisted, or married a movie star, Silliphant drew coverage in columns, TV, reviews, and publicity because of who he was: the highest-paid screenwriter in Hollywood. When the average Writers Guild member was lucky to get $30,000[1] for a script, he had a one million dollar, three-picture deal with Warner Bros. He worked every day on an electric typewriter, often writing one project in the morning and another in the afternoon. He wore a green eyeshade because he thought it looked cool. He kept several offices throughout LA so he could multi-task psychologically—though some were doubtless reserved for extramarital flings. He was on the A-list's A-list, yet when the Beverly Hills party circuit became boring, he moved to Mill Valley in Northern California to stare out at the bay. He drank fine wines, collected stamps and Lalique crystal, and, when he liked the feel and design of Gucci bags but thought the logo garish, he had the company custom-make his without *Gucci* on them.[2]

As with his best writing, there were many levels to the man. He was a strong union member who marched picket lines with the Writers Guild, a social progressive who pushed his agenda through his work, a passionate opponent of American wars in Southeast Asia, and a fierce critic of the very television industry that kept hiring him. Yet he also voted Republican and supported the first Bush Gulf War. He was a diligent collaborator, a generous teacher, and a quotable pundit. But he could also churn out work strictly for the money, turn his back on projects that went sour, and snap at people who didn't measure up to his expectations.

Silliphant is associated with four widely differing periods in American film and television: he wrote the majority of scripts for the 1960-1964 televi-

1

sion series *Route 66*; he was there for the beginning, the middle, and the end of the "disaster film" cycle of 1972-1980; he nurtured Bruce Lee and arguably godfathered the kung-fu craze; and he spent immense personal capital chronicling the Vietnam war from the Vietnamese people's point of view, a torch that would be borne by his widow after he died.

If you grew up in the 1960s, as I did, you couldn't help notice his distinctive name in the credits of TV shows like *Naked City* or *Route 66* (in those days, the networks were proud of who made their shows and didn't squeeze them to the side of the screen) or in movies like *Charly, Village of the Damned*, and *In the Heat of the Night*. There was always something extra in what he wrote, some spark in his characters. In late 1974, I became New England publicist for *The Towering Inferno*, which he had written, and my duties included taking him on publicity interviews. He traveled with his new wife, Tiana, and it quickly developed that they had come to town not only to tout the picture but to visit Sparkman and Stevens ship builders on Boston's historic waterfront to see how their new yacht was coming along. A master at working the Hollywood ropes, he had contrived to make the studio pay for the trip.

Over dinner at Locke-Ober restaurant—which Stirling paid for because he knew the studio would reject my expense tab—he and Tiana spoke of their love, their friendship with Bruce Lee, and their plans for an unflinching TV mini-series about Vietnam, to be titled *Fly Away Home*. We reconnected in 1992, when I wrote his monograph for *Backstory 3*. By then, the Silliphants had relocated to Bangkok, and we interviewed by fax: I would send him questions in the morning and he would return his answers that night, always neatly typed, spell-checked, and immensely quotable. One day he faxed that Tiana had just completed a documentary called *From Hollywood to Hanoi* about her life between two cultures. It was going to be shown at Harvard Square's historic Brattle Theatre, and, since I lived a stumble away, would I look after her as a personal favor? Tiana and I hadn't seen each other since that two-day press tour nineteen years earlier, and I saw that she was a whirlwind of energy, charm, and determination.

Stirling and I stayed in touch, not only by fax but in a surreptitious visit he made to Los Angeles in 1994 after I had relocated there from Boston. We met at Shutters, a posh hotel on Santa Monica Beach. He entered the cafe looking like a plantation owner in a white linen suit, a yellow shirt, and a Panavision smile. After our meal, we were met by his son, also named Stirling, who was attending UC Santa Cruz, and together we drove to the airport to see him off to Bangkok. I never found out why he had come to Los Angeles or why he alerted so few people, but I felt honored to have been one of them. Sadly, he died in 1996, before our *Backstory* collaboration was published in 1997 (academic presses make glaciers look like avalanches). After settling some estate matters in Thailand, Tiana moved back to Los Angeles and asked me to help collect his papers for his Special Collection at UCLA. She said many times that it was one of Stirling's last requests that I tell his story. When you turn the page, you will fulfill that wish.

This is not an objective book, but it is, I hope, a fair one. I am less concerned with the minutiae of a filmmaker's life than I am with the creative process and the events that fuel it. This is not a scholarly dissection of Silliphant's oeuvre. First, I doubt how much of that sort of thing is valid in the collaborative world of commercial filmmaking; Second, it would bore me insensate. Scholars wishing to deconstruct Silliphant's work and dredge for arcania are reminded that, in Hollywood, the writer may write the words but he seldom has the final one. Nevertheless, our unedited interviews are among my papers at the UCLA Performing Arts Special Collections.

Another purpose for this book is, in part, to amend that 1997 *Backstory* monograph in light of information that has emerged since Silliphant's death. It carries the same title and refers to a 1963 *Time* magazine article in which an admiring television producer said Silliphant was "almost inhuman… a writing machine… the fingers of God."[3] At the time of *Time*, Stirling was writing simultaneously for *Naked City* and *Route 66*. Over those series' runs, he would contribute over 150 teleplays. The Writers Guild of America notes over 200 screen credits, which are cross-referenced in Appendix A with IMDb listings. This does not include his unproduced work (see Appendix B), workshops, script doctoring, lectures, and voluminous correspondence. With all that writing, it's a wonder he found time to live. But live he did, and his life informed his work.

In addition to those who graciously granted interviews, on and off the record, I appreciate my unflappable agent, Agnes Birnbaum of Bleecker Street Associates, Andrew Abbott, Stephen Bowie, Donovan and Claire Brandt of Eddie Brandt's Saturday Matinee, Tom Brown, Kevin Corcoran, Rick Dailey, William Froug, Christopher Hampton, Reg Grundy Productions, Barry Krost, Yon G. Lee, Russell Leven, James Robert Parish, Carter Potter, Melanie Rose, Susy Smith, Dr. Tanya Stoddard, Allan Taylor, Douglas Thompson, Michael Ventura, and John M. Whalen.

Martial arts expert and historian John Corcoran, author of *The Martial Arts Encyclopedia*, provided significant help with information on Silliphant and Bruce Lee. I deeply value the counsel of David Morrell, whose knowledge of All Things Silliphant was generously given. I owe a long-standing debt to Patrick McGilligan for providing me the opportunity to reconnect with Stirling for *Backstory 3*. My appreciation as well to Tom Hyry, Peggy Alexander, Brandon Barton, Robert Montoya, and Cesar Reyes of the UCLA Performing Arts Special Collections for access to the Silliphant papers; the staff of the Margaret Herrick Library and to Laureen Loeser of the Academy of Motion Picture Arts and Sciences; Karen Pedersen of the Shavelson-Webb Library at the Writers Guild Foundation; and Jenni Matz of the Emmy Foundation of the Academy of Television Arts and Sciences. In an industry that lies about its past as well as its present, these diligent professionals and their institutions preserve the truth.

To Tiana Silliphant; his sons Stirling Linh Silliphant and Stirling Rasmussen; and to his half-brother Allan Silliphant I owe incalculable gratitude for sharing memories that were at times joyous and at times difficult, but were always helpful.

Finally, a very personal thanks to Ami, Ivanna, Adam, and Joseph (JB) Benjamin Lahmani for their love that, every day, I strive to deserve.

– Nat Segaloff, Los Angeles, 2013

Prologue: In the Heat of the Oscars

APRIL 10, 1968, should have been the best night of Stirling Silliphant's life. Dressed in his own tux, he sat on an aisle seat at the Santa Monica Civic Auditorium, one of seven men nominated for the five films competing for the Academy Award® for "Best Screenplay of 1967 based on material from another medium."

This year, the "Best Screenplay" and "Best Picture" nominees didn't match. Out of the 250 or so films that were released theatrically during 1967, and thus had qualified for consideration, the general membership of the motion picture Academy had selected *Bonnie and Clyde, Doctor Dolittle, The Graduate, Guess Who's Coming to Dinner*, and *In the Heat of the Night* as contenders. The screenplays, however, were chosen by the craft-savvy writing branch of the Academy, and they were slightly different: *Cool Hand Luke, The Graduate, In Cold Blood, In the Heat of the Night*, and *Ulysses*.[4] Silliphant had already won the Golden Globe and the Mystery Writers of America's Edgar®, and had been nominated for the Writers Guild of America award, for his clever adaptation of John Ball's mystery novel, *In the Heat of the Night*. But who could tell how the balloting would go once the entire 5,000 member Academy voted? After all, most of them were over forty and slavishly loyal to old fashioned, conservative, big-studio fare (they nominated *Doctor Dolittle*, f'r Chrissake), not a scrappy, race-conscious cinema provocateur.

Even as Hollywood congratulated itself on its night of nights, it was in transition.[5] In 1966, Jack Valenti, who was then President Johnson's close advisor, had been persuaded by MCA/Universal Chairman Lew Wasserman to leave the White House and take over the industry's rudderless trade organization, the Motion Picture Association of America. Faced with competition from foreign films and a blossoming domestic independent cinema, both of which reflected the sexual and political liberation of the times, Valenti began constructing a letter-based rating system that would, in November of 1968, replace the starchy Production Code that was introduced in 1930[6] to whitewash a series of Tinseltown scandals and stave off official censorship.

Moreover, film schools were opening all over the country to churn out hip young filmmakers. New York University (NYU), the University of Southern California (USC), and the University of California at Los Angeles (UCLA), among others, were grooming an emerging generation that was poised to take movies to the next level, whatever that would be. So far, only Francis Coppola had emerged from one of these schools; tyros like George Lucas, John Milius, Randall Kleiser, Robert Zemeckis, Basil Poledouris, Donald Glut, Walter Murch, and their peers were still making student films. If they had any connection with the Oscars®, it was watching them on TV.

The original screenplay nominees were the oracles of change. Robert Benton and David Newman's *nouvelle-vague*-influenced *Bonnie and Clyde* led the pack of originals. A sympathetic look at Depression-era spree bandits, the film had caused a sensation by first being buried by its studio, then resurrected to become a beacon among young audiences who embraced its exuberant anti-social message. The original screenplay for *Divorce, American Style,* by Robert Kaufman and Norman Lear, looked like a glossy studio movie, but its insights and attitudes were as subversive as those in *Bonnie and Clyde.* So was Frederic Raphael's brittle, time-bouncing *Two for the Road*, which showed the dissolution and regeneration of a marriage through a succession of motor holidays. And finally, Jorge Semprun's *La Guerre est Finie*, which most Academy voters doubtless read only in subtitles instead of its original French.

The race for "Best Adapted Screenplay," in which Silliphant was running, was even more diverse. *The Graduate,* from Charles Webb's thin novel, was about an older woman seducing a younger man, and it became a surprise box-office phenomenon in the growing "youth market." *Cool Hand Luke* was an unrelentingly brutal chain gang drama, which continued star Paul Newman's string of anti-hero hits and coined the catchphrase, "What we have here is failure to communicate." *Ulysses*, based on the oft-censored James Joyce novel, drew its own controversy for using the word *fuck. In Cold Blood*, from Truman Capote's non-fiction novel, brought shattering documentary realism to the sordid story of a multiple murder and the duo responsible for committing it. William Rose's *Guess Who's Coming to Dinner*, about how two sets of traditional parents—one white and one black—react to their children's impending marriage, was an actors' field day. Its seasoned director, Stanley Kramer, described it as a fairy tale because the intended husband, played by Sidney Poitier, was so perfect that the only reason to oppose his marriage to white Katharine Houghton was racism.

The anomaly among the nominees was *Doctor Dolittle*, the plodding screen adaptation of Hugh Lofting's sprightly children's books about a Victorian veterinarian who talks to animals. It was widely whispered that producer Arthur P. Jacobs and Twentieth Century-Fox had bought a nomination through parties and gifts to Academy members.

In the Heat of the Night drank from two streams. Its timely racial theme brought it close to *Guess Who's Coming to Dinner*, which, thankfully for Silliphant, was nominated in another category. But it was also an old-fashioned murder yarn. Years before mystery writer Walter Mosley created Ezekiel "Easy" Rawlins, John Ball conceived detective Virgil Tibbs, a black homicide detective struggling to keep his calm, not to mention his life, when he is impressed into solving a murder in a southern town that can't accept a Negro (sic) as a human being, let alone as a highly competent out-of-town police officer. It was directed bravely and with coiled urgency by Norman Jewison, an industry favorite and a Canadian; shot by Haskell Wexler, whose political credentials were as strong as his photographic skills; and edited by Hal Ashby, who was about to become a director in his own right. The picture had been a box office hit and had scored well with the critics, but had, like *Cool Hand Luke*, become celebrated for a single line of dialogue barked by an outraged Poitier at Sheriff Bill Gillespie (Rod Steiger) when he'd had enough redneck condescension: "They call me *Mister* Tibbs!"

The film was a contemporary blend of new ideas and a classic genre, and Silliphant was the perfect—though not the first—choice to write it. His scripts, hitherto primarily for television, caught the drama of characters in conflict with each other and within themselves. The emerging New Hollywood, however, was about people in conflict with the world around them, heavy on plot but developing only just enough character to serve the action.[7]

Silliphant knew things were changing. He knew he had to keep up with the changes in order to survive. But first he had to get through the evening. Accompanied to the Oscars by his third wife, Margot, he looked around the auditorium while Rod Steiger and his actress-wife, Claire Bloom, read the adapted scriptwriting nominees and then announced him as the winner.

"I can recall that night, every second of it," he said.[8] "Mostly my disbelief to hear Claire Bloom call my name. And then I was whizzing down the aisles past all those smiling faces—wondering why are THEY smiling?—and, as though fast-forwarded, I was in front of the mike and mesmerized by the backdrop of faces and tuxedos and great boobs of all the dazzling ladies who'd spent all day getting their hair done—all looking up at ME and awaiting something more than 'I want to thank, etc.' Not having expected to win (would you—competing against *Bonnie and Clyde* and *The Graduate*?) I had prepared absolutely nothing. I do remember mumbling something about, 'We members of the Writers Guild are not allowed to write on spec—and so I have nothing prepared.'[9] That seemed to do the trick—the audience gave me a warm sweeping feeling of love and support—and I may or may not have said thanks to Norman and Sidney and Walter [Mirish] and especially to [agent] Marty Baum, who got me the job. At least I hope I said that—then I was whisked off with my Oscar®, far heavier than I had imagined—but, then, when had I ever imagined I'd be holding one?"

In hindsight, the 1968 Oscars were a watershed moment for Hollywood. The Best Picture nominees (the winner was *In the Heat of the Night)* were not only wildly eclectic, they showed the confusion of a sixty-year-old industry roiled in creative and commercial panic.

But Silliphant refused to panic. Instead, he changed, as he had changed his entire career, from journalist to publicist to novelist to producer to television writer to screenwriter. He'd seen television go from a writer's medium to a producer's medium, and movies go from escapism to realism and back to escapism. He'd watched Hollywood change from a town where everybody knew everyone else to a place too big to know anybody. And he'd watched America change from a nation of innocents to a country where people were starting to acknowledge their place in the world and the responsibility that came with it.

"I've been writing and producing films for thirty years," he said, looking back on his continual metamorphosis. "I'm into my third decade. It used to be that a decade could last you pretty well. You wouldn't have to change too much from the start of year one to year ten; as a writer. I find now that I have to change as a writer, in terms of my style, my attitudes, my own internal relationship to life, about every ninety days. I am no more the same person I was in January of this year in any respect than some stranger. Well, that's kind of frightening. But if I'm going to stay at the top of the heap or the head of the market, I must do that. So I'm constantly re-forming myself. It's a good idea for any human being to constantly re-form himself, but at the point where it becomes a desperate scramble to keep up with what's happening, it becomes alarming. When I first started as a writer, for the first ten years, I was sort of dumb and happy, and I just kept doing my work and some things were good and some things weren't. In the second ten years, it began to accelerate, and I began to see that the world around me was changing faster than I was. So I had to get up to it first, and then ahead of it. That's what kind of bothers me sometimes.[10]

But at this moment in 1968, his *In the Heat of the Night* Oscar still warm, he was the newly anointed Scribe-in-Chief of an industry that was heading for disaster. Ironically, in a few short years, he would create a series of screen disasters that would steer it back on course. But first he had other things on his mind.

1

The Blank Page

STIRLING SILLIPHANT HIT THE ROAD even before he drove a car. The man who would make Route 66 a national metaphor practically lived on it and other highways until he was seven, riding with his parents, not because they were homeless, but because it was how his father made a living. Lemuel Lee Silliphant was a traveling salesman for Chicago-based Princess Pat Cosmetics (supposedly named after one of Queen Victoria's daughters) and purveyed to his share of the 40,000 independent pharmacies, general stores, and beauty parlors that sold makeup in the 1930s before the Depression and chain stores put them out of business. Stirling would recall that the family car always reeked of face powder, and, when his father opened the trunk to remove his wares, the smell of rouge, lipstick, and other ladies' paint supplies was overpowering. It was also a pheromone for Lee's female clientele, who doted on him at each sales stop. This, rather than boredom with being a housewife, inspired Stirling's vivacious mother, Ethel, to make it three for the road, keeping an eye on Lee as well as to teach the baby how to read. She was good at both; by three, little Stirling had picked up the skill, and the marriage held.

Lemuel Lee always had an independent streak. Born in Kensington, Prince Edward Island, Canada, in 1894, he crossed to America just after World War I, arriving in Detroit. The family name has several variants and two possible origins. *Silliphant* is the most common in America, but there are also Sillephants and Sellifants. Stirling always claimed it was of Norman origin and could be traced back to William the Conqueror. "It used to be Silliphanté," he told interviewer Reed Farrell. "My father was constantly reminding me that he was very proud about that lineage. 'We conquered England.' He seems to think we must have done it single-handedly."[11] According to his half-brother, Allan, its roots connect to Donal Cam O'Sullivan,

9

the "last prince of Ireland," who stood bravely but unsuccessfully against the English crown to preserve his country's independence at the Battle of Kinsale in 1602. The phonetic Gaelic is "O-sool-le-phan," which became, over time, *O'Sullivan* on the one hand and *Silliphant* on the other.[12]

His mother, Ethel May Noaker, born February 25, 1898, in New York, was the daughter of a large New York clan from English, Dutch, and German stock. When she married Lee in 1916, the couple rented a house at 155 East High Street in Metamora, Michigan, sixty miles north of Detroit. She was eighteen, he was twenty-one, and Sterling (sic) Dale Silliphant was born on January 16, 1918.[13] Soon after, they moved to Detroit proper, settling into a home on Pingree Street.[14] A second son, Leigh Arlington, was born there in 1921.

Lee was a charismatic and restless man with varied interests, traits that he passed to his sons. By 1925, he abandoned Princess Pat and had taken the family to seaside San Diego, California. Though only seven at the time, young Stirling remembered, "I got my first boat in San Diego—a surfboard. I learned more about sea swells and wind and tide aboard that board than they can teach you at Annapolis. Then I cranked my way around San Diego Bay in a Sabat and learned about wind-shadow from passing aircraft carriers. A Sunfish taught me to enjoy capsizing."[15] From San Diego, the clan moved to a house on Linden street in sleepy Glendale, just north of Los Angeles.

With Ethel now tied to a home and two children, Lee started seeing other women; by 1930, Ethel found out about it and the couple divorced. She would later marry Fred Wellershaus, leaving the boys to be raised by an aunt, Lucy Sun, who was chief nurse at Burbank Community Hospital (near Glendale), and her husband, Mont. They were enrolled in the Gardner School for Boys in Glendale.

Lee kept the Silliphant name alive with two more marriages yielding one more family. His second ended in tragedy when his young wife suffered a fatal aneurysm. His third, in 1935, to Virginia Mary Abraham, age twenty-one, produced two sons, Robert, born 1937, and Allan, born 1941. In between, in 1938, he became an American citizen.

He was always restless; in years to come, he would do a stint with Canada's World At Home Circus, was Chairman of the Speakers Bureau at the National Association of Manufacturers, tried acting, and had a radio show in Long Beach, California.[16] When Stirling and Leigh outgrew the Gardner School, they were sent to the San Diego Army and Navy Military Academy. The exile affected him profoundly; although he stayed close to his mother, he would cite his father's emotional distance and recognized that he had absorbed that trait himself, struggling to overcome it later in life. This may have been Stirling's own perception of Lee, because, by the time Lee married Virginia, he had become a warm and giving father to their two new sons. "He was a very, very good man," Allan Silliphant stated. "We'd give him a back massage and he'd make up radio plays of 'Jack and Bill,' and he'd always leave a cliffhanger. My dad was very articulate and he was into a lot of romantic history novels, always reading things like swashbuckling and so forth. My mother was even smarter than him, and he was brilliant. He knew history inside and out. He could quote poetry and Shakespeare. My mother founded a group that now has thousands of women volunteers in the fifty-two Shriners hospitals, a group called the Fatimas."[17]

Transferring to Herbert Hoover High School in Glendale, Stirling took up fencing. "I always had swift reflexes and sharp eyesight," he told writer and martial arts historian John Corcoran in *Kick* magazine, "and because I always had a sense of other people's auras, bio-rhythms, and movements, I was able to respond to my opponents' moves with exhilarating ease—almost precognition." He chose fencing, he explained, because, "I was fascinated with self *defense* as opposed to *offense* as early as age six or seven."[18] The sport likely appealed to the romantic in him, with its conjuring of the Knights of the Round Table and their chivalric code.

Ethel's early reading lessons paid off. When Stirling was five, he wrote a short story called "Little Whisperers"[19] and, by the time he was at Hoover, he was freelancing to *The Los Angeles Post* and *The Los Angeles Times*. He was was graduated in the winter of 1953 with honors from the California Scholarship Federation. A scholarship brought him to the University of Southern California, where he not only continued to write for the *Times* but joined USC's three-foil fencing squad and "[scoring] ninety percent of my *touchés* via counter-attacks. An opponent would make a move and I'd counter it while he was still engrossed in having delivered it—and skewer him where he stood." He was also a member of several USC health care service fraternities and served as president of the Quill club. After three years, he was graduated *magna cum laude* and *Phi Beta Kappa*.

The Friday after Silliphant received his diploma, he married Iris Garff, twenty, a teacher from Salt Lake, Utah. The pair had met when Silliphant visited the city in 1936, and their friendship resumed at Yellowstone National Park the next summer where she was working a summer job as a chambermaid in one of the lodges. Iris was graduated from the University of Utah, dabbled in dramatics there, and was the daughter of Mr. and Mrs. Reginald Garff. The ceremony was performed June 10, 1938, in the Garff home, and Stirling's brother Leigh was his best man. Ethel attended, Lee did not.

After a honeymoon in the Grand Tetons, the Silliphants returned to Glendale, where Stirling took a publicity job at the nearby Walt Disney Studios. With the phenomenal success of *Snow White and the Seven Dwarfs* in 1937, Disney had begun an ambitious slate of films including *Pinocchio*, *Bambi*, and *Fantasia*, and needed to keep a curious world at bay. In those days, the Disney studio was still a homey, if increasingly cramped, campus on Hyperion Avenue in the Silverlake area northeast of LA proper. The handsome, garrulous Silliphant fit right in.

On August 8, 1940, Iris and Stirling produced a son, Stirling Garff Silliphant.[20] "She was raised a Mormon," the boy recalled of his mother, "but by that time had started an intellectual quest that moved her away from her dad's more rigid interpretations. Funny thing is that, because of her travels in the world (Turkey, Japan, Bangladesh, and India), she wound up religiously in the same place my father did, very Buddhist-like. She even recalled in detail several reincarnation experiences."[21]

In 1939, Disney moved lock, stock, and mouse to the company's present site on Buena Vista Street in Burbank. But, by then, Silliphant had moved on to a publicity job at Twentieth Century-Fox where he survived until 1942, when he entered the Naval Air Service in World War II. As Lt. (j.g.), he did not see combat, but was stationed at Treasure Island, San Francisco, in the Navy's informational services unit. With his fellow informational officer, Raymond Katz (later to become one of Hollywood's leading talent managers and producers), Silliphant went to Pearl Harbor, New York, and other cities as their services were required. As men in uniform during the war, they also had their pick of women.

While Silliphant was thus occupied, Iris and little Stirling Garff moved to New York, then San Francisco. When the boy was in the first grade, Iris sent him to live with her family in Salt Lake City, while she went to New York to get her Master's degree in Psychology at Columbia.

After the war, the Silliphants reunited in New York, and Stirling resumed his Fox job where he was exposed to studio operations and Hollywood politics. He was also exposed to Spyros Skouras, the bombastic businessman who, in 1935, had helped finance the merger of Darryl F. Zanuck's Twentieth Century Pictures with William Fox's floundering Fox Pictures. When Zanuck went off to fight Hitler in 1942, Skouras took over the studio and, in a series of business decisions not inaccurately called a Greek tragedy, nearly buried the company until Zanuck returned.[22] By 1951, Silliphant was running Fox's east coast publicity, a position that placed him in close touch with book publishers and national magazine editors. It was here that he perfected his ability to pitch stories that met the needs of each individual reporter or editor, a talent that not only sharpened his narrative skills but would make him a confident, compelling salesman of his own material to network and studio brass.

Skouras made Silliphant his personal assistant in addition to his PR duties, and Silliphant learned to write in character to take the edge off his boss's penchant for mangling the English language. The Silliphants and the Skourases (Spyros and Saroula Bruiglia Skouras) also spent time together away from the office on the Skouras yacht. On one occasion, Spyros approached Iris to become his mistress. She declined. "Lovely place, Hollywood," her son appraised.[23]

But the marriage was already crumbling when Skouras offered to breach it. Stirling and Iris divorced in 1946. Their son stayed in touch with his grandmother, Ethel, and would later reconnect with his father, but his mother never did. "I have a picture of her, years later, standing overlooking Yellowstone Falls," he said, "that, to me, represents that she never lost the love for my dad." In 1947, Iris met and married James Rasmussen, whose surname young Stirling took to become Stirling Rasmussen. It was just what the boy needed.

"Jim was a solid, loving person," he said. "He was a civil engineer, also a graduate of USC. They met in 1947 and married then. By the time I was in fifth grade, we had moved to La Cañada, California, and Jim became the city engineer for South Pasadena. When my mother then wanted to travel, he got jobs overseas. In 1955, we moved to Japan where he built airfields for the US military. We were there for a year and a half and for me it was a marvelous time." Family travels broadened the boy's horizons.

"In 1959 they were off to Turkey," he said. "In 1960, taking a year off from college, I joined them. I played basketball on a Turkish basketball team. I taught English as a second language for the Georgetown University English language program, with students twice my age from the Turkish military, business and writing worlds who were going to head to the States for extended projects. After I returned to the States, they moved on to Bangladesh, where Jim built sea walls, a very necessary item there. During that time my mother spent time in India, going to the area where the Tibetans had come across, and there met the Dalai Lama, and helped them set up their initial education program. India made a large impression spiritually. Jim died in the mid-1980s."

Following his divorce, Silliphant's man-about-town status in New York made him a visible, attractive catch. "He was a very handsome guy at that age," said Allan Silliphant. "He looked a lot like some of the lead characters that he hired later on, like James Franciscus. There was something about the brightness of his eyes. He looked for people he could identify with and then he would create a character based on his affinity, like having a puppet."

His single status did not last long: that same year he married Ednamarie Patella. "Pat" Patella had been a successful cover girl for national fashion magazines. She was glamorous and exuded an earthy sexuality. She put her career on hold to become a wife and mother, but disenchantment simmered inside the Sicilian beauty. They would have two children: a son, Loren, born in 1951, and a daughter, Dayle, born in 1955.

"I could see that wasn't gonna to last after a couple of years," Allan said, "and I guess he was trying to get away from someone who thought they were a world-class glamour symbol. She didn't choose to be a celebrity, she just was a natural celebrity. That wasn't a happy situation."

"There was the time she made this elaborate meal for him," recalled Stirling Linh Silliphant—Silliphant's son by his fourth wife, Tiana. "He had cheated on her and she was going crazy, so she was waiting for him to come home one night. She cooked this elaborate meal—a sumptuous meal, as it was described—and, as he sat down to eat, she wrapped everything off the table and threw it in the trash."[24]

Meanwhile, Silliphant's Fox duties included taking movie stars around on publicity interviews. For *Deadline, USA* (1952) the studio sent him Humphrey Bogart, who had just won the Academy Award® for *The African Queen* and easily attracted press attention. "This is a bit presumptuous of me," the thirty-four-year-old Silliphant asked Bogart as they were getting out of a cab, "but I hope to be a screenwriter. What do you think is the key to success in Hollywood?" Said Bogart, "One word: survival. Stick around long enough and everybody else will die or retire. Just hang in, kid, and you'll end up with all the awards and all the cups."[25]

Bogart's cynicism notwithstanding, it did little over the years to dampen Silliphant's attitude toward youthful competitors. "I like younger people," he would come to say, even at a time when the young Turks who had taken over Hollywood had forgotten who he was. "Because I worry about them. I hope they can have what I have had and continue to have. But the chances are they won't. And so I want to help them. And they are invigorating to have around because they have more eyes than I have. With them around, I can see as the bee or the fly sees—through multiple and peripheral mirrors."

More philosophically, he added, "The most dangerous thing anybody can do is to live, and, since living is a daily peril which we all share, whether we are seventy or seven, I have never been threatened by anyone younger than I for the simple reason that I am superior to them, in the sense that I have achieved something they may never achieve: a lifetime of more years than they have had. And they may die, be killed, diseased, stricken tomorrow at five thirty for all anybody knows. So why should I envy them? Actually, I pity them."

In 1953, Fox had a major upheaval. *The Robe*, the first film released in the wide-screen CinemaScope process, was crucifying the box office competition. More importantly, it was knocking out television. The studio announced that, henceforth, all of its films would be in 'Scope.[26] Silliphant cringed. "I was detesting my job despite the fact that, even in those days, I was being paid $500 a week, had a department of forty people, assorted assistants, and two secretaries. I decided it was time either to write or be unhappy for the rest of my life."

But first he had to tell his boss. Not surprisingly, Skouras roiled, "You'll be back. You'll come back crawling, but you'll be back some day." And, indeed, Silliphant did come back to Fox one day, but it wasn't crawling, it was to make *The Poseidon Adventure* and *The Towering Inferno*, the box office successes of which saved the studio. But by then Skouras was long gone.

"I heard from somebody in publicity at MGM in New York that their studio was looking for a script for Joan Crawford," Silliphant said. "I got a copy of some of our Fox scripts to see what the physical layout of such work looked like. Then I wrote a romantic story, the Joan Crawford role built around a Pulitzer Prize-winning poetess seeking love in Cuba and in the oil city of Maracaibo, Venezuela. I wrote the script in two weeks, working all night every night, doing my Fox publicity job in the daytime. Then I rushed the finished script over to MGM to a sort of godfather of mine, Oscar Doob, who was Metro's VP in charge of advertising-publicity, and 'submitted' it to him to send along, if he thought it was worthy, to his studio. He told me he'd be happy to read it, but he knew nothing of the studio looking for a Joan Crawford script. Where had I heard that rumor? 'From friends in your publicity department,' I replied. Right then and there he called the studio in Culver City. Result: nobody, but nobody, was either looking for or wanted a script for Joan Crawford. At least at MGM.

"So there I was, script in hand, no market. A week later, while at lunch with Roger Straus (Farrar, Straus publishing house) I told him the story and joked about my gullibility. 'Let me read the script,' he suggested. I sent it to him and the following day he called to tell me he thought it would translate into a pretty fair novel. Did I know how to write a novel? 'Well,' I said, 'three weeks ago I didn't know how to write a screenplay, so I might as well see if I can't also find out how to write a novel.'"

But first, he embarked on a producing gambit. He secured the life story rights from heavyweight boxing champion Joe Louis and landed financing from Walter P. Chrysler, Jr. (son of the founder of the Chrysler Corporation and a well-known art collector and benefactor) and William Zeckendorf (the real estate developer who would make the deal with Spyros Skouras to build Century City). They hired Robert Sylvester—a columnist friend from *The New York Daily News* and a fight buff—to write the screenplay. He engaged workmanlike director Robert Gordon and secured promise of release from United Artists, and then found himself doing the one thing he hated to do most: wait.

"It never occurred to me to write the film, only to produce it," he said. "Only when Bob failed to give me some of the scenes I felt were essential did I step in and write them myself. Later, when I watched the completed movie, I saw that the several scenes I had written were far and away the best ones in the flick—at least to my considerably prejudiced opinion. But, even more, I had discovered the pain of having to sit there and *wait*—as a producer—for the writer to deliver. What the hell, it struck me, why not be the guy everybody's waiting for rather than the guy who's going crazy waiting?

"As I recall, Bob wrote the mother-son violin scene. The scenes I wrote were the later John Marley scenes and virtually all of the Joe vs. Maria marital scenes, along with the 'finding himself' wind-up. The gutsy, fight and ring-side stuff is all Bob's. My scenes are the more personal, intimate moments, which, for some reason, evaded Bob in his writing of the draft."

Joe Louis, the "Brown Bomber," is credited with bringing new excitement to boxing following the retirement of Jack Dempsey. But Dempsey was white and Louis was black: something that made no difference to Silliphant, but did to some of his advisors who were not bashful about showing their racism.

"The flack from 'friends' of mine, southern exhibitors, was an eye-opener," Silliphant sighed. "They called long-distance to tell me I was out of my mind to make my feature debut with a 'race' movie. And what was that scene where Manny [played by John Marley], Joe's trainer, is sitting there with Joe's *black* daughter on his lap? That's gotta go—or it'll never play in *our* theatres." The pressure increased when Chrysler's and Zeckendorf's funding proved insufficient. "From the beginning I never was fully funded," Silliphant confessed, "but I went ahead and shot anyway—even while I was still out drumming up money. We got a life-saving infusion half-way into the shoot from one of the few black businessmen who came through for Joe. This gentleman was Harlem's leading abortionist and obviously business was good uptown." *The Joe Louis Story* was released on September 18, 1953. When its copyright was not renewed, it slipped into the public domain and has enjoyed a wider distribution on home video than it ever had in theatres.

Two years after *Joe Louis* saw *5 Against the House* (1955), a taut heist tale from a *Good Housekeeping* magazine story by Jack Finney, author of *Invasion of the Body Snatchers,* among other classics. Silliphant put up his own money—his fee from *Maracaibo*—and established Dayle Productions (named after his daughter) with writer-director John Barnwell. This time he wrote the script, which was later polished by William Bowers and Barnwell, and had Phil Karlson—a fine action hand—direct the no-nonsense story of four college buddies planning on robbing a Reno casino just to show it can be done, and one of them double-crossing the others by planning on making off with the loot. Guy Madison, Kim Novak, and Brian Keith starred. Although Silliphant produced, this was his first screenplay credit, and it brought him in contact with one of Hollywood's true moguls: Columbia Pictures's monstrous boss, Harry Cohn.

"I only met Harry Cohn once," Silliphant recalled, "in his office. He was courteous and businesslike, but that could be because I was the only goy in the shop and young and wide-eyed, and he knew instinctively he could have me for breakfast on the worst day of his life, so he spared me. And, yes, he [ordered] us to cast Kim Novak in *5 Against the House.* But who cared? She couldn't act, but the role didn't require a Shakespearean capability. All she had to do was to slink and roll those eyes. And, yes, Mr. Cohn was definitely running things when I was there. But I preferred that hands-on, rough-and-tumble control to today's push-button executions from offices in distant skyscrapers. Today you never quite know who ordered your death. With Harry around, you never had any doubt."

As he would do so often, Silliphant purposely over-extended himself. He kept a private journal marked "Income From Writing" listing everything he worked on in 1956. He set personal goals of $40,000 from screenwriting (demanding of himself $1,000/week for forty weeks), $20,000 from sales of originals, and $5,000 from books. By year's end he had amassed a pre-tax total of $73,354.53 derived from a staggering number of projects. Not all were produced (*), but all were paid:[27]

SCREEN

*Nightfall**	4,000
Squaw Fever	5,000 (for Raoul Walsh)
Last Man at Wagon Hound	3,000 (for Clark Gable)
*Damn Citizen**	9,500
Pakistan	19,666 (for John Wayne)
*Rachel Cade**	14,000 (*Sins of Rachel Cade*)
Angel's Twenty	2,000
Wherever You Are	4,000 (for Donna Reed)

TV

"The Thread"*	1,250 (*Jane Wyman Theatre*)
"Never Again"*	500 (*Hitchcock Presents*)
"The Warriors"*	875 (*Chevron Show of Stars*)
"The Hunted"*	1,250 (*G.E. Theatre*)
"The Idea Man"*	1,250 (*Ford Theatre*)
"Fan Dancer's Horse"*	2,500 (*Perry Mason*)
"Not for the Rope"*	1,000 (*Zane Grey Theatre*)
"Mr. Cinderella"*	1,100 (*Heinz Playhouse*)
"Jonathan" (polish)*	500 (*Hitchcock Presents*)
"The Manacled"*	1,250 (*Hitchcock Presents*)
"We Fly Anything"	1,350 (unproduced pilot)
"A Bottle of Wine"*	1,250 (*Hitchcock Presents*)
"Juvenile Delinquent"	800 (*West Point*)

During this period, he sold, for $7,500, a screenplay called *Huk!,* about Communist guerillas fighting land owners to free the Philippines from imperialism. The film was directed by John Barnwell and saw brief United Artists release in 1956. Not wanting to leave any revenue source untapped, he also novelized the script, as he had *Maracaibo*, into a paperback, this time for Popular Library.[28]

All of this enabled him to move to pre-Castro Cuba. "I rented a house on the beach, a place well outside of Havana—Playa Tarara, I believe it was—and there, working nights only (the days were spent scuba diving) I [finally] turned the aborted film script [*Maracaibo*] into a novel, which Farrar, Straus published in 1954, and which my then-agent Ned Brown of MCA sold to Universal for what to me (in those days) was a small fortune—either $37,500 or $47,500. I have the feeling it was probably the lesser figure, but since I could live in Cuba on that much money for three or four years I had suddenly become rich. So this is a long answer to How did I learn [to write scripts]: I just jumped into the water and swam." *Maracaibo*[29] was eventually filmed by Cornel Wilde, who also starred; the screenplay is credited to Ted Sherdeman. The "Joan Crawford" role was played by Jean Wallace, who was married to Wilde at the time.

When Silliphant returned from Cuba, he got a call from an old friend in the Disney publicity department. Walt was about to start a TV show aimed at kids, something called *The Mickey Mouse Club*, and was desperate for material.

2

The Mouse

EVEN THOUGH WALT DISNEY would have his finger firmly up the pulse of the public until his death in 1966, in 1938 his investors had so little faith in his company's future that they tied the construction of his new studio to a bizarre condition. The bank leaned on Roy Disney, Walt's financially savvy brother, to design the building with halls and doorways wide enough to admit hospital beds so that, if the studio failed, it could be sold to St. Joseph's Medical Center across Buena Vista Street as an infirmary. Completed in 1940, the studio's old art deco animation building—which now houses administrative offices—stands as testament to the Disneys' vision and the bankers' myopia.

The Mickey Mouse Club was a different animal. Debuting on ABC-TV on October 3, 1955, it was created in the wake of the successful *Disneyland* TV series, which had begun on the alphabet network in 1954. Financed by an arrangement with ABC that also had the network invest in the Disneyland theme park being built in Anaheim, California—the show was an instant hit.[30] The hour-long *Club* aired weekday afternoons just as kids were getting home from school. It was heavily formatted: Monday was "Fun with Music Day," Tuesday was "Guest Star Day," Wednesday was "Anything Can Happen Day," Thursday was "Circus Day," and Friday was "Talent Round-up." Each program featured songs and dances by the teenage Mouseketeers, Disney cartoons that had never before aired (Walt refused to sell to TV), newsreels of kid-oriented activities, educational shorts hosted by Jiminy Cricket, and serialized adventures with youthful casts ("Spin & Marty," "Corky and White Shadow," "The Hardy Boys," etc.).

Told by a former colleague that Walt was looking for additional segments, Silliphant pitched Disney an idea that had children taking a crack at what they wanted to be when they grew up. Trans-World Airlines, which was

19

an exhibitor at Disneyland, agreed to let kids into their Kansas-City-based training center to learn what it took to become a pilot (Duncan Richardson) or flight attendant (Pat Morrow). The series, for which Silliphant was writer and production supervisor, was called "What I Want to Be" and ran for ten weeks beginning October 3, 1955, in the third quarter-hour of *The Mickey Mouse Club.*

For all his genius as an innovator and story editor, Disney the man was a ganglia of contradictions. As a result of having been cheated out of the first cartoon character he created, Oswald the Lucky Rabbit, he was paranoid to a fault about everything else his studio turned out. He would roam the office after his workers had left, leaving notes for them in blue ink and rifling through their trash cans in case they had discarded an idea that his genius would know how to save. But he also wanted to discover if any of them was working for anybody else on his time. When Silliphant realized this was going on, he started leaving cryptic and misleading material in his trash can to see what Walt would do. Perhaps as a result, when Silliphant pitched Disney on future episodes, discord developed between the men and both the series and Silliphant's employ were canceled.[31] "What I Want to Be" was replaced by "Adventure in Dairyland," in which Mouseketeers Annette Funicello and Kevin "Moochie" Corcoran appeared. As for Silliphant, he never worked for Disney again.

Meanwhile, *Maracaibo* was published to reviews that were good enough to warrant a call from *Collier's* magazine "about my interest in submitting a short story for consideration," Silliphant said. "Having no short story conveniently in stock, I sat down that very night and wrote 3,500 words and called it 'Under Capricorn.' The title comes from one of the lines in the human palm, which, in the case of murderers, is to be found under the mound of Capricorn.[32] The *Collier's* editor, upon receiving and reading the short story, rejected it with a vehemence, which I found quite disturbing [calling it] 'the most horrible story she'd ever received.'" Undaunted, he took off the rejection slip and mentioned the story to agent Ned Brown. "He promptly sold it for $750 (more than I would have received from the niggardly *Collier's* crowd) to a new TV show called *Screen Director's Playhouse.* "I said, 'How long has *this* been going on?' and I was in television."[33]

The story was never produced, but that hardly mattered; Silliphant had cracked TV. The first four titles in his imposing Writers Guild of America credit roster are for *Alfred Hitchcock Presents,* which filmed at Revue—the TV arm of MCA—in 1956. Peggy Robertson and Norman Lloyd handled the day-to-day chores as associate producers. Silliphant's first script for them was "Never Again" (airdate: April 22, 1956), which had a twisted history: it was based on a story by movie columnist Adela Rogers St. John, with earlier attempts by Gwen Bagni and Irwin Gielgud. Silliphant applied the final polish.

Apparently it shone like a beacon because he was hired ten more times over the course of three years but seldom got to work with the Master of Suspense himself.

"Except for one meeting with Hitch to discuss my scripting a one-hour *Suspicion*," Silliphant said, "I never, over the two or three seasons I wrote for the show, met the man.[34] My meetings were always with Joan Harrison—with nobody else—not even with Norman Lloyd, although I did see him a few times around the office at Revue. Joan would simply call me up and tell me she was sending me a story to read and if I liked it to come in and we'd talk about it. I don't recall ever having written an original for the show—only adaptations—and all based on stories given to me by Joan. This lady had a prodigious talent and… one of the keenest story minds of any producer with whom I ever worked—I have always preferred to work with women producers—they are more complex, more insightful, I have found, than ninety-nine percent of the male producers I've known. I can tell you, without any question, had it not been for Joan, Hitch's show wouldn't have stayed on the air ten minutes, for he had less to do with it than any of the several writers Joan used as her backstop for the scripts which she then produced. It wouldn't surprise me to learn that Hitch probably didn't even screen ninety percent of the episodes. Or that he never read a single script. Believe me, it was Joan and Lloyd who made that show. Hitch was their book-end. *Nada mas.*[35]

"I must tell you an amusing (though to me it wasn't at the time) story about Joan and me. After I'd written several episodes for the extravagant sum of $500 for each half-hour *Alfred Hitchcock Presents* script, I heard that she'd paid one other writer, one of her New York stable—I forget his name, but I believe he wrote more episodes than I did for the show—$750. That did it. I demanded $750 hereafter, or else.

"'Or else *what?*' Joan asked with that sweet bitchiness which I so loved about her.

"'Or else I don't write any more episodes for you.'

"'I'll miss you,' she smiled, and I was out the door. Seven—maybe more—months went by while I was busy elsewhere. Then she called. 'I have a simply marvelous story for you,' she told me. 'It's called "The Glass Eye" and you're going to love doing it.'

"'For how much?' I asked.

"'Well,' she said, 'I think in this instance I can probably scrape up the $750.'

"'Sorry,' I said, 'my price has gone up to $1,000.'

"'Please read the story, Stirling,' she urged. 'I'm sending it right over.'[36]

"I read it—I loved it—I called back. 'Okay,' I said. 'I agree—it's a fabulous story and I'm going to write your single best episode—but only for one thousand dollars.' Well, happy ending—I got the thou—and from then a thousand for all subsequent half-hours. I think the price jumped to $2,500 for each of the one-hour *Suspicion*s I wrote for Hitch. Robert Stevens, the director of 'The Glass Eye,' won the Emmy that year for the episode. I won nothing—except the raise.

"Now, my single meeting with Hitch: Joan told me the Master was actually going to direct one of his TV shows—this one his very favorite story—'The Voice in the Night'—to be the flagship episode for his one-hour *Suspicion* series on NBC.[37] Joan drove me to his home, up Bellagio Road, one of those canyon streets off Sunset Boulevard where you drive through a gate. Hitch was charming. Congratulated me on the scripts I'd done for the half-hour *Alfred Hitchcock Presents* shows, personally made me a Scotch and soda and sat me down with my yellow pad.

"I wouldn't trade the hour that followed for anything I can think of at the moment, except possibly—no, not even that. The man was *brilliant*. He fucking dictated the script to me, shot by shot, including camera movements and opticals. He actually had already *seen* the finished film. He'd say, for example, 'The camera's in the boat with the boy and the girl. The move in is very, very slow while we see the mossy side of the wrecked schooner. Bump. Now the boy climbs the ladder. I tilt up. I see him look at his hand. Something strange seems to have attached itself. He disappears on deck. Now the girl starts up and I cut to the boy exploring the deck. I'm shooting through this foreground of—of *stuff*—and I'm panning him to the cabin door. Something there makes him freeze. He waits. Now the camera's over here and I see the girl come to him. Give me about this much dialogue, Stirling.' He holds up his hand, thumb and forefinger two inches apart. I jot down, 'dialogue, two inches.'

"As I say, the whole goddamned film—shot by shot—no dialogue—just the measurements of how much dialogue and where he wanted it. He left its content to me, since there is no dialogue in the entire short story. It's all introspection and the memory of horror and the writer didn't want to spoil it with dialogue. Lotsa luck, screenwriter. 'Give me an inch of dialogue right here.' I went away and wrote what I still consider a rather neat piece of work, but lo and behold Hitch decided to shoot a movie, and his presence was denied to us. [Arthur Hiller directed it]."

For Hitchcock, Silliphant also wrote the classic "The Crystal Trench" from A.E.W. Mason's haunting short story about a young couple who go mountaineering. The woman's fiancé is killed when he falls into a trench in the ice. Out of love and loyalty to him, she remains single over the decades that it takes the slow-moving glacier to reach the foot of the mountain and deposit his perfectly preserved body. When it does, he is wearing a locket. She opens it. Inside is the picture of another woman. The grotesquely chilling episode was broadcast October 4, 1959.

In today's world, when everybody seems to be writing scripts, it's worth noting that, years ago, good, solid, fast script writers were hard to find. Silliphant was one of them. "Back in the '50s and '60s thirty (or so) of us were writing eighty-five percent of prime-time TV," he reported. "I don't know if I can explain why this was, it just was. Whether you were freelance or staff, it seemed essential, in order to meet the deadlines." And there was another, more pragmatic reason: money. "Dean Martin was signed to guest star in a *Rawhide* episode and my agent got me the assignment to write for Dean. This was the first time I was ever paid $10,000 to write a one-hour show. We're talking back in the time when $4,500 was considered *top* money for an hour episode. I may be wrong, but this could have been the highest per-hour episode fee paid up to that time for a Hollywood-based TV show."

It may seem strange to struggling screenwriters, or to those who are aware of current industry scruples, but there was a time when film and television producers actually *wanted* to read material and had story departments constantly on the lookout for it. Silliphant entered the game at that exact moment when TV was desperate for scripts and even more desperate for grown-ups (Silliphant was in his mid-thirties at this time) who could churn them out quickly. "At the time there was an obverse Greylist," he later remarked. "There was a prevailing policy at the studios *not* to hire the bright young blokes all the studios are now searching for. I don't believe that age—whether the writer is young or old—is an issue. Only the work matters. There are millions of old coots who can only write mediocre material and millions of young minds who can't do any better. If anything, the odds are in favor of the younger guys simply because they are writing for a medium which can seldom tolerate 'excellence'—a medium which only wants 'hot' or 'trendy' or 'best seller'—and we all know that those requirements can only be met by mass appeal comic strips disguised as motion pictures."

During this period, Silliphant also wrote the script for the feature film, *Damn Citizen*, based on a true story of corruption in Louisiana and told with a semi-documentary style popularized years earlier by Louis de Rochement. Universal-International Pictures sat on it for a year and then dumped it into a few theatres on March 1, 1958.

One of the stranger collaborations—strange in that it was not a collaboration—occurred with *Nightfall* (1957), an atmospheric crime thriller directed by Jacques Tourneur. Tourneur had distinguished himself as a genre filmmaker with *Cat People* (1942) and *I Walked with a Zombie* (1943) at RKO and was prepping *Curse of the Demon* (1957) when Columbia handed him Silliphant's script of Robert Goodis's novel of the same name. "All I remember of this gentleman [Tourneur] was that he seemed much too gentlemanly to be a director," Silliphant offered. "He fits elusively in the remote backcountry of my recall as a courteous person. He simply showed up on time at Columbia, took my script (which, incidentally, had Anne Bancroft in it), and went out and methodically shot it. If he was distracted prepping *Curse of the Demon*, I was never aware of it."

Nightfall has Aldo Ray falsely accused of a bank robbery and a murder, and he must clear himself not only with the police but with the actual robbers/killers. It sounds stock, but its gyrating narrative is immensely appealing, and the darkness itself, as befits a Tourneur film, becomes a separate, threatening character.

At that time, Silliphant—who had been writing episodes of *Suspicion, Chicago Manhunt, Alfred Hitchcock Presents, West Point,* and *Perry Mason*— linked with director Donald Siegel to script one of the best films that either man would make, *The Lineup (1957).* Siegel had directed the pilot for CBS's *The Line-Up* TV series in 1954, and when Columbia decided to spin off a feature film, they removed its hyphen and brought back Siegel, who brought in Silliphant. The story has to do with a heroin ring that smuggles smack into the city in unsuspecting travelers' unguarded luggage, but when they stash some in a little girl's doll that then vanishes, all hell breaks loose.

Siegel and Silliphant instantly hit it off. "I *loved* the guy," Silliphant said. "I found him immensely competent, in total control of his craft. If Don ever had any doubts about what he was up to, I was never aware of them. If you had fought in a platoon in Vietnam, Don would have been the kind of lieutenant you'd have hoped you were lucky enough to have been leading your scared ass. I was with him in San Francisco on location when he shot *The Lineup.* I remember being somewhat apprehensive about his reaction to my script when it was first given to him. I had created an off-the-wall character (played by Robert Keith—Brian's father)—an agent for Eli Wallach, one of the country's top hit men. The idea of a killer having an agent appealed to me immensely, since the connection to Hollywood was immediately symbolic. As Wallach proceeds through my script, blowing people away in successive killings, each time he'd return to the waiting line and the eager agent, Keith, would ask him the inevitable question: 'Well, what were their last words?' Keith was an avid collector of such closing statements. Eventually, his insistence on knowing last words provokes his client to shoot him; Wallach is fed up with this philosophic shit. Back in the 50s, this was hardly your average screenwriting, if I can be somewhat immodest, and so I was shaken about Don's reaction. Well, he fucking went out of his mind—hooted with laughter—and shot it all with relish."

Silliphant's filmography during this brief period from 1956 to 1959 includes sixty-eight episodics and five features (*5 Against the House, Huk!, Nightfall, The Line-Up,* and *Damn Citizen*). That's three scripts per week, not counting the movies. "Things in TV were immeasurably different than they are today," he understated. "In the 60s and 70s, for one thing—and this is *key*—the network commitment to a producer for any given series achieving airtime was for a far greater number of episodes than the networks now allot. Half-hour shows usually scored a 36-episode season. Hour shows seldom less than 24 episodes. For this reason, when a producer turned up a writer with whom he resonated, he was more likely than not to ask (even beg) that writer for multiple commitments. Apparently I was such a writer when I was freelancing. For example: the series *Tightrope*, starring Mike Connors, produced by Clarence Greene and Russell Rouse. I believe I wrote four episodes for *Tightrope* and the producers wanted me to write even more, but I wasn't free after those four. For *Route 66* I ran up an almost ridiculous score. Similarly for the half-hour *Naked City* season when I wrote 32 out of 39 episodes. When we got to the hour-long show I couldn't maintain that pace, since I had to write *Route 66* simultaneously. So the combination of having my own shows, plus the then-common practice of producers trying to grab the 'hot' writers for multiple assignments, plus the much-larger-than-now numbers of episodes per season—all these elements made it easy for me to pile up the kind of score I did."[38]

It was no accident that his scripts were actor magnets. "When I first got to Hollywood, I attended acting classes for three years, then I went back every few years—right up until I left town. I wanted to understand the acting process so I could write for actors. Watching them, I learned how to streamline my dialogue—where to hesitate—where to rush—so that the writing itself would give the actor all the clues he needed to find his way under the skin of the character I'd written. Why should I tell him to speak a line 'defiantly' when he might be more effective, out of his own life, to play defiance by seeming to be meek—or seeming uncaring—or all the other infinite shades of human reaction? So not only is such writing presumptuous, it is short-circuiting. It is denying the potential for magic to happen.

"Believe me, I had to *learn* this, because I used to write that way too—feeling like God, telling my actors how they were going to conduct themselves in the presence of the nuggets I was giving them—until I put myself on the same stage with the actors and realized how goddamned hard it was to *be* an actor and that the last thing he needed was some half-assed writer telling him how to do his job.

"And I had great teachers. Once, in a *Naked City*, at the top of Act II, I wrote two inches of dialogue for Lee J. Cobb that I felt should have been carved in marble on the Lincoln Memorial. Lee took me aside before the scene was shot and asked me if he could play the scene with *no* dialogue. I was appalled. Jesus, Lee, not say all this good stuff here? Let me show you something, he said, and he *acted* out my words with a few simple movements, not mime, just body language which spoke far more eloquently than my precious words.[39] George C. Scott—when we did *Mussolini: The Untold Story*—gave me a refresher course in the same way—a look rather than the words—a shift of shoulder rather than the words. In little snippets in parentheses beneath the dialogue. Just the dialogue. And you've even got to watch that.

"But do not think that I didn't have to go through exactly the same process that freelancers have to deal with today in TV. Yes, I had to go meet the producer. I would even have to sit in the projection room and run the pilot or be given the pilot script and be expected to read it. I was then asked if I had any storyline in mind which might fit into that specific format or program which had just been ordered by a network or was under development at a studio. Either I pitched a story at that first meeting or I'd come back the next day and make the pitch.

"For some reason—maybe it was those earlier years in publicity trying to convince bored movie editors at the New York papers to please for Christ's sake, Bosley [Crowther], give me a break this Sunday—can you give us the right-hand column and a four-column cut for this piece of shit opening at the Roxy next week? For some reason I seem to have a talent for pitching stories and telling just enough to whet the producer's appetite without telling him too much and revealing I haven't yet worked the fucking story out to whatever its ending might be. I don't recall ever going to a pitch meeting (in those days, not now) from which I didn't emerge with an assignment—or a multiple deal—before I'd written *fade in*.

"But I never worked with the story editor of any series. I always felt these guys were either jealous or were saving an assignment for their second cousin. I met only with the show's creator (usually the producer) or with the Boss (e.g., Aaron Spelling) or the v.p. of TV development at a given studio or the network v.p. in charge of development. I always regarded story editors as extremely low on the totem pole.

"For me the proof of this is that virtually all of my television writing—which I consider in many instances to have been my best writing for the medium—has been original—the stories, the people, the thematic element—all these came from within the cosmos of my own life experience in one way or another. The attitudes and beliefs expressed began in my own psyche. How much simpler to write out of one's self than to address an alien piece of material and find in it those elements which impelled the producer to acquire the property in the first place, then to try to dramatize those properties for the actor and the camera, and yet still try not to submerge within this foreign stew your own personal feelings and beliefs."

The irony is that Silliphant, who preferred to write originals and distinguished himself by doing so, would wind up becoming one of Hollywood's highest-paid adapters of material from other media. But that was before he moved back to New York for a gambit that made that great city's streets a character in one of the most celebrated TV series ever produced. It also put him in business with a colorful rogue who would later take him for a ride on Route 66: Bert Leonard.

3

Eight Million Stories

NAKED CITY **HAD BEEN ON THE AIR** for three years when *MAD* magazine chimed in with their twist on the TV show's regular closing line: "If there are eight million stories in the Naked City, how come all the re-runs?"[40] What they didn't know at the time was that Stirling Silliphant and Herbert B. Leonard, who produced the series, were asking themselves the same question.

"The line was first used in Mark Hellinger's black and white *film noir*," Silliphant reported. "New York was less populous at the time Mr. Hellinger produced it, [so] the closing line was 'There are *five* million stories in the Naked City—this has been one of them.' By the time we geared up, New York had grown, hence we notched the count up to eight million stories. Each week, as I faced the daunting task of coming up with a new episode, Bert and I would have lunch and kick ideas around. I remember saying to him on several occasions, 'Bert, if there *are* eight million stories in the Naked City, why in the fuck can't we come up with even *one*?'"[41]

The motion picture *The Naked City* (1948) had been directed by Jules Dassin from a screenplay that Albert Maltz and Malvin Wald had written from Hellinger's original story. Hellinger, a street-savvy newspaperman who brought that gritty sensibility to such movies as *The Killers* (1946) and *Brute Force* (1947), didn't romanticize New York, but he didn't flinch either. He constructed a drama (and narrated it too) about the murder of a young woman that leads to the exposing of a ring that deals in stolen jewels. What lifted it above the level of a standard cops-and-robbers picture was its attention to the details of police work and the spectacular use of New York City itself as a character, in part inspired by the work of photographer Weegee (Arthur Fellig) in his 1945 book of the same title. The film, which is now regarded as a classic, was doubly jinxed as it neared its March of 1948 release, first, by the blacklisting of writer Albert Maltz in the wake of the October, 1947 HUAC

(House Un-American Activities Committee) hearings, and the December, 1947 death of Mark Hellinger.[42] Doubtful of the film's commercial potential and frightened of right-wing pressure against Maltz, Universal Pictures considered burying the film until Hellinger's family reminded them of a mandatory release clause in Hellinger Productions's contract.

When Bert Leonard acquired the rights from the Hellinger Estate, he took it to Screen Gems, the television division of Columbia Pictures, where he had been an independent producer on *The Adventures of Rin-Tin-Tin* (1954-1958) and *Circus Boy* (1956-1957). The Screen Gems connection was not a slam-dunk. Although Leonard had a profitable track record with the company, he also had a belligerent one. But, then, he had a belligerent relationship with nearly everybody.

A charming man with a dangerously casual manager about his own affairs, Leonard combined the buccaneer bravery of early Hollywood moguls with the business savvy of the bean counters who were taking over the industry just as he was coming into producing prominence. The catch was that it was only his own beans that he counted. Born in New York City's Hell's Kitchen in 1922, he was a Navy fighter pilot in World War II. After the war he and his brother, Roger, spent time in Mexico living a sybaritic life until he moved to Los Angeles eager to get into the film business as well as the starlets who were drawn to it. He succeeded at both. Although his uncle was Columbia Pictures's vice president Nate Spingold, Leonard chose to go it alone, linking with Sam Katzman, the prolific exploitation film producer, from whom he learned filmmaking from the bottom (where Katzman fed) up. In 1953, he felt confident enough in his own talent, and confined enough by Katzman, to make a deal with Lee Duncan, the discoverer and trainer of Rin Tin Tin (sic), to star the charismatic canine in a TV series.[43] The original Rinty had saved Warner Bros. from bankruptcy in the silent days when Darryl F. Zanuck was running the studio and also pounding out innumerable scripts featuring the noble German Shepard. But that was three decades earlier; the current Rin-Tin-Tin #4 was a shadow of his talented great-grandfather, and Leonard—who sold the show to Screen Gems and ABC-TV—had to work around his limitations by using doubles. Leonard's ingenuity and tenacity created a hugely successful series, but his constant arguing with the studio brass over budget, quality, and scripts continually threatened to scrap the deal. Uncle Nate Spingold tried to quell the conflict, with scant success. The fact that Leonard was generally correct in his judgments only made the studio executives dig in.

Nevertheless, when Leonard sold *Naked City* to ABC-TV, he set it up at Screen Gems; both companies may have been irritated, but they were not stupid. The half-hour series bowed on ABC on September 30, 1958 with Silliphant's hostage drama, "Meridian."

Naked City holds an unusual place in television history. Along with *The Defenders, Coronet Blue*, and a small number of other hold-outs, it continued to shoot in New York City when production was relocating to Los Angeles. "I came in at a time when we were going to film," he told interviewer Elwy Yost.[44] "Way back in those days it was tape versus film, and film was winning. *Naked City* and *The Defenders* were the two key shows on in New York in the late '50s, which was right at the end of the golden age when everyone went to film. [Reginald] Rose wrote nearly all of [*The Defenders*]. We were highly competitive.... . We didn't like their show and they didn't like our show. We felt they were too preachy and we were very sharp, like today."

Naked City was set in Manhattan's fictitious 65th Precinct, which was actually located on West 54th. Street between Eighth and Ninth Avenues. But the show's verisimilitude came from its seasoned New York production crew knowing every alley and cul-de-sac in the city's five boroughs. As with the 1948 feature, *The Naked City* (the *The* was dropped after the first season) looked at the procedural aspects of crime fighting as it followed Detectives Jimmy Halloran (James Franciscus) and Lt. Dan Muldoon (John McIntire) on their dangerous, but often boring, duties.

"Arriving at the main characters was a joint creative effort between my partner Bert Leonard, who had acquired the rights to *Naked City* from Mark Hellinger's estate, and me," Silliphant said. "It seemed so simple—a gruff precinct boss (now a parody character), a young, idealistic detective, and a street cop partner with flattened ears and a busted nose. When I wrote them, they didn't seem like stereotypes. Today they simply wouldn't do." Silliphant also created meaty roles for guest stars, a device that allowed them to cast New York stage actors in the same way that "golden age" live TV dramas in the 1950s reaped the bounty of Broadway. Continuing the tradition of the producer doing the narration, Bert Leonard performed Hellinger's voice-over chores.

Silliphant wrote thirty-two of the first season's thirty-nine episodes. "It was easier just to write the damn things than it was to waste time interviewing other writers and trying to get them to catch what we were after, then having to rewrite them, something I truly hate," he said. He was paid $1,500 for a half-hour script and $2,500 when the show bumped up to an hour. He also collected $500 on those occasions when he polished somebody else's work.[45] Additionally, eight of his teleplays were adapted into prose by Charles Einstein and published in a Dell First Edition paperback with the unusual arrangement of carrying Silliphant's byline on the cover and Einstein's byline within.[46]

Although the show was extremely well received by the critics, at first, audiences did not respond. Moreover, there was discord on the set. Some sources say that McIntire grew tired of location shooting in New York and wanted to live on his Montana ranch. Others say that he was irritated by his costar Franciscus's egotism. Whichever it was, Silliphant arranged for Muldoon to die in a car crash in "The Bumper" (March 17, 1959) and be replaced by a presumably more malleable Lt. Mike Parker (Horace McMahon). Harry Bellaver was added as Sgt. Frank Arcaro. Emboldened by reviews, Leonard protected his series like a lion guarding its young. He shot himself in the foot, however, for the June 23, 1959, broadcast of "A Wood of Thorne." In a two-hander of steadily increasing tension, Halloran intrudes on Lois Heller (Cara Williams) as she celebrates the impending execution of convicted murderer Philip Hone, even though both she and Halloran know that her boyfriend, Nikki, is the real killer, and only she can make the call to stop Hone's execution. The electrocution process is described vividly, yet it's all offscreen, which makes it even more riveting.[47] ABC wanted to pull the episode, but Leonard flashed his contract and forced them to air it. In retaliation, the network canceled the series entirely in June, and only the intervention of the sponsor, tobacco company Brown & Williamson, saved it.[48] On its fall revival in October of 1960, it became an hour-long drama with Bellaver and McMahon returning, but Franciscus jettisoned in favor of Paul Burke as Detective Adam Flint and Nancy Malone as his actress-girlfriend, Libby.

Silliphant hadn't intended to return to television when Screen Gems and Leonard asked him to write the *Naked City* pilot, but when three of his screenplays[49] were bought but not produced (that kind of waste "destroys your whole reason to work," he said[50]), he took the assignment and, when it sold, he found the changes the medium had undergone to his liking. "A Case Study of Two Savages" (airdate: February 7, 1962) is emblematic of this rekindled interest. "We had a thing where Rip Torn plays a killer from the south, he shoots everyone up all over New York City, he's making it with Tuesday Weld, and finally he's gunned down in Grand Central Station. He's lying there in a pool of blood and Tuesday Weld is crying, and Paul Burke says to her, 'Why?' And she says, 'For the hell of it.' That's pretty advanced back in those days, but we felt that was the justification. I mean, wanting a big speech about his mother left him and father went to jail? They would do all that on *The Defenders;* we didn't. We went for the action and the sharp line. It's hard to get to that point where you can end the film—she looks up—I'll never forget the shot—tears in her eyes, she screams out, 'For the hell of it.' And you know they'd kill twenty more people if he weren't dead on the floor. We had no compromises on that show. We never pandered to nice people or giving an easy solution. We really showed it the way it was, and the way it is."[51]

Other episodes are remarkable for their varied mood and character interplay. Scattered examples are "The Bloodhounds" (airdate: May 25, 1959) in which detectives use a traffic accident victim's lost dogs to find a missing girl, to "The Canvas Bullet" (airdate: June 16, 1959), in which a prize fighter takes to the ring even though he knows it may cost him his life. Real-life champs Rocky Graziano and Jake LaMotta appeared in the character drama, which was directed, as were many episodes, by Stuart Rosenberg (*Cool Hand Luke,* 1967). "The Rebirth" (airdate: April 21, 1959) has a scrubwoman, Betty Sinclair, robbing a bank and discovering that money will not relieve her loneliness, so she turns herself in. And "Fire Island" (March 3, 1959) costars a pre-*Route 66* George Maharis, along with Henry Hull, Michael Conrad, and Guy Raymond, in a shoot-out between police and off-season bootleggers. There was also the remarkable "Four Sweet Corners" (airdate: April 28, 1959) in which Maharis, as a returning soldier, decides to drive around the country with a service buddy, Robert Morris. It's a setup that, if it was not a pre-pilot for *Route 66,* certainly inspired the latter series.

Naked City ran four seasons and 128 episodes between 1958 and 1963, but Silliphant left, for all intents and purposes, after season one to do *Route 66,* although he wrote the hour-long reboot, "A Death of Princes," and three additional hours: two in 1960 and one in 1962. He was replaced by the equally industrious Howard Rodman and Arnold Manoff, the latter working under a pseudonym because he, like the original film's director, Jules Dassin, was blacklisted.[52]

Although *Naked City* helped American television grow up, the country and the medium still had a long way to go. Silliphant and Leonard would give it another boost with a series that remains part of the cultural landscape even as its actual namesake has faded.

4

Pilgrim's Progress

STIRLING SILLIPHANT AND BERT LEONARD had more in common than a hunger for stories about New York City. Both were sons of salesman fathers, although Bert's was a ne'er-do-well and Stirling's was industrious; both traveled the country when young; both were keen observers of human nature; and both could weave tales with the seductiveness of Scheherazade. When Leonard proposed the idea to Silliphant for *Route 66*, he said it came out of the relaxed odyssey that he and his brother, Roger, had taken around the country and into Mexico after the world war. For his part, Silliphant referred to the series as a "*Pilgrim's Progress*, 1962,"[53] alluding to John Bunyan's 1678 allegory in which a man abandons his family to seek the Celestial City. Leonard's earthy synopsis perfectly complemented Silliphant's literary allusion, and the public agreed, because the series ran for 116 episodes between October 7, 1960, and March 13, 1964.[54] Silliphant wrote seventy of the shows himself. It was produced by Lancer-Edling Productions, Lancer being Leonard's company and Edling being Silliphant's.[55] In a September 20, 1961 joint agreement, Silliphant put up $160 for sixteen percent of the proceeds and Leonard put up $840 for eighty-four percent. Each would also receive a producion fee. Leonard also hired his then-wife, Willetta, as Assistant to the Producer (himself).

Route 66 combined two genres: the road picture and the anthology drama.[56] The former was both simple and elastic: two young men—Tod Stiles (Martin Milner) and Buz Murdock (George Maharis[57])—tool around the country in a red (actually brown) 1960 Corvette and become involved in dramatic conflicts at every stop.[58] Buz was a fighter from Hell's Kitchen, Tod a Yale-educated scion of a ruined businessman whose only legacy is the car his father willed him. The two were opposites who attracted not only trouble but an audience. Halfway through the third season, Maharis departed, and his place was taken by Glenn Corbett playing Lincoln "Linc" Case, a former

Army Ranger who had completed a tour of duty in Vietnam. His backstory was not only a manifestation of Silliphant's growing concern over American involvement in Southeast Asia, it is believed to be the first continuing character in a U.S. network TV show who reflected the emerging Vietnam experience.

At the same time, the people with whom Stiles, Murdock, and Case become involved at each detour have their own stories, which the travelers may or may not help resolve. This made each episode something of a stand-alone drama. The concept is Zen-like: are Tod, Buz, and Linc characters other people's stories? Or are other people characters in Tod's, Buz's, and Linc's story? The blend was a clever way to broaden the protagonists' characters by throwing them into conflict with a constantly changing array of guest stars.

That show drew a roster of the finest established and up-and-coming talent of the era: Edward Asner ("Welcome to the Wedding," "Shoulder the Sky, My Lad," "The Mud Nest," "The Opponent," "The Man on the Monkey Board"), Beulah Bondi ("Burning for Burning"), James Caan ("And the Cat Jumped Over the Moon"), Joan Crawford ("Same Picture, Different Frame"), Robert Duvall ("Birdcage on My Foot," "The Newborn," "Suppose I Said I Was the Queen of Spain"), Barbara Eden ("Where There's a Will, There's a Way," Parts 1 and 2), Anne Francis ("A Month of Sundays," "Play It Glissando"), Tammy Grimes ("Where are the Sounds of Celli Brahms?"), Joey Heatherton ("Three Sides"), David Janssen ("One Tiger to a Hill"), Ben Johnson ("A Long Piece of Mischief," "Like a Motherless Child"), Boris Karloff ("Lizard's Leg and Owlet's Wing"), Buster Keaton ("Journey to Nineveh"), DeForest Kelley ("1800 Days to Justice," "The Clover Throne"), George Kennedy ("Black November"), Cloris Leachman ("Love is a Skinny Kid"), Jack Lord ("Play It Glissando"), Tina Louise ("I'm Here to Kill a King"), Dorothy Malone ("Fly Away Home," Parts 1 and 2), E.G. Marshall ("Three Sides"), Lee Marvin ("Mon Petit Chou," "Sheba"), Walter Matthau ("Eleven, the Hard Way"), Darren McGavin ("The Opponent"), Lois Nettleton ("Suppose I Said I Was the Queen of Spain," "Some of the People, Some of the Time," "The Opponent"), Julie Newmar ("Give the Old Cat a Tender Mouse," "How Much a Pound is Albatross"), Dan O'Herlihy ("To Walk with the Serpent"), Susan Oliver ("Fifty Miles From Home," "Hello and Goodbye," "Welcome to Amity"), Suzanne Pleshette ("Blue Murder," "The Strengthening Angels"), Robert Redford ("First Class Mouliak"), Michael Rennie ("Fly Away Home," Parts 1 and 2), Burt Reynolds ("Love is a Skinny Kid"), Janice Rule ("But What Do You Do in March?," "Once to Every Man," "A Lance of Straw"), William Shatner ("Build Your Houses with Their Backs to the Sea"), Martin Sheen ("...and the Cat Jumped Over the Moon"), Sylvia Sidney ("Child of a Night," "Like a Motherless Child"), Lois Smith ("Who In His Right Mind Needs a Nice Girl?," "Only By Cunning Glimpses," "Go Read the River," "Incident on a Bridge"),

Rod Steiger ("Welcome to the Wedding"), Ethel Waters ("Goodnight, Sweet Blues"), and Tuesday Weld ("Love is a Skinny Kid") among dozens more.

"The series did attract some of the best actors from both New York and Hollywood," Silliphant agreed. "I remember Joan Crawford called us personally and asked if she could appear in an episode. I wrote a show just for her: 'Same Picture, Different Frame.' But we must remember that we had one of the most brilliant casting talents in the business working on the show: Marion Dougherty. And she was working out of New York where her judgment was based on performance, not fan mail."

The casting and production (see the next chapter) were helped immeasurably by two things. First: CBS gave Leonard and Silliphant an order for twenty-six one-hour episodes at a single time, allowing them to plan ahead and amortize budgets; second: then they left them alone. Neither happens any more.

"Bert... and I had creative control in our contracts," Silliphant told fellow writer William Froug. "We had right of approval. The networks didn't. This was the last time that ever happened.... . We were able to force the networks to put our work on the air. Now that gave us a sense of exhilaration and freedom, and responsibility. In those four years I think I really learned my craft because there were no rules. There was nothing I couldn't do. Nothing I couldn't experiment with, and it was such a heady thing, and such an inspirational thing, that I look at some of those scripts today with wonder."[59]

Even though the network couldn't control content, they held the on/off switch over broadcast, and this occasionally brought them into conflict with Silliphant's experimentation and Leonard's protectiveness. The most bizarre instance involved the May 5, 1961, episode called "The Newborn." Said Silliphant, "I wanted to see how George and Marty could help an Indian girl about to have a child in the desert of New Mexico. How do you help a woman bear her child when you're miles from medical facilities and have nothing but the Corvette? The problem centered around the umbilical cord: how do you sever it without a knife (shoelaces, obviously) and what do you do about the placenta, etc. etc.? Well, the network went *ape* when I devoted about six minutes of prime time to this area. They insisted we cut all that *stuff* out. We refused, once more waved our contract, and I fired off a memo accusing CBS types of having been born without navels, hence their sensitivity to that little hollow above their balls. We almost won that one. *We* didn't cut anything out and they put the episode on—but *they* cut out the footage and we had to run end titles for about four minutes."[60]

Not only did Silliphant write *Route 66* from his heart, he wrote it on the road, traveling to locations just ahead of the production caravan. He would scope out interesting filming sites, meet local residents, hear their tales, and then sequester himself in a motel room to churn out the pages that Leonard and company would shoot when they caught up with him, by which time he was gone. Life was a succession of motel rooms, and he was not always alone in them. "Remember, this was a time when the orgies were going on," said Tiana Alexandra-Silliphant, whom he married in 1974. "He was in a different city every two weeks. He was casting, and his producer was screwing around too. It's a fun life. You get fans. Every day your ego is going to be massaged. If you're a writer, you may not have the money like directors, but women think you can write them a part. Little do they know, don't fuck the writer!"[61]

Each fifty-two-minute script took an average of nine days to write while, at the same time, he did rewrites and polishes on previous pages, and discussed new stories with Leonard. The leapfrogging went on for the entire run.

"When we were doing *Naked City* and *Route 66*," he explained, "Bert Leonard and I were accountable to no one except ourselves. We would go out to lunch and we would say, 'We need a story for next week. What are we going to do?' 'Well, let's see; what haven't we done?' 'We haven't done anything about jury fixing. Why don't we do something about jury fixing?' 'Okay, that's not a bad idea. Now let's see. We haven't done a story for two weeks about a girl. And we'll get so and so to play the part. Just a minute, I'll call her and see.' Now you pick up the phone and call X and say, 'Stirling wants to write a *Route 66* for you.' She says 'Groovy, what's the story?' 'We don't know, we're just sitting here kicking it around. But are you going to be free on such-and-such a date?' So we'd book the shows this way. We've had the best actors and actresses in the business and we got them without scripts. We know who the actor or the actress is, and we'd write for them. That was what made it so great, because I was able to write for specific people.[62]

"The characters came out of the writing—the casting then came out of the character. For example, I wrote an episode called 'Kiss the Maiden All Forlorn' which required a debonair actor of clearly established class—and Marion signed Douglas Fairbanks, Jr. for the part. Bert Leonard flew him from London to the location in Texas. In the case of the two-parter, 'Fly Away Home,'[63] directed by Arthur Hiller in Phoenix, we were so far behind in getting scripts ready that I *told* the plotline to some of the stars we had decided we wanted in it—in this case thinking of them almost simultaneously with the story. We wanted Dorothy Malone and Michael Rennie and a couple of other fine New York stage actors, so I called each of them on the phone and 'talked' the story—and such was their confidence in the show that all of them accepted without having seen the script. Actually, when they arrived on location in Phoenix, they only had the first hour (of two) in hand. I was still writing the second hour in a hotel room in Phoenix and feeding pages out to the location."

Silliphant admitted to giving his guest stars the juiciest parts, "as witness Anne Francis in 'A Month of Sundays' or Julie Newmar in 'How Much a Pound is Albatross' or Tuesday Weld in 'Love is a Skinny Kid' or Bob Duvall in 'Bird Cage on My Foot.' But look also at George Maharis's cry of anguish when, at the end of 'A Month of Sundays,' Anne Francis whispers, 'I was alive, wasn't I? I lived.' And she dies and George screams—over the honky-tonk carnival sounds behind him. No! Without George and the impact of Anne's death upon *him* the story would not have been as affecting."

With such stunning guest stars, wasn't there a risk in taking the series leads for granted? Not at all. "I never felt impeded by or burdened with our two main characters," Silliphant stated, "and, yes, we could have done many of the stories without them—as witness the fact that for almost two seasons I had to write without having George Maharis with us any longer. But the stories, somehow, worked *better* with Marty and George involved. In a sense, *they* were the viewer—bringing the viewer into a new town, meeting new people, becoming involved, having the involvement either affect or not affect their own search for identity. Rather than feel they were a drag on the stories, I can tell you clearly that I would have been lost without them and their reactions and interplay."

Tales of Silliphant's efficiency were legendary. In one, *Route 66*'s production manager, Sam Manners, asked if he had a spare script that they could shoot in the same city where they were because a company move to another location would cost $75,000. Silliphant didn't have anything to send, so he wrote an original one-hour show in three days.[64] Likewise, Silliphant and Leonard were not averse to saving money in other ways. Depending on how the budget looked for any given week, Silliphant could be paid as little as $902 or as much as $3,340 for a script, plus customary residuals.[65] (Ownership of the series would become a contention in future years.)

The show attracted its share of fans quite apart from the beefcake appeal of its stars. One such aficionado was David Morell, then in high school, who sent Silliphant a handwritten letter at Screen Gems asking how to do what he does. "One week later," Morell said, "I received an answer from him—two densely typed pages that began with an apology for taking so long to get back to me. 'I'd have written to you sooner,' he said, 'but when your letter arrived, I was out at sea in a boat.' He revealed no secrets and refused to look at anything I had written, but he did tell me this: The way to be a writer is to write, and write, and keep writing." Morrell did just that, and, to date, has published over thirty-five books, among them *First Blood* (1972), which became the basis of the *Rambo* movies. Morrell and Silliphant became friends and, "All these years and millions of words later," he says, "I'm still writing."[66]

"For me and my friends," wrote another admirer, journalist Michael Ventura, "*Route 66* was not a television show, it was a promise. A weekly training film. A way out and through and over. [Tod and Buz were] looking not for adventure, but—and they were quite explicit about this—for meaning. Remember that this was 1962, when pundits were saying that rebellion was done in America, that dissent was over, and that kids were interested in nothing but conformity and money. So imagine how it sounded when, in an episode called 'Go Read the River,' an engineer, John Larch, said: 'Somewhere, somehow, a simple beautiful thing, a single morality, a single set of standards was smashed like an atom into 10 million separate pieces. Now, what's right for a man can be wrong for his business. And what's right for his business can be wrong for his country. And what's right for his country can be wrong for the world.'"[67]

Route 66 earned a reputation as a "dark" show—this was before "edgy" became an adjective and well before it became a cliché—not just because of the personal changes its creators were undergoing, but because of those that were pounding away at the country. The 1950s were dead; the 1960s brought Camelot, assassinations, the blossoming of the Civil Rights struggle, and the emergence of an unholy war in Vietnam. America was maturing. Confirmed Silliphant, "We [dealt] with ideas which were out there on the cutting edge at the time and, with few exceptions, we never had a moment's problem with CBS. With two notable exceptions: 'The Newborn,' which I wrote, and 'Don't Tread on Me,' (aired as "To Walk with a Serpent") an episode written by Leonard Freeman, who was producing for us that season. Leonard's story savaged the John Birch Society and it turned out that somebody high up in the General Motors hierarchy (Chevrolet bought half the show for the entire four years) must have been a Bircher, because all hell broke loose. Jim Aubrey (head of CBS) flew out to meet with Bert and me and demanded we withdraw the episode, but Bert pulled the contract, which CBS had signed, granting us total creative freedom, the network's power [being] only that of not exhibiting the episode, but having to pay for it whether they approved it or not. So we won that one. Other than these two incidents—and one more beef about the violence in an LA street gang story I wrote ('Most Vanquished, Most Victorious')—and we won that one too—we sailed through the seasons."

Ultimately, the series was a catharsis for Silliphant as well as a crash course in writing, something that came easily to him—perhaps too easily for him to respect his own talent. That changed when he looked back in his later years.

"I have always felt that the most original—and, if I may be permitted the conceit, the most effective in the sense of touching the feelings of many, many other people—writing I have down in the filmed media was done in the period 1960 to 1964 when I wrote the majority of the one-hour *Route 66* filmed-on-location shows for CBS. These shows caught the American psyche of that period about as accurately as it could be caught. I wrote all of them out of an intense personal motivation, each was a work of passion and conviction. It was actually (if truth be known) a dramatization of my personal four-year psychiatric exhumation of all the shit that was bubbling inside me, and it's hard to assign that one to another writer. There were few of the stories I wrote for *Route 66* during those four years which did not spring out of my own life."

A painful case in point was the 100th episode called "The Stone Guest," which starred Jo Van Fleet as a single woman whose ill-chosen affair with a married man, Lee Phillips, is exposed when they are trapped in a mine cave-in. The episode, which aired on November 7, 1963, "with its bitter attitude toward marriage, is another example," Silliphant said. "My marriage [to Ednamarie Patella] at that time was a battle zone, so I wrote 'The Stone Guest' out of quiet fury."[68]

Because the episode holds so much significance, it bears examination. Its inspiration was a fair-sized shouting match the Silliphants were having and, in the middle of it, Silliphant went for his typewriter, saying, "Wait a minute, I've got to get this down." The marriage lasted nine more months. In the story, Tod and Linc get jobs in a Colorado mining town: Linc in the mine and Tod, atypically, working stage crew for the local opera company's production of *Don Giovanni*. When a mine cave-in traps a spinster, Hazel Quine (Jo Van Fleet) with the town's Lothario, Ben Belden (Lee Philips), the mismatched pair is forced to confront their pasts while hoping rescue workers can save them. At the same time, Belden's neglected wife, Nora (Marion Ross), is giving birth to their daughter alone; his school-aged son, David, has fought to uphold his father's unwarranted honor in a playground brawl; and Hazel is strangely liberated by the desperation.

It's a busy script but all of its plotlines converge in the need to face Truth (in the existential sense). Did Silliphant model the philandering, cost-cutting, belligerent Belden on himself? Did he use Ednamarie as a template for the lonely, desperate, self-sacrificing Hazel? Or is Beldon's abandoned wife closer to his sense of her (Nora confesses to having babies as a way to hold onto her husband)? In their time trapped, Belden comes to see Hazel as a redeemer for his misspent life, but what will he come back to on the surface? Did Silliphant regard forced confinement as the only way to reconcile the events that were destroying his marriage? The mine collapse is the result of Belden's shoddy construction; was Silliphant accepting blame for his shoddy marriage (that nevertheless produced two children)? Tod's explanation to David of the plot of *Don Giovanni* is a way of explaining (though not excusing) the character of David's father; was Silliphant trying to reconcile with his own children? In the end, Belden sets off a huge dynamite charge in an attempt to free himself and Hazel, although "free" can be taken both as enabling them to leave the mine as well as to end their haunted lives. It turns out to be the latter.

On August 13, 1964, Ednamarie (40) sued Silliphant (45) for divorce, claiming that, since 1960, he had spent "over $100,000" on "a dozen" women with whom he was having extramarital affairs.[69] The divorce was granted on

September 30, 1964, but the details of the settlement would drag on for years. Even after the decree, Ednamarie harbored resentment not only for Silliphant but for their daughter. The tension grew to the point where, according to sources, she once attempted suicide by cutting her wrists, not in her own bathtub, as might be expected, but in their daughter, Dayle's.

As usual, Silliphant worked out this conflict on the page. "This is the truest thing I will ever tell you," he said of his *Route 66* episode, "Kiss the Maiden, All Forlorn." "Why did I write it? Because my sixteen-year-old daughter announced one morning she was going to become a Catholic nun—the order of BVM—Blessed Virgin Mary—in Peoria.[70] Gulp! And she did. I had to deal with this. It was not easy. So I researched the subject. Until that moment I had never, never talked to a nun. I wouldn't have known what to say to one. The outfits intimidated me. But by going to several orders and *learning*, I found that the Church is not out hustling prospective sisters. You really have to have a calling to arrive at the decision my daughter had arrived at. This gave me new understanding and gave a credibility to the script, which had I written it from the outside, rather than out of my own anguish at having to surrender a daughter to an institution I had always regarded with distrust, still bearing in mind the screams of those who died during the Inquisition, of all the hundreds of thousands of Jews who went to their deaths, unprotected by Rome, would have not had the power this finished episode had."[71]

Midway through the third season, George Maharis left the series. Various statements at the time attributed his departure to displeasure with the grueling production schedule, relentless travel, and health issues.[72] Although his replacement, Glenn Corbett, was also attractive and competent, there was no way he could slip into the backstory that Maharis and Milner enjoyed, and the series was canceled after its fourth season.

Suddenly it was over. Not just *Route 66*, but the way in which television was produced. The networks had long bristled at putting up the money for the shows they ran only to have the producers, and not them, control the content. And if not the producers, the sponsors. Beginning with FCC Commissioner Newton B. Minow's 1961 observation that television was a "vast wasteland" of sub-level programming, both critics and politicians went on the attack—critics for quality, and politicians, as they are wont to do, for publicity.

"[Television] changed," Silliphant noted," because Senator Dodd[73] brought those ridiculous accusations against the networks back in the sixties that we were corrupting the youth of America and we were doing all kinds of naughty things and making people violent and inspiring crime by our comic strip stuff. The networks, instead of fighting that, kissed ass. They let it happen for a very good reason: they wanted control of the programming."[74]

And they got it. Before long, network executives whose hands-on experience had been limited to changing the channel were demanding to approve not just finished teleplays but story ideas, casting, locations, production crew, and even the costumes and wallpaper. Instead of deciding in one pitch meeting what script to write, the process began to take weeks. Focus groups replaced intuition and experience. Inspiration and diversity suffered. Today, despite having 500+ channels, television content is controlled and engineered by six huge communications conglomerates, none of which, thanks to FCC deregulation, has any responsibility to serve the public.

As popular as it was, *Route 66* had to end somewhere, which it did with a two-parter called "Where There's a Will, There's a Way" on March 6 and 13, 1964. Tod and Linc wind up in Tampa, Florida among an eccentric family (including Chill Wills, Nina Foch, Patrick O'Neal, and Barbara Eden) fighting over an estate. Having toured the country for four years, the pair head off to Houston, but independently, their odyssey completed and they, themselves, presumably now fit to face the world.

As uncertain as their futures might have been, the fate of *Route 66* became even more vague. After a summer of reruns, it faded from network schedules and went into syndication on local stations. Through a succession of sales, swaps, and licenses that would make a Gordian knot look frayed, Bert Leonard, as best as can be determined, sold off various aspects of the show—rerun, foreign, remake, feature film, home video—whenever he needed money. Likewise, Silliphant may or may not have sold Leonard his ownership shares (but not his residual rights as co-creator and writer); the paperwork seems to have vanished along with a clear chain of title.

The location of the original negatives, so essential to preservation, has also been hard to pin down. For years, tapes of episodes were at a premium; many circulated on Betamax and VHS among fans who recorded the show on rerun and syndication. Even Silliphant, who presumably had access to pristine courtesy copies, had a hard time prying them from CBS, and his correspondence includes letters reminding friends who'd borrowed them to be sure to bring them back.[75] His collection includes off-air dubs like anyone else. Exhaustive research by television historian Stephen Bowie[76] reveals that, toward the end of his life, Leonard transferred his copyrights to former attorney James Tierney in settlements of debts totaling $1.5 million. The video rights to *Route 66* were carved out to the distribution company Shout! Factory, after an earlier gambit with CBS Home Video, and *Naked City* went to Image Entertainment. The TV remake rights to *Route 66* were licensed by Columbia Pictures Television, which produced a reboot in 1993 that aired on NBC. The new series starred James Wilder ("Nick Lewis") who, like Tod Stiles, inherits his father's Corvette and picks up a drifter, Dan Cortese ("Arthur Clark"), and together they have adventures. More precisely, they had four adventures, because NBC pulled the series when it didn't immediately catch on. Since then, the rights have been in flux.[77] Sony claimed TV distribution rights under license from CBS; for a while they were under lien by Leonard's attorney James B. Tierney;[78] in 2007 they were acquired by Kirk Hallam of Roxbury Entertainment;[79] and in 2011 Hallam disclosed that he was in partnership with the show's video distributor, Shout! Factory, on a TV remake and possibly a feature film.[80] He also had acquired the finegrain dupe negatives ("They're in vaults all up and down the east coast") but decided against using the original negatives that were still in Sony's vaults, a choice that created controversy within fandom when he issued the first DVD sets through Shout!.[81]

Bert Leonard fell on hard times in his later years but he never gave up; like *Route 66*, the life was an open road full of promise. He produced a number of TV movies and feature films. One of his pet projects was *River of Gold*, a Rin-Tin-Tin story that parked briefly at Disney before the budget scared the studio off. By the 1990s, at financial odds and in declining health, he lived for a while with stunt coordinator-director Max Kleven, then his daughter Victoria, then his daughter Gina. Soon the cancer that had taken his larynx returned and ate away at the rest of his body, but not his spirit. He died on October 14, 2006 at the age of 84.

Route 66 remains the iconic television series of the 1960s. Its strength is that, like the highway itself, one does not need to follow the series from the start in order to enjoy its drama. Each episode is a separate experience, and the sum of them is a portrait of a nation in transition, aimless perhaps, but always headed into the future with a seductive blend of optimism and pragmatism—not to mention a golden era when gasoline was 29¢ a gallon.

5

Under the Hood

ON STIRLING SILLIPHANT'S PILOT SCRIPT dated October 27, 1959, appears the title *The Searchers*. While there has been speculation that he later changed it to avoid confusion with John Ford's 1956 masterpiece, he and Bert Leonard might just as accurately have called it *The Seekers* if that's where their minds were headed. But Interstate 66, which had opened in 1926 and ran from Chicago to Los Angeles, was called variously the Mother Road, Will Rogers Highway, and the Main Street of America. Route 66 was a ribbon of both commerce and romance, the lifeline of a nation. Even when the show veered away from its namesake and into other cities, its mission stayed intact. Travelers drove it to the beat of Bobby Troup's 1946 hit song "(Get Your Kicks) On Route 66," first recorded by Nat "King" Cole. But it was Nelson Riddle's jazzy piano and string version, orchestrated by Gil Grau, that glided into television history.

In fact, Silliphant's pilot script is so specific that it calls for just the kind of theme that Riddle would write. An inspection of his teleplays for the series reveals that he was, in essence, directing the show on paper, not just the music, but tone, verisimilitude, and sometimes even the street corner.

"Frequently, when I was writing episodes for *Route 66* at the rate of one every nine days," he said, "I would shorthand the exposition by telling the director to, for example, 'give us a three-minute fight here, which makes the fight in *Shane* look like a Girl Scout dance.'" It was clear from the start that he was in charge. At the front of his pilot script, which was subtitled "The Wolf Tree," (which aired on October 7, 1960, as "Black November"), is a list of "don'ts" that he wanted the series to observe:

1. No smoking or displays of any type of tobacco product.
2. No use of matches or mechanical lighters.
3. No use of beer or alcoholic beverages of any kind.
4. No drunkenness.
5. No shaving or display of shaving equipment.
6. No derogatory treatment of food or food products, household appliances, or automobiles.
7. When such props are required, no use of identifiable brand features of any food, drug, or appliance products, either on labels or in peculiarity or uniqueness of shape or design.

Although some of these cautions were ultimately ignored, they show the producers' awareness that the series had to appeal to sponsors as well as viewers, not only during its network run but later in syndication, and they didn't want to drive away any potential advertisers with conflicts of interest.

One of the most surprising discoveries in the pilot script is that Buz and Tod aren't driving a Corvette: their wheels are described only as "a sports car." And although many people recall the car as being red, the series was shot in black and white, so there's no way to tell it was actually brown.

Running slightly longer, at seventy-eight pages, than usual hour-long teleplays, which usually go between fifty-eight and sixty-four pages, "The Wolf Tree" had the task of not only establishing the main characters but also setting their motivation and milieu. Here Silliphant is clever; only *after* Buz gets into a brawl is it revealed that he has a roughneck heritage (even though Tod is the one who gets battered most of the time), and not until page thirty-two is it noted that Tod's father gave him his car before he died. The rest is left to considerable development and occasional revelation in succeeding episodes.

Like *Naked City*, *Route 66* was filmed on location. Unlike *Naked City*, however, *Route 66*'s locations spanned the contiguous 48 states and Canada. The places and people (many credited at the end of the episodes in which they appear) offered the kind of detail that a writer stuck in LA could never know. For "Child of a Night," set in Georgia, which aired January 3, 1964, from a teleplay dated two months earlier on November 9, 1963, (which gives some indication of how close to airdate they were shooting), Silliphant includes a page thirty-three note to associate producer Sam Manners, "I found this road out Victory Drive, out toward Bonaventure Cemetery on the way to Fort Pulaski…" In a note on page 55 in "A Cage in Search of a Bird," involving a flashback sequence in modern-day Denver (written June 3, 1963, and airing on a leisurely November 29, 1963, thanks to summer reruns), he again asks Manners:

> Now, Sam, comes the trick of the century. If you can manage to clear this vital traffic area of today's Denver for one mag-

nificent shot of a 1930 Buick—alone—traveling across the Civic Center—with the Capitol in the b.g.—you deserve an Emmy for Creative Management. If you can't, then, as soon as Julie says, "… up toward the Capitol," we cut out of shot, in any event…

In this script, as in others, Silliphant establishes location by describing camera moves ("a long tracking shot from high, high up, starting at the golden dome of the State Capitol, then panning over to Broadway, where we pick up the tiny speck, which is the Corvette…") and even calls for close-ups, two-shots, and angles favoring one character in the frame. This is precisely the thing that modern screenwriting gurus caution their students never to do, but it was the way that *Route 66* kept the visions of its creators intact regardless of how many directors worked on the show.[82]

The real trick in writing a series is keeping the main characters interesting enough to hold the audience, deep enough to challenge the actors, and consistent enough to sustain the germ of the show. Revealing too much too soon blows the show's wad; being too vague makes it frustrating. Silliphant cleverly meets this task by dropping hints about Tod's, Buz's, and Linc's past whenever they meet a new character who inspires a revelation. "It comes to me now that, with all the places I've been, I still haven't found a place where I'd like to wake up every morning for the rest of my life," confesses Tod in "A Cage in Search of a Bird," which is a particularly rich show. In "Like This it Means Father…Like This—Bitter…Like This—Tiger" (written November 24, 1963; aired January 17, 1964), it is revealed that Linc spent time in Saigon and learned Chinese. And so on, layer by layer, week by week. The proof of these decisions can be found in the finished shows, and a selection of them reveals the alchemy that made *Route 66* the testament of its times.

It is impossible to comment on all seventy-three episodes that Stirling Silliphant wrote; numerous books and fansites address the series with insight and passion. For now, some of the more notable entries—gleaned from conversations with Silliphant and the pleasure of multiple screenings—include (caution: spoilers):

"Black November" (pilot airdate: October 7, 1960): *Seeking a shortcut back to the main highway, Buz and Tod are stranded with a broken axle in a small Mississippi town. Their presence sets off a melt-down involving Caleb Garth (Everett Sloane), the man who owns everything and everybody; his haunted son, Paul (Keir Dullea); a storeowner, Jim Slade (Whit Bissell); Slade's terrified daughter, Jenny (Patty McCormack); and various townspeople, all of whom seem to have something to hide. They do: the town's deadly secret is that, years ago, Garth murdered a German youth as payback for his own son's death in World War II, and then killed the preacher who tried to protect the German. It all took place under a huge wolf tree whose shade has kept everything beneath it from flourishing. Once the truth is out, the tree is felled, the Corvette gets its axle fixed, and Tod and Buz hit the road again.*

Blessed with a superb cast that also includes Malcolm Atterbury and George Kennedy, shot by Ernesto Caparros (who also shot *The Miracle Worker*), and rich with such production values as crane shots and night photography, this episode does a great deal of heavy narrative lifting. Philip Leacock's controlled direction of Silliphant's detailed script allows the fine cast to flourish. Casting note: Silliphant and Leonard hired Dullea instead another newcomer named Robert Redford.

"A Month of Sundays" (airdate: September 22, 1961). *Broadway star Arline Simms (Anne Francis) has returned to her hometown of Butte, Montana, to die. At first cold and distant, she slowly warms up as Buz pursues her, yet refuses his marriage proposal without telling him why. When Tod learns of her illness, he urges Arline to marry Buz anyway. She does, but collapses shortly after the ceremony and dies, exhorting, "I was alive! I really was alive!" as Buz cries in anguish.*

Francis delivers a solid performance that ranges from bitchy and angry to warm and sensitive, and director Arthur Hiller encourages openness from all the actors. Among dialogue gems is Tod's advice to Arline, "Only when we lose our fear of death can we defeat it—and we can make every hour of our existence really count."

"Birdcage on My Foot" (airdate: October 13, 1961): *When Tod and Buz see Arnie (Robert Duvall) trying to steal the Corvette, they want to press charges, but, when they realize that he is a drug addict, they try to intervene in his recovery.*

Saying that Robert Duvall is a fearless actor is like saying that water is wet, and in this early role he sidesteps the cliché mannerisms of movie junkies and shows a vulnerability that binds the entire episode together. Elliot Silverstein's unflinching direction allows Milner and Maharis to step up to Duvall's level.

"The Newborn" (airdate: May 5, 1961): *Frank Ivy (Albert Dekker) holds a pregnant Indian girl, Kawna (Arline Sax), hostage so she can deliver his dead son's child on his property, after which he*

*intends to keep her from seeing the baby again. When she escapes
Ivy's grasp, Tod and Buz find themselves her custodian and must
deliver her child in the middle of nowhere. Kawna dies, and Tod
and Buz turn the baby over to her tribe as Ivy fumes.*

Cited (above) by Silliphant as the victim of CBS censorship, "The Newborn"—
which also features Robert Duvall as a psychotic ranch hand bent on killing
Tod and Buz—not only lacks a coherent childbirth sequence, but Duvall's
accidental death happens as the camera pans away carelessly rather than discretely. Arthur Hiller coaches Dekker into a stern, clenched performance.
Contrary to Silliphant's recollection, the show (seen on Columbia House
video) runs to full length.

> "And the Cat Jumped Over the Moon" (airdate: December 15,
> 1961): *Social Worker Chuck Briner (Milt Kamen) dies when he
> fails off a rooftop trying to fix a "hit" ordered by Packy (Mar-
> tin Sheen), the scrappy leader of the Missiles street gang. Packy
> and his boys are bent on killing Johnny (James Caan) because he
> left the streets to go with Marva (Susan Silo), whom Packy now
> deems his property. A game of rooftop chicken between Johnny
> and Packy ends when Packy blinks and the gang breaks up over
> his cowardice.*

Youth gangs had captivated TV and movie audiences since *The Blackboard
Jungle* (1955) and *West Side Story* (1961) but Silliphant, adapting a story by
Frank L. Moss, adds the twist of making the bad guy a psychopath. Set in
Philadelphia, the rooftop scenes are harrowing and authentic-looking. Sil-
liphant unfolds the story indirectly—the viewer has to play close attention
to wrest narrative clues from the action—and Elliott Siverstein keeps it edgy.
Notable as Sheen's first TV role, an early role for Caan, and for the presence
of Susan Silo, who later became a highly a respected casting agent. Nelson
Riddle's jazz score is particularly effective.

> "Lizard's Leg and Owlet's Wing" (airdate: October 26, 1962):
> *Boris Karloff, Peter Lorre, and Lon Chaney, Jr. meet at a Chicago
> motel where Buz and Tod are working. They want to, in Karloff's
> words, "strike out in a new direction: adult horror" for TV, and
> they test their theory and make-up on unsuspecting women. A
> Halloween show, this is not just a vehicle for three venerable hor-
> ror movie stars, it's a way to take a swipe at television program-
> ming executives, and it succeeds at every level.*

Journeyman actor-director Robert Gist gets out of the way of the scenery chewing, and Silliphant covers his bases by writing a script note describing a scene in which Chaney, made up as his trademarked werewolf, frightens a group of secretaries: "Milk them, Bob—with individual coverage of Lila, Beth, and the others—spilling drinks, screaming, fainting, etc." Martita Hunt, more arch than usual, adds a lovely turn. A splendid example of Silliphant's ability to write for specific actors when they're booked to do a show, he describes Lorre as "wearing dark glasses and his lightweight trench coat is up around his ears in the murky manner of a Balkan intelligence operative" and creates such dialogue as, "My boss always says a high voice goes with a low income."

> "A Lance of Straw" (airdate: October 14, 1960): *Passing through Grand Isle, Louisiana, Buz and Tod sign aboard a shrimp boat run by budding feminist Charlotte Duval (Janice Rule) whose jealous suitor, Jean Boussard (Nico Minardis), tries to warn them off. The shrimping is good, but a hurricane intervenes and Charlotte manages to save Jean's boat. Having proven her proficiency in a man's world, Charlotte at last accepts Jean's proposal as Tod and Buz drive on to their next adventure.*

Directed with an eye toward action by Roger Kay, the second episode in the series stresses fighting and a storm at sea on top of the sexual tension unleashed by sultry Rule. At this point the series had not yet gained its form—it rings heavier on plot than character—but it clearly displays its strength in its location settings.[83]

> "Across Walnuts and Wine" (airdate: November 2, 1962): *The unexpected arrival of Autumn Ely (Nina Foch) in the Oregon City home of her sister Maggie Carter (Betty Field) and her husband Van (James Dunn) upsets her sullen nephew Mike (Robert Walker, Jr.) who actually owns the house and is in the process of evicting them. Mike is already at odds with the town tough (Dick Theis) for dating Theis's sister, and it develops that Autumn, who is a teacher as well as a religious zealot, was fired from her job, feels useless, and wants better for Michael.*

Directed crisply by Bert Leonard (the only time he directed for the series), this is a brooding story of shame, isolation, responsibility, and redemption. Buz and Tod serve as narrative catalysts more than story participants, but the balance works as the character drama escalates.

"Somehow It Gets to Be Tomorrow" (airdate: February 15, 1963): *Driving through Corpus Christi, Texas, a solo Tod is latched onto by a conniving orphan, Joby Paxton (Roger Mobley, the go-to child actor in the 1960s), who wants Tod to help him and his annoying kid sister, Susie (Leslye Hunter), escape their foster home with social worker Evan Corelli (Martin Balsam) in pursuit. More specifically, they want Tod to be their adoptive father.*

A wise script, part bleeding heart and part hard truth, it touches all the emotional bases in honest ways. The engaging Balsam may spout aphorisms ("You know, Stiles, there's a saving grace about a dilemma: you can't get tossed on more than two horns") and teach gentle lessons, but in the end reality wins out and nobody gets off easily in this bold, downbeat episode directed by David Lowell Rich.

"The Stone Guest" (airdate: November 8, 1963): Cited elsewhere by Silliphant.

"Kiss the Maiden, All Forlorn" (airdate: April 13, 1962) *Fugitive embezzler Charles Clayton (Douglas Fairbanks, Jr.) returns to America to see his daughter, attracting the law and involving Tod and Buz in a kidnapping (by Michael Tolan, Elena Verdugo) contrived to throw the police (James Brown, who starred in Bert Leonard's Rin-Tin-Tin TV series) and press (Walter Hill) off the scent. He cannot understand why his daughter, Bonnie (Zina Bethune), is becoming a postulate nun.*

Silliphant admitted that he wrote the show to work through his concern over his daughter Dayle's decision to go to convent. It's an emotionally complex script, starting with Fairbanks, who is no crook with a heart of gold but a cynic who even tries to buy off Mother Superior (Beatrice Straight).[84] Is Bonnie atoning for her father's sins? Or does she indeed have the calling? It's Fairbanks's show, and his scenes with Bethune will tear your heart out. In the end, it's Silliphant's understanding that makes it ring true. Once again, Tod and Buz are mostly along for the ride.

"Between Hello and Goodbye" (airdate: May 11, 1962): *Tod gets involved with a troubled woman, Chris (Susan Oliver), not knowing that the destructive blonde is a dual personality with her repressed, dark-haired sister, Clair.*

Although the condition is obvious to anyone who had seen *The Three Faces of Eve* (1957) or read *Dr. Jekyll and Mr. Hyde*, Silliphant and director David Lowell Rich do an effective juggling act that gives Oliver a vivid showcase for her character's psychosis. One especially riveting scene has Chris launch a tirade about the social and financial pressures that befall married couples (given the torment building in Silliphant's own marriage, it's a doubly remarkable scene). But because the words came from a mentally ill person, nobody noticed its subversiveness.

> "A Fury Slinging Flame" (airdate: December 30, 1960): *Scientist Mark Christopher (Leslie Nielsen) leads a community of families into Carlsbad Caverns, California with every intention of living there until World War III, which he says will start in two days, subsides. Tod and Buz are drawn in because Christopher gave them his house trailer en route, and a newspaper science reporter, Paula Shay (Fay Spain), latches onto the story as the press gathers to await zero hour.*

The Cold War comes to prime time the same year that Soviet Premier Nikita Khruschev sank the Paris summit peace talks, U.S. flyer Francis Gary Powers was shot down during a spy mission over Russia, and John F. Kennedy defeated Richard Nixon for the Presidency. Although America wouldn't start building home fallout shelters until the October, 1962 Cuban Missile Crisis, this episode reflected the public's growing nuclear paranoia. Director Elliot Silverstein objectively keeps a lid on what could have become farce, and Nielsen relishes a prolonged monologue that's a model of controlled insanity. James Brown appears as the stern park ranger trying to quell the whirlwind. Actual reporters Larry Barbier, Bill Fiset, Marlin Haines and Bob Lardine appear in publicity-inspired cameos. The title comes from a poem by Tennyson. Spoiler Alert: The world didn't end.

> "Mon Petit Chou" (airdate: November 24, 1961): *Lee Marvin appears as Ryan (ID'd as "Glenn Ryan") who is so possessive of the French cabaret singer, Perette Dijon (Macha Meril), whom he is building into a star, that he refuses to see that she loves him. Moreover, he won't admit that he loves her (he was devastated when his previous protégé jilted him). Only when Tod beats the stuffing out of him does he accept the truth and turn his pain into affection.*

The odd aspect of this episode is that is really doesn't need Tod or Buz. It's one of a number of stories (see also "One Tiger to a Hill") in which a central character hides his sensitivity behind a veneer of violence. Marvin is commanding in a complex role, and Bert Remsen, as his friend and chauffeur, Higgy, is equally skillful. It's directed by Sam Peckinpah with none of the touches for which he would become known, although the Ryan-Tod slugfest on a narrow balcony is carried off in a space so cramped it's a wonder there was room for the cameras. Publicity releases at the time pointed out that Milner broke Marvin's nose in Peckinpah's search for realism.

> "Some of the People, Some of the Time" (airdate: December 1, 1961): *Maximilian Coyne (Keenan Wynn) is a scam artist who runs fake Hollywood talent pageants, but his past catches up with him in Boiling Springs, Pennsylvania once he hires Buz and Tod to be his advance men.*

Directed by Robert Altman (who, like Peckinpah, had not yet blossomed), this twist on Meredith Willson's *The Music Man* starts off going in one direction but winds up unexpectedly but satisfyingly in another.[85] The main story has Coyne using his wiles to sidestep fate, but while that is entertainingly going on, Buz tries to rig a Cinderella contest so a plain-looking young waitress he likes, Jahala (Lois Nettleton), wins. When she does, she reveals that she was one of Coyne's ringers, but this is the first time she actually has been made to feel special. The skill of the writing is that, even though the guest stars completely con the series stars, everyone emerges with his and her integrity intact. So maybe it *is* a Robert Altman film after all.

> "Where There's a Will, There's a Way" (airdates: March 6 and 13, 1964): *The two-part series finale was written as "Don't Kill Us, We'll Kill You" in teleplays dated January 17 and 21, 1964. Set in Tampa, Florida, the contrivance is that a millionaire has died and willed his $4 million estate to his surviving relatives on the provision that his daughter, Margo (Barbara Eden) marry Tod. The multi-plotted story also includes Russian spies, greedy kin, and Linc and Tod donning a succession of disguises in order to foil everyone's dastardly schemes.*

Silliphant was not known as a comedy writer, and these two episodes, directed by Alvin Gazer (who worked with Leo McCarey and Preston Sturges before switching to TV) are loopy at best. Considered one of the first TV series to produce a definitive ending, *Route 66* thus concludes with a married Tod driving to Houston with Margo in the Corvette, and Linc heading there on his own to reunite with his estranged family. Linc's long walk down a driveway after one last caress to the 'Vette was scripted as a melancholy wrap to 116 episodes, an effect somewhat diminished by being immediately followed by a promo for the first re-run. While not one of the series' best, it can safely be said that there was no shark-jumping associated with the final fade-out.

Even today, *Route 66* remains a breakthrough series. Considering that America in the early 1960s was nowhere near as permissive as it would become in the late '60s, here was a popular network show that pushed the boundaries of broadcast standards with episodes on heroin addiction ("Birdcage on My Foot"), survivalist zealots ("A Fury Slinging Flame"), Fundamentalists ("Aren't You Surprised to See Me?"), mercy killing ("A Bunch of Lonely Pagliaccis"), LSD ("The Thin White Line"), terrorist hate groups ("To Walk with the Serpent"), and an almost all-black cast ("Good Night Sweet Blues"). It was the power, the taste, and the tenacity of Silliphant and Leonard that goaded the series, no matter who the writers were, into the fast lane of social observation.

Route 66, the road, was officially removed from the United States Highway System on June 17, 1985. *Route 66*, the series, drives on.

Ethel May Noaker, Stirling's mother.

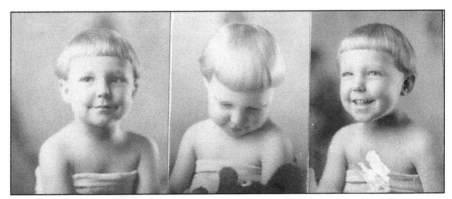

As a child, Stirling traveled with his parents on his father's sales calls.

Entering Gardner public school. Even then he had a fondness for sailing.

As a young cadet at the San Diego Army and Navy Military Academy.

Stirling and his younger brother Leigh
as cadets.

Graduation photo from Glendale's Hoover
High School

A lettered student at the University of Southern California.

Stirling and his mother while he was at USC.

Top left: At Yellowstone the summer after graduating from USC in 1937.

Top center: Stirling meets Iris Garff at Yellowstone, Summer, 1937.

Top right: Iris Garff.

Botttom lef: Iris and Stirling married, June 10, 1938.

Leigh, Stirling, Iris, and her sister Lois at Stirling's and Iris's wedding, June 10, 1938.

Top: Stirling in his Navy uniform. He was based in San Francisco but got around.

Left: Stirling in his Navy Uniform. He spent the war in public information.

Top: Young Stirling and
his father, Stirling,
in uniform

Right: The two Stirlings
stateside during World
War Two leave.

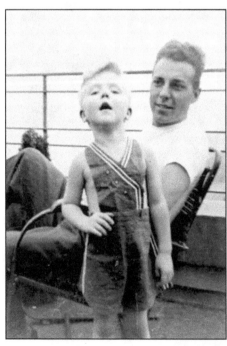

Left: Father and son relax
stateside during the war.

6

Man of Two Worlds

WHEN *ROUTE 66* RAN OUT OF GAS, Silliphant had less work and more to do. Although he had never concentrated exclusively on a single project, being relieved of the obligation to turn in one script every nine days, plus rewrite the old ones, plus plan the new ones, meant that he could make a new play for the movies. That was where the money was and, more than that, the prestige.

Strictly speaking, he had never really left features, although *Huk!*, *Maracaibo*, and the other early attempts were not going to put him on Hollywood's "A" list. As a matter of fact, when *Route 66* had been fueling up in 1959, he delivered a stealth science fiction classic that was rushed into production for 1960. Based on John Wyndham's 1957 novel *The Midwich Cuckoos*, the resulting film, directed by Wolf Rilla, was released by MGM as *Village of the Damned.* It was a major hit, and a major struggle.

The story is profoundly creepy: One afternoon the entire British village of Midwich falls asleep for several hours. Months later every fertile woman in town delivers a blond, hauntingly intelligent child that may have been "fathered" by extraterrestrials who visited earth while everyone was unconscious. Only local scientist George Zellaby (George Sanders) is able to gain the trust of these hybrid progeny who can read and control human thoughts. He learns that other cities around the world had similar visits, and he vows to destroy the tow-headed monsters. Distracting the telepathic children by concentrating on the image of a brick wall, he annihilates them—and himself—with a bomb hidden in a briefcase.

Silliphant was hired by MGM for $5,000 on July 8, 1957, to write a screen treatment (in prose) from the book "of not less than fifty (50) pages."[86] The screenplay came next. By the time it was released, it was credited to Silliphant, Wolf Rilla (later the author of the widely read text *The Writer and the Screen*), and George Barclay, who wrote elsewhere under the name Ronald Kinnoch. There's a story there. Originally bought by MGM on a pitch from Wyndham, who also wrote 1961's classic *The Day of the Triffids, Cuckoos* was intended as a production by MGM's home studio in Culver City to coincide with the book's publication. Reported Silliphant, "MGM's New York office was so high on the book that they airmailed me microfilm of each page of the manuscript as the author finished writing it so that I could get a jump-start on the script. My producer was Milo Frank. We offered the script to Ronald Colman, who accepted. Unhappily, this fine gentleman died before we could advance the production. At that point an incredible thing happened. The then-head of MGM, Robert H. O'Brien, who was Catholic, apparently actually read my script and flipped—*negatively*. The idea of human females being impregnated by ETs and bearing laser-eyed young'uns sent him into a religious cartwheel; what the fuck were we trying to say here? Were we making a mockery of the Virgin Mary? Or something to that effect. Bottom line: *Village of the Damned* got cancelled so fast Milo didn't have time to pack his briefcase and leave the lot. As for me, I was so pissed I left features (for a while) and went over to TV. That's when I went into business with Herbert Leonard and did the first year of *Naked City* for ABC.

"In any event, the script hung in limbo for months, then suddenly it surfaced in England as an MGM English project and that's when Rilla and Barclay were brought in. They did little, if anything, to change my script, but in those days our WGA didn't have power over English writers and there was nothing we could do about their credit-grab, which, to this day, I regard as a form of larceny on the part of these two British highwaymen. What they did was to make the dialogue more English than my American, which is why some of my dialogue ends up sounding like ersatz Noel Coward. In terms of the mood, I would say the filmmakers can make little claim to adding that. The mood came out of the original novel and I zealously preserved it in my draft. But that entire concept of George Sanders erecting the image of a brick wall in his mind in order to block the thought penetration by his 'son' is mine mine *mine*. I spent a week cerebrating over that one. In short, this is one the Brits got away with because our Guild had not yet extended its arbitration machinery to those precious writers over there. Otherwise—and I speak with the objectivity of decades—I would have been awarded the solo credit I merited."

In addition to its nod to the myth of the virgin birth, *Village of the Damned* has also been seen as a metaphor for a Communist takeover of the west. Silliphant dismissed that as well. "If anybody ever came up with the theory that this film was a metaphor for pulverizing Communism at whatever cost," he said, "it would have to be the Brits, since nobody in Culver

City would ever have had the imagination to concoct so zany an idea. As the guy who wrote the script, I can tell you my only thought was how to blow away these little bastards with the luminous eyes and their sickeningly blond Dutch haircuts. As a matter of fact, I had a dialogue passage in the script about the Soviets nuking their ET kids.[87] If anything, I wrote this out of simple admiration for the fact that the Sovs seemed always to have a better grasp of the harsh realities of existence than some of our Christian lads—especially heads of studios who are devoted Catholics."

Village of the Damned (released in the U.S. on December 7, 1960, after a July UK release) was enough of a box office success that it spawned a sequel, *Children of the Damned* (1964). It was remade in 1995 by John Carpenter with a $22 million budget. The original had cost $200,000.

Silliphant's first produced script after *Route 66* was one that could have been a *Naked City* episode. Based on a *Life* magazine article by Shana Alexander about a suicide prevention hotline in Seattle, Washington, *The Slender Thread* marked the feature directorial debut of Sydney Pollack and was produced by Alexander's husband, Stephen Alexander. Adapted, if not wholly invented, by Silliphant, the plot has a distraught Anne Bancroft phoning a suicide hotline manned by a lone Sidney Poitier after she has taken an overdose of sleeping pills, and Poitier's efforts to keep her on the line while he has the call traced so a detective (Edward Asner) can track down her husband (Stephen Hill) and her shrink (Telly Savalas) to intervene. The title is symbolic of both the phone connection and the line between life and death.

"Actually, *The Slender Thread* was not the original title," Silliphant recalled. "I believe my original title was *The Willow Plate*, which was based on a scene in one draft where Bancroft breaks up the willow plate pattern set of china in her dining room as a futile rebellion against her stifling marriage. But Howard Koch, then head of Paramount, didn't like my title, so he offered me *The Slender Thread*, which I rather liked (without mulling its metaphoric significance) and I took it. The studio had bought a novel, which was entitled *The Slender Thread*, and had shelved the book, but now saw a chance to recycle the title of the un-shot book." Other names fielded for the project were *Voice on the Wind*, *Call Me Back*, and *Cross Your Heart and Hope*. Elizabeth Ashley was signed when it was called the latter, but the studio insisted on Bancroft, who had recently won the Academy Award® for *The Miracle Worker*. Silliphant noted that Ashley "was bitter about this and, in a book she wrote subsequently [*Actress: Postcards From the Road*, 1978], she goes into major detail about the incident, blaming me for playing along with the studio, doing their bidding, and 'dumping' her on their orders rather than fighting for her. I got cut up rather badly in her account."[88]

Ironically, Sidney Poitier's "Best Actor" Oscar for the previous year's *Lilies of the Field* had been presented to him at the 1964 ceremony by Anne

Bancroft. The moment was significant because the two actors kissed on national television, marking an interracial milestone for people who mark such things.

"I didn't see the 1964 Oscars," Silliphant said, "and therefore did not see Bancroft kissing Poitier, hence this trans-racial contact had nothing whatsoever to do with the casting of these two fine actors. We picked each one because we felt there was no one around who could better portray what I had written for each. Yes, race was totally ignored. That's what appealed to me, that neither hero nor heroine could see each other—therefore they did not and could not bring to their brief relationship any prejudices or pre-set standards of evaluation. Their mutual humanity is purely that—the relationship of people without the impact of race, religion or societal pressures—people free to relate to each other on the simplest level of humanity: self-preservation. For this reason, at the end, I elected to have Sidney *not* want to see the woman. Because he *knew* seeing her would diminish the magic which they had experienced, divorced from each other except for their connection by phone—their linkage heart to heart. The character elects to savor the triumph—to preserve it, unspoiled, in his memory."

The screenplay's sleight-of-hand has been overlooked, but it is worth mentioning that Bancroft's story is told from Poitier's point of view. "It shouldn't work," Silliphant agreed, "and, in some instances in the film, I'm not sure it did. But it worked well enough in total to validate the attempt to try something different."

In his autobiography, Sidney Poitier credits his agent, Martin Baum, with discovering and nurturing the property. "He read the script and found a part he thought I could play, although again the part was not designated for a black actor. Through a determined effort, Marty sold the producer [Stephen Alexander], who in turn sold the film company [Paramount], who in turn gave permission for Sydney Pollack to hire me to play that part opposite Anne Bancroft, Steven Hill, and Telly Savalas. *The Slender Thread* experience gave me great satisfaction. Anne Bancroft was simply fantastic, and Telly, of course, is an infinitely better actor than *Kojak* allowed us to see."[89]

The Slender Thread holds up today, but, at the time, it nearly stalled the career of everyone involved with it. "In TV I was a comet, blazing across the heavens," Silliphant appraised. "In features, who he? So the film was vital to me; it had to make its mark—*or else*. But it didn't, in one sense. And in another, it did. We previewed in Encino [a valley community north of Hollywood] and, as I watched the film and 'felt' the audience, I knew I had failed. The picture was *not* giving off sparks. I felt it drag and drag. The subject seemed depressing, and the audiences palpably depressed. End titles up, lights on, the audience virtually limped out, nobody jazzed up, nobody talking. Christ, I thought I'm still in TV, that's for goddamned sure. This ain't no comeback, baby! I remember sitting alone in the theater while the Paramount execs, including the always ebullient and affable Howard Koch, were out in the lobby trying to strongarm the rapidly fleeing patrons into filling out reaction cards. A fella with a big smile and red hair suddenly appeared in my row as though he had materialized from the ceiling. He sat down next to me. 'A bomb, huh?' he suggested. 'Yep,' I agreed. 'A fucking bomb. From start to finish. I doubt that any single person in America will ever bother to buy a ticket to this flick.' 'You have to get another screenplay assignment before the word gets out,' he counseled. 'Yeh?' I asked. 'And how do I do that?' 'I'm Martin Baum,' he said. 'I represent Sidney Poitier.'

"I knew Marty Baum represented Sidney along with a lot of other top actors, writers, *et al* and that he was one of Hollywood's most prestigious agents. 'So you're Marty?' I asked. 'Yeh,' he said. 'And I want you to know something: Sidney doesn't blame you for this picture.' 'Maybe Sidney doesn't,' I said, 'But *I* do. I wrote the thing.' 'Well,' he said, 'I find that refreshing, that *somebody* in this town can admit he blew it. Look, I'm going to get you a job—fast. It has to be fast—because the minute word gets out about this turkey—forget it.'

"Then he disappeared. Still heavy-hearted, not believing a word of what I had been told, I forced myself to go out to the lobby where I discovered the studio execs congratulating themselves on having a hit. They showed me a half dozen cards marked 'excellent.' What they didn't show me, but what I saw, were the piles of cards they'd thrown away: 'stinks' was the average comment. There were a few kindly 'boring's. But it was downhill all the way."

Silliphant is being unduly harsh on the picture, which, though it set no box-office records, confirmed Sydney Pollack's transition from television to features. He followed it with *This Property is Condemned* (1965), marking his first movie with Robert Redford and beginning one of the most enduring and productive collaborations in cinema.

Personally, Silliphant was adrift. On October 1, 1965—a year after his divorce from Ednamarie and two months before *The Slender Thread* opened—he married Margot Ruth Gohlke. Although the divorce from Ednamarie was finalized, the settlement dragged on for another four years and tied up Silliphant's funds to the extent that he had to seek bridging loans from the City National Bank in Beverly Hills. This, despite pulling in $20,000 a month. Ever the optimist and self-assured as a writer, he needed work, and the Baum/Poitier connection was promising. Still, in Hollywood, you can die of encouragement. So he waited.

7

It Happened One "Night"

IT's AN AXIOM THAT GOOD BOOKS MAKE BAD MOVIES, but bad books have a shot at becoming good ones. And then there's the middle ground of books that contain underdeveloped seeds, which perceptive filmmakers can nurture into something that transcends the original without detracting from it. This is what happened with *In the Heat of the Night*, and it made screen history.

Turning books into movies is easy to do but hard to do well, and few screenwriters did it better than Silliphant. For example, practically the entire canon of Stephen King (with the notable exceptions of *Stand By Me, Misery, Carrie*, and *The Shawshank Redemption*) has arguably been mangled en route from page to screen because the adapters, including at times King himself, think the plot is more important than the subplot. In shorthand, the *plot* is what *happens* in the story but the *subplot* is what the story is really *about*. In King's stories, his plots are usually about weird goings-on, but his subplots—which most film adaptations ignore or suppress—are about challenges to human sensibility and to society's ethos. (This is why he is not only a popular writer but one whose work is more profound than is generally acknowledged.)

Getting from page to screen is more than just removing the *he said* and *she said*. Take a simple line of prose: "John so longed for Mary that he couldn't sleep for all the yearning he felt in her absence." That single written sentence introduces John, limns his situation, and offers a hint of backstory. But it is internal, told *about* John rather than *by* John. How to make it cinematic? Imagine the camera on John asleep—pan over to show his hand resting on a photograph of a woman pressed into the pillow of his half-empty double bed—move in closer to the photograph and it's inscribed, "To John, I'll never leave you, love, Mary." And the photograph is torn in half. Describing the shot takes more words than the original sentence, but it makes the point that movies need to *show* things in the visual language of cinema.

Silliphant often said that he preferred originals to adaptations. "Number one," he compared, "originals come out of my own experience and feelings. Number two, you don't have to waste time reading somebody else's work. Number three, you seldom get a really fine piece of material to adapt, since the best-written material is usually not able to be adapted. How would you like to take a crack at Proust's *Remembrance of Things Past*, for example? In discussing originals, we start with a handicap: *What* originals? I may have seen, over a lifetime of moviegoing, only a handful of what, to me, were films with stories different from the mainstream ammo line fired off by all the Hollywoods of the world. One shining example of an original piece of filmmaking is the Wim Wenders film *Wings of Desire*. Another was the original Kurosawa *Seven Samurai*. Another is [Kaige Chen's] Chinese film *Life on a String*. One or two of Bergman's films would qualify, and possibly one or two of Godard's early ones. We all have our private lists, but my point is that, even being as charitable as one's standard of judgment may permit, you would be stressed to name *fifty* films *ever* written which might hope to compete in a contest of quality with *fifty* of the best pieces of literature ever produced by man.

"So, setting aside that sense of the word *original*, let us proceed to the nuts and bolts of the film biz, by the rules of which an original screenplay is one cooked up as a 'concept': by a studio, a money group, a producer, or a director or writer—or by *anybody*: A screenplay *not* explicitly based on a published novel, article or stage play suggesting a narrative line, characters and dialogue already written. It is my contention that adapting the work of another writer is far more trying and requires infinitely more professional ability than writing one of these so-called 'original' screenplays."

And that's exactly what Silliphant faced in turning John Ball's short (184 pages), crisply written, Edgar®-winning 1965 novel into what became an Academy Award®-winning film. The process—and it was not easy—shows what can be done when a committed screenwriter and relentless director agree from the start on what kind of movie they want to make, then keep plugging away until they reach it.

Set in the fictitious small town of Wells, South Carolina, *In the Heat of the Night* begins with a highly trained homicide detective from Pasadena, California—Virgil Tibbs—waiting at a railroad depot for a connection home on the night an important businessman, Enrico Mantoli, is murdered. White police officer Sam Wood takes Tibbs into custody not just because he's a stranger but because he's black. The friction increases when Wood and the town's new police chief, Bill Gillespie, realize that Tibbs's investigative skills can solve the killing, but they must also admit that a Negro (sic) knows more than they do. Pressure is applied by City Councilman George Endicott, who comes from the North and wants Tibbs to stay and help. Complicating matters, Patrolman Wood has eyes for Mantoli's daughter, Duena; exhibitionist Delores Purdy accuses him of rape; Wood and Gillespie wrongly accuse local man Harvey Oberst of the crime; and various rednecks attack Tibbs before the actual killer is caught.

Silliphant was not the first to adapt the book; how he was drawn into the project is an example of Hollywood deal-making. It started when H. N. "Swanie" Swanson, who represented novelist John Ball, sent the manuscript to agent Martin Baum hoping for the involvement of his client, Sidney Poitier, who was America's top African-American (technically, Caribbean-American) star. Poitier declined to commit without seeing a script, so Baum sent it to producer Walter Mirisch, who had a deal at United Artists. Mirisch sent the novel to Robert Alan Aurthur, who had written *Edge of the City*, the 1957 waterfront drama in which Poitier had scored a career-building success. Aurthur completed a treatment for Mirisch but, after turning it in, informed the producer that he was leaving *In the Heat of the Night* to take on the bigger-budget *Grand Prix* for director John Frankenheimer, MGM, and Cinerama. This was in late 1965.

Then came the fateful screening of *The Slender Thread* and Baum's promise to line up something quick for Silliphant. Clever agent that he was, he probably already had *In the Heat of the Night* in mind, because, a few days later, Baum sent him to Mirish, who gave him the Ball book and informed him, "Sidney Poitier brought this in to us and we plan to develop it," not telling him that he was counting on his script to cinch the deal. Poitier would be paid $200,000 and twenty percent of the profits and Silliphant would receive $35,000 with an additional $15,000 if he was accorded sole screen credit (he was). His hiring was announced on December 22, 1965,[90] even though the paperwork wasn't formalized until September of 1966.[91]

Now all they needed was a director.

George Roy Hill, who had just made *Hawaii* for Mirisch, was keen on the project when he heard the producer describe it on the plane to their picture's Minneapolis sneak preview in early 1966. But Hill—a meticulous craftsman who would later direct *Butch Cassidy and the Sundance Kid* and *The Sting*—had let *Hawaii* get away from him, and Mirisch was not eager for another collaboration.

Meanwhile UA was having qualms. Although the company had benefited heartily from its association with the brothers Walter, Marvin, and Harold Mirisch,[92] and despite management's strong liberal beliefs, they feared that the racial tension that drives *In the Heat of the Night* might spook southern exhibitors who were fearful of pickets or too entrenched in their own personal racism, and they might refuse to book it. That meant that it would have to recoup its costs above the Mason-Dixon line. Defensively, UA allotted only $2 million (though some sources say $1.5 million), which bought only a tight forty-day shooting schedule and no location frills. The final budget would slightly escalate to $2.09 million.[93]

Here memories differ. Mirisch says he wanted Jewison to direct; Jewison says Mirisch tried to dissuade him from directing because he thought the impossibly low budget would be an unwise career move. But Jewison, a Canadian by birth and a Progressive by choice, had unusual passion for the story's milieu. When he was eighteen, he had hitch-hiked through the South and, when he reached Missouri, he heard about a lynching that had taken place there. He later learned that the truck that had given him the ride was the one that had been used to drag the victim to his fate.[94]

Despite the tight budget (Mirisch planned to shoot it cheaply on sets at the Goldwyn Studios in LA), Jewison felt the film deserved to be more than a potboiler, and it was on a family ski trip in the winter of 1965-1966 that he got the ammunition to notch it up. On the slopes, the Jewisons happened to meet Robert Kennedy and his family and, when the director told RFK the story of *In the Heat of the Night*, the former Attorney General urged that he make the picture the way he intended, exhorting, "The time is right for a movie like this. Timing is everything in politics, in art, and in life itself."[95] Mirisch capitulated but kept the budget where it was.

As soon as his deal was firmed, Silliphant hit the ground typing. He turned in a 22-page "Revised Step Outline" on January 7, 1966.[96] Coming to it already familiar with the film, one sees that it reads like the movie on fast-forward. The storytelling is lean and evocative, yet allows for embellishment. Even at this stage, Silliphant has made telling changes: Tibbs is no longer from genteel Pasadena, California but from the rougher Phoenix, Arizona. Endicott becomes a manipulative racist. The murder victim is no longer a music producer but Philip Colbert, a Chicago businessman who is building a factory in town. And Sam Wood no longer yearns for the victim's daughter, Duena, whose name is now Louise. The book is explicit in its representation of racism, and unfolds from several points of view, a technique that heightens the tension while diminishing the drama, as Silliphant immediately corrected.

"I found the story more compelling in its opportunities to exploit the situations of the contending characters than I could generate any kind of enthusiasm for what is essentially a very thin and pale little mystery yarn with little surprise or suspense," he reasoned. "The centrality of the story for me lay clearly in the wonderful concept John Ball had of putting a city-trained BLACK homicide detective in a rural, southern cracker small town where everybody and anybody is a potential enemy—even the Sheriff. I determined to tell this story and this story only."

To do so, Silliphant made an inspired change: "The main problem was that the book lacked a conflict between two equally matched characters that could drive the plot. The central character is a patrol cop who falls in love with the daughter of the murdered man. I relegated the cop to a minor role and concentrated on building Bill Gillespie's character. Sheriff Gillespie is a minor character in the novel. I made him a southerner, but from a different state [Texas], so that he was as much an outsider to the town as Sidney Poitier's character was. They had this alienation from the others as a common bond." In enriching Gillespie, Silliphant created a man who saw that he needed to change but had nothing in his background that told him how to do so, especially from Tibbs. "Gillespie is beginning to find a manhood in Tibbs far more significant than a skin coloration, a manhood he knows—or hopes he knows—exists deep within himself." Voicing Gillespie's thoughts, he wrote in the treatment that it was the "first time he's ever had to plead with a Negro. Damned humiliating, but he had to make the effort. He decides to play smart with this colored boy."[97]

Other changes deepened the virulence of the town's racism. Endicott is no longer the one who is pressuring Gillespie to have Tibbs continue the investigation, but is now an entrenched bigot. "We unpeel Endicott slowly," Silliphant explained, "leaving the condemnation of Tibbs to other more outspoken racists." Endicott, he added generously, shows "the dilemma of the thinking, sensitive southerner of the better class—a man who regrets the passing of the old ways but begins to realize a new time is coming and that nothing can hold it back." He achieves this with a scene (which was scripted but didn't make the final cut) among civic leaders, most of whom are crackers and all of whom revere the elegant Endicott, "in which Endicott recalls how things were with this land at one time—how lovely and lost those times were—and, against this, play the short-fused tempers of the poor whites who only hear that part of what Endicott says, which they can use against Tibbs." Several later take to their cars to ambush the detective.[98]

The Endicott subplot pays off in a scene that has become one of the most significant in American cinema. Tibbs, believing Endicott killed Colbert, visits Endicott's plantation greenhouse with a puzzled Gillespie in tow. When Endicott realizes that Tibbs suspects him of the murder, he gives Tibbs a firm slap across the face. Tibbs immediately slaps him back, harder. Gillespie witnesses it and refuses to act, and the cards shift. The return slap has come to be regarded as the first time a black man gave it back in kind to a white man in a major American film.

"I couldn't play a part where I'm asking a chap a legitimate question and he slaps me," Poitier said. "I told the people who were making the film that I have no interest in it if that is what I have to endure—that he slaps me and I just take it and walk away. No, I will *not* take it and walk away. So pass me and I hope you find someone. And they were very understanding. They had their sessions with the United Artists people. They said they would take care of it and I told them that 'taking care of it' means that either I do it that way or I don't do it; it's just against my value system. So they said that they would shoot it that way. That's about the size of it."[99]

And it was. Although rumors have circulated that the slap exchange was in jeopardy of being cut as a sop to southern audiences, it was, in fact, shot and released the way it was born on page sixteen, scene twenty-five, of Silliphant's treatment. The slap is Silliphant's creation: it's not in the Ball book.

"The slap scene was in the script," Director of Photography Haskell Wexler confirmed, "the producers knew, everybody knew. There were questions even if the film should be made, and the producer was considered brave. It is hard for some people to realize what was considered daring for Hollywood at that time."[100]

"Wonder of wonders," marveled actress Beah Richards, who appeared in the film, "a white man [was] actually slapped, which must have blown minds all over the United States and Europe."[101]

"Imagine, for me" Silliphant enthused, "to go from being told that I can't put Joe Louis's child on the lap of his white trainer to a scene in which Sidney Poitier slaps, as hard as he can, a rich, white land owner in the Deep South. That is progress."[102]

The 166-page first draft script dated January-February, 1966, which Silliphant delivered, shows the writer's savvy in knowing whom he was writing to attract—at this stage Poitier had not agreed to star—by describing Tibbs as "well-dressed, despite the heat. His nose seems the nose of an aristocratic white man, the line of his mouth slender and well-formed. The eyes are even more remarkable. Something dances behind them, a kind of banked fire." In other words, a starring role.

As for Gillespie, the script clearly states his unresolved status as Wells's police chief. "I'm new here," he says on page seventeen, "going on my fourth week. Come up from Texas to take over the department." The final film will remove this backstory, including a moment when one officer tells another that their boss is still in his trial month. Instead, various civic leaders remind him every now and then that his future depends on solving the murder, adding to the pressure to do so. A March 1966, polish was apparently enough to secure Poitier's consent. Next it was Jewison's turn.

"It wasn't, then, an especially elegant piece of writing or plotting," the director recalled, "but what it had going for it was, at its core, a compelling confrontation. For this period, this was incendiary material, the notion that a black was in any way superior to whites. It had the potential to make a provocative and progressive statement about race in America. But it wasn't perfect." How does a thirty-nine-year-old director, hitherto mostly of frothy comedies and TV variety shows, explain this to a seasoned forty-eight-year-old writer with 150 acclaimed titles to his credit? Jewison used psychology. He put check marks beside lines he thought could be improved, only he didn't explain what they meant, hoping Silliphant would feel the need to make changes on his own. Silliphant bit. 'That line you marked on page forty-two, Norman?' he said the next day. 'I got thinking about it last night, and it's too perfect for a movie. It's overwritten, just too pat. I fixed it.'"[103]

"It turned out that he had planned it all along," Silliphant confirmed. "Well, six months later I was still working on that script. And he was fantastic about that. He made you *want* to change it. He challenged you. He would just guide you from one thing to the other. That's a talent—Norman has that great talent."[104] And so went the best collaboration of both men's careers.

By July of 1966, a 140-page script was not only shorter, it was sharper. Now Tibbs was from Philadelphia, a northern city with a more substantial black population than Phoenix. Leslie Colbert is no longer the murder victim's daughter but his wife, which reduced the prominence of Sam Wood and made Gillespie the primary antagonist.[105] Above all, the moment is refined in which Tibbs, having been hauled into Gillespie's office from the train depot, is taunted by the Chief, who sees his wallet bulging with cash, "Now just what do you do up there in Pennsylvania to earn that kind of money?" to which Tibbs, at the end of his (and the audience's) patience, says, "I'm a police officer!"

"At that moment," Silliphant grinned, "the film *explodes* into life and doesn't stop until the final moment—at the train station—when the Sheriff reaches for—and Tibbs surrenders to him—Tibbs's bag—two human beings have bonded. We protracted that moment of initial impact as long as we could—right down to the precise frame of film at which point we felt we might be teasing the viewer *too* long.[106] This was from the beginning the intent of my screenplay and anything which did not advance that dynamic was ruthlessly rejected.

"This may be the most 'controlled' and 'deliberate' piece of craftsmanship of all my work," Silliphant admitted, adding quotation marks to show disdain for such calculated construction. "Usually, in writing, I let emotion and feeling dominate, lead me down unknown and, for me, still-unexplored pathways." But *In the Heat of the Night* demanded precision. "In discussions early on with Norman Jewison, we agreed that, if the crime story were plotted as the alphabet, from A to Z, how much of it could we pull out and play off-screen without ever seeing or making any reference to? We kept A and jumped to F, then from F jumped to L and from L to P—then from P to Z-and then we tried to see how we could still pull more exposition out of that fragmentary crime-story structure. We applied this principle to every scene: wherever we could, any explanation or exposition, we stepped on it. The result of this withholding of information was to compel the viewer to invest attention to the least detail. Maybe there was a clue in the look Gillespie gave Virgil—maybe not. But we'd better watch and see."

Although Poitier was to receive top billing, the film needed an equally strong presence to play Gillespie. Mirisch first asked George C. Scott but, as the deal was being finalized, the mercurial actor decided to do a play in New York with his temporarily ex-wife, Colleen Dewhurst.[107] At one point *Daily Variety* even ran a squib that Raymond Burr, best known for playing Perry Mason on TV, had been approached.[108] Rod Steiger was Jewison's second choice and he consented to do the film after he wrapped the Russian *Napoleon* in Italy.[109] He was paid $150,000.[110]

With all the fireworks surrounding the racial theme of the film, another equally significant casting decision went almost ignored: Lee Grant. Grant had been nominated for an Academy Award in 1951 for her first film, *Detective Story*, and then found herself on the Blacklist when she refused to testify against her husband, Arnold Manoff, before the House Committee on Un-American Activities.[111] For the next twelve years she found it hard to get work, and playing Louise Colbert—who, unpoisoned by racism, is the person, rather than Endicott, who pressures the town to listen to Tibbs—helped revive her career. Warren Oates, as Sam Wood, was another notable addition. Though the Kentucky-born Oates had appeared in countless television episodes and movie westerns, this was the first time he had a chance to hint at his acting potential. Likewise, Scott Wilson made his film debut; his next role would be in Richard Brooks's memorable *In Cold Blood*.

With Jewison winning the battle to shoot on location, the problem then became, "What location?" The authentic Deep South was out; even though the Civil Rights Act of 1964 had been passed two years earlier, the region's attitudes had not measurably improved. Besides, only a short time earlier, Poitier and Harry Belafonte had nearly been killed by Klansmen while on a civil rights mission to Mississippi. After scouting upwards of 200 northern townships that might pass for Dixie, Jewison and production managers James E. Henderling and J. Howard Joslin settled on Sparta, Illinois, sixty miles southeast of St. Louis, Missouri. Serendipitously, when the advance construction crew arrived to change the signage from *Sparta* to *Wells*, they discovered that it was so pervasive that it was easier to change the script, so Wells, South Carolina became Sparta, Mississippi, courtesy of Sparta, Illinois.

Production started on September 26, 1966, during an uncharacteristic cold snap.[112] Director of Photography Haskell Wexler was no stranger to the south or the Civil Rights Struggle; he had made the heralded 1965 documentary, *The Bus*, about a group of activists driving to the August 1963, demonstration in Washington, DC. He and Jewison decided to shoot their film with low light levels, not only to achieve a *noir* mood but in order not to wash out Poitier's dark skin, as often happened in studio movies, whose high key lighting favored Caucasian actors. The result was a gritty, yet assured, verisimilitude.

The company was billed in Belleville, Illinois and bused forty miles on the state highway every day to Sparta. Even while keeping a low profile, the filmmakers' presence was constantly monitored by the townspeople. "We had a situation in the motel," recalls Wexler, "where some white guy—Southern Illinois is like the Deep South—said that his wife was shacked up with someone in the film crew. The guy was drunk and came to the motel and one of the rooms he knocked on was Rod Steiger's room. When he banged on Rod's room, Rod quickly got out and said, 'No she's not here' and went over to Sidney's room, which was a couple down, 'cause if that guy got anywhere near Sidney at that time...'"

The production did, however, venture briefly into Jim Crow territory for the Endicott/Tibbs slap that needed to be shot on a cotton plantation for authenticity. True to Poitier's concerns, there were incidents with local thugs knocking on doors at the crew's Dyersburg Holiday Inn and a general chill from the town's residents, so much so that the company left a day and a half ahead of schedule, forcing them to finish their scenes on matching sets at LA's Producers Studio (now the Raleigh Studio). "We felt we weren't getting the cooperation we needed," Jewison understated diplomatically to *Variety*'s Army Archerd.[113] Principle photography wrapped on November 8.

Despite its age, *In the Heat of the Night* remains astonishingly modern; the only elements that date it are the cars (which might well still be on the road in Sparta) and, surprisingly, Quincy Jones's original score, parts of which sound like canned music from a '60s TV cop show. The interplay between Poitier and Steiger is breathtaking. Jewison suggested that Steiger chew gum in addition to sporting yellow sunglasses and an overhanging gut. At first, he resisted the gimmick, but he quickly discovered that he could convey Gillespie's mood by how fast he chewed at any given time. A Method actor, he stayed in character throughout the shoot, causing Poitier to marvel, "I was on the threshold of discovering what acting really was."[114]

Their symbiosis led to a scene that has been the subject of ongoing, though good-natured, controversy ever since it was shot. Scene 296, starting on revised page 123 and dated September 28, 1966, takes place at night in Gillespie's functional apartment. He is drinking as Tibbs waits for word that will lead him to Mama Caleba (Beah Richards), an abortionist who may unwittingly know who the killer is. "They'd eaten a poor meal of bread, butter, pork, and beans," Silliphant's script indicates. "Gillespie is pouring the fourth or fifth bourbon for himself."

"You're the first colored I ever sat in a room with like this," Gillespie says. Feeling comfortable enough to be sarcastic, Tibbs responds, "You can't be too careful." Hitting the Wild Turkey again, Gillespie says, "You know everything, don't you, boy? What do you know about insomnia?"

"Bourbon can't cure it."

"Thirty-seven years old. No wife, no kids. Scratching for a living in a town that doesn't want me. A fan I have to oil for myself. Desk with a busted leg." He looks at the wallpaper. "This place." He looks at Tibbs. "Know something, Virgil? You're the first person who's been around to call. Nobody else has been here. Nobody comes." Then, writes Silliphant, "In a sudden spontaneous gesture of compassion, Tibbs reaches out, touches Gillespie on the shoulder, a simple and moving human contact. But it only infuriates Gillespie, who barks, 'Don't treat *me* like a nigger, Tibbs!'" Tibbs stiffens at the rebuff. In the film, the line becomes, "Oh, now, don't get smart black boy. I don't need it."[115]

"It would have been good if Gillespie said *nigger*," Wexler explained clinically, "because that's what he would have said. There were all kinds of words that you couldn't say on many films. The thing about the film is the concept. What was happening at the world at that time was far advanced to what *In the Heat of the Night* was, but *In the Heat of the Night* was far advanced for what movies were."[116]

Added Silliphant, "To me that's what Lenny Bruce must have felt when he used obscenities to make the point that the problem is not with the words, the problem lies in our dirty little minds. It's a cultural imprint and nothing more So by getting the word *nigger* out there and looking at it simply as a word, not as a pejorative term, I think you can get air into it. Air and hopefully sunlight—and maybe the need to use it will disappear as the impact of the word itself becomes diminished."

The "Gillespie apartment scene" has, over forty years, become a point of contention, Silliphant said. "I have heard that everybody claims to have written that scene—Haskell Wexler, Rod Steiger, and, Lord knows, even the generator man. I can only assure you that I conceived it and wrote it. Rod did switch a couple of words around, but with an actor of his talent I made no objection."

Indeed, Silliphant was not present on location, so director and actors felt free to change his words when necessary. When, for example, Gillespie asks Tibbs where he's from and Tibbs responds, "Philadelphia," Gillespie asks, "Mississippi?" Not only was the southern town of Philadelphia, Mississippi the first thing a southerner would think of, it's also an allusion to the place where civil rights workers James Chaney, Andrew Goodman, and Michael Schwerner were murdered by Klansmen in 1964.

Not long after the apartment scene, the mystery is solved: Ralph, the night man at the town diner, accidentally killed Colbert in a robbery to pay for Delores Purdy's abortion. Next day, Tibbs boards his train back to Philadelphia. The script has the two men saying a perfunctory goodbye; in the film, however, Gillespie turns and says, "Virgil? You take care, you hear?" The men trade careful smiles—editor Hal Ashby cuts between them twice to cement the unspoken bond—and Ray Charles sings the exit theme.[117]

The film premiered in New York on August 2, 1967, and in Los Angeles on August 23, after which it went into general release, collecting nearly $11 million in rentals. The reviews were strongly positive, but it encountered a strange backlash from three distinct, yet overlapping, audiences. First, Poitier had been facing growing resistance from the African-American community for his frequent casting as a near-saint despite the barrier-shattering strength of his roles. Then the film itself suffered from critics who, while applauding its craft, got picky about how easy it was to take sides. Then there was the audience who, the filmmakers hoped, would see the movie as something more than a racial polemic. Silliphant bristled when they didn't.

"I have been quoted and misquoted on this point for two decades," he said with a measure of impatience. "What I was referring to was the fact that the film had never been appreciated for its craftsmanship or for its unique and polished style of holding back, holding back, but was judged on the level of its black-white content. I felt then and still feel that such a judgment is overly simplistic and, for that reason and that reason alone, I made the statement that getting plaudits for *In the Heat of the Night* was like waving the American flag or pushing Mom's apple pie. It was just too damn easy to manipulate people in issues which, for the moment, have flagged their attention. It was impossible *not* to like *In the Heat of the Night* at that time. Today's phrase is 'politically correct.' I hated to be politically correct since I felt there was no validation for the work in such a posture, but only a knee-jerk reaction on the part of a populist majority opinion on what happened by chance to be the subject matter of the film."

"I think [he] was reflecting the revolutionary changes America had gone through since he wrote his script," opined Poitier, "and so, in some way, he was apologizing for something he couldn't have helped. At the time he wrote the script, most of America was where he was, and, to my mind, it was a very forward-looking piece of material; naturally, there were things in it that black people would have preferred to see more of, but, on the whole, it was revolutionary as mass entertainment."[118]

Perhaps these controversies, as well as the film's genre (mysteries seldom win "Best Picture" Oscars despite such outstanding examples as *The Maltese Falcon, Chinatown, The Long Goodbye, Night Moves, L.A. Confidential*), combined to deny Norman Jewison a directing Oscar. Even Arthur Penn, whose *Bonnie and Clyde* revolutionized American cinema, was passed over that year. Academy voters gave their directing statuette to Mike Nichols for *The Graduate*, marking one of the rare times that the Picture-Director awards have been split.

"About Norman Jewison, both the talent and the man," Silliphant stated, "he is superb in both departments. I adore him—did from the beginning, always will. He was a magnificent sport when the Academy passed him over. I can only tell you that those of us who went up to get our Oscars felt little personal triumph because Norman—who made it all possible—wasn't up there with us. For that matter, neither was Sidney. But then the Academy had to decide: Sidney or Rod. It couldn't be both."[119]

Naturally, Silliphant was approached to write a sequel. His files contain a blue, loose-leaf notebook with forty-five pages of character and story notes, quotes from Dick Gregory and others, a highly personal deliberation about Black Power, and a six-page unsigned letter/summary to Walter Mirisch dated May 20, 1968. Nothing came of it.

Ball's book, boosted no doubt by the success of the film, led to six more Virgil Tibbs novels and two short stories. There were two film sequels sans Silliphant (*They Call Me Mister Tibbs!*, 1970, and *The Organization*, 1971) and a seven-year television adaptation that cleverly cast Carroll O'Connor against Howard Rollins. In 2011, a stage adaptation by Matt Pelfrey titled *John Ball's In the Heat of the Night* used the original novel (thus the possessive title) but not Silliphant's script. Its New York production was not enthusiastically received. Silliphant received no compensation from any of these.

8

Silliphant, Inc.

EVERYONE WHO WINS THE ACADEMY AWARD goes back to work the next day carrying Hollywood's best-kept secret: although an Oscar brings money and power, it does nothing to erase the self-doubts that creative people carry with them every moment. Silliphant was no exception. He confessed that, "Every [new] one is, 'Can I do this one?' It's what an actor must feel. Most of my friends are actors, and I know, even when they're superstars, when they go on the set, they're very, very uptight. You know you *can* do it but you're not sure how *well* you can do it. Each one is a new challenge."[120]

Following *In the Heat of the Night*, Silliphant was offered every old, dusty project that the studios had on their shelves, and was asked to revamp it by adding a black character. He reacted haughtily by saying that using token blacks in films is "dangerous" because it portrays American racism as being a thing of the past, which, in fact, it was not. He even went so far as to call the film companies' attitude toward blacks a "modern slave trade."[121]

Only someone on a post-Oscar roll could have dared such a charge, but Silliphant was too busy to care. The same year that saw the release of *In the Heat of the Night,* he also wrote the pilot and two episodes for MGM Television's series *Maya*, about a boy and his elephant, based on their 1966 theatrical film. Both the feature and the series were produced by the King Brothers, the low rent siblings who had earned a place in movie history for having hired blacklisted screenwriter Dalton Trumbo under the name "Robert Rich" to write *The Brave One,* which won Trumbo a 1956 Oscar that he was unable to claim until 1975.[122]

By the time *Maya* aired in September, Silliphant was already at work adapting Daniel Keyes's short story, "Flowers for Algernon," into what became the 1968 movie *Charly*. Cliff Robertson had starred in the live February 22, 1961, broadcast of CBS's "The Two Worlds of Charlie Gordon" on *The United States Steel Hour*. He was taken with the star-making role and felt it could lead to a movie career. But he was painfully mindful that his starring role in *Playhouse 90*'s October 2, 1958 production of "Days of Wine and Roses" had gone to Jack Lemmon when the lush property had become a feature. Robertson made sure that wouldn't happen to "Flowers for Algernon" by buying the screen rights to the story and producing it—and, of course, starring in it—himself.

Published in the April 1959 issue of *The Magazine of Fantasy and Science Fiction* after several rejections from other periodicals because Keyes wouldn't change his ending to a happy one, "Algernon" unfolds through the diary entries of a thirty-seven-year-old janitor with an IQ of sixty-eight who works in a box factory. Charlie Gordon is the subject of taunts from his coworkers, whom he thinks are merely giving him attention. He takes an adult education course from Alice Kinnian so he can "get smart" but, when this fails, she introduces him to research scientists who have had luck increasing the intelligence of a laboratory mouse, Algernon, and are ready to try the experiment on a human. The procedure works and Charlie becomes a genius but, when Algernon's newfound intelligence decays and the mouse dies, Charlie realizes that his own mind will go too. On the verge of reverting to his old self, he asks Miss Kinnian to please leave flowers on Algernon's grave.

Keyes expanded his short story into a novel in 1966, adding a backstory about Charlie's parents, a subplot about a sexual liaison with a neighbor, and a drinking habit that parallels his rising IQ. Over the years the book has faced numerous censorship assaults from groups who think it stigmatizes mentally disabled people when, in fact, Keyes wrote it to humanize them.

Bent on turning the novel into a feature, Robertson ignored James Yaffee's 1961 teleplay and approached a young novelist he had met through his cousin, and whose energy and interest had impressed him. This was William Goldman, who would become one of the screen's most honored writers.[123]

Goldman tells it a little differently, reporting that Robertson had read the manuscript of his 160-page, 1964 novel, *No Way to Treat a Lady*, and was misled by its short chapters into thinking it was a film treatment.[124] When the actor asked him to write "Flowers for Algernon," Goldman says, he didn't know what a screenplay looked like, and even when he found a how-to book on the subject, it made no sense. "To this day," he writes, "I remember staring at the page in shock. I didn't know what it was exactly I was looking at, but I knew I could never write in that form, in that language."[125]

But Goldman managed. He eventually called Robertson, said he had finished, and wanted to give him the script of what was to be called *Charly*.

Robertson came to Goldman's Manhattan apartment and picked up the story in his Archive of American Television interview: "He said, 'You can go in the other room and read it.' I said 'No, I wouldn't do that to you, I'll take it home.' I lied. I took it down to the corner delicatessen. and I'm looking through it, and although he's a brilliant writer, he somehow had missed it. I wasn't about to say that to him. But I went home and I swallowed my pride—well, best-laid plans—I have to get somebody else. I called Bill and said, 'Bill, I just don't think it's gonna work.' He said, 'But you paid me.' I said, 'I know.'"[126]

Says Goldman, "The next event of consequence was when I found out that I was off the project and Stirling Silliphant was doing the screenplay. (And wonderfully, too, without a scintilla of mine in the finished work.) I couldn't believe it. Getting canned is always two things, shocking and painful. I was rocked. I'd never been fired before. No one ever told me specifically what was wrong with my work. But if I were forced to guess, I would say, odds on, my screenplay stunk."[127]

"So that's how Stirling Silliphant got involved in *Charly* the movie," Robertson continues, "and I worked with Stirling very closely through the whole picture. I might add that Bill was misquoted later on in an article about Hollywood where he said I fired him. I never fired Bill. I never fired anybody in my life. But he was quoted as saying that I fired him, you know, from *Charly*, but I didn't fire him, and he'll admit that. I simply paid him the money and it wasn't gonna work out."[128]

Silliphant's first problem was a major one, the one that, if it didn't play, would sink the whole film: the surgery that increases Charly Gordon's intelligence. "Okay," he explained, "*what* surgery? If it exists, why aren't surgeons sawing away night and day at the unfortunate mentally deficient? I didn't want to write a science fiction piece. I wanted—and Ralph Nelson, our director, wanted—and Cliff Robertson, our Charly, wanted—all of us wanted to make this a film dominated by the sense of real life, of reality. So I had to understand for myself—even if I never used any of the research—how the brain works. Imagine my astonishment, after digging into towering stacks of medical works and after meeting with numerous neurosurgeons and other experts, to discover that nobody really knew too much about the human brain. That is, knew for *sure*. And the more research I did, the more I found that each successive writer had somehow slightly poached on the work of a previous writer, and that, ultimately, if you traced this pyramid to its foundations, everybody was borrowing from a few seminal sources.

"For this reason, I arrived at the wondrously devious answer to my problems: when in trouble, punt. I dismissed everything I had learned and summed it all up in a simple scene between Claire Bloom (Kinnian) and Cliff in which she asks the poor chap, still in his moronic stage:

Kinnian: Would you like an operation like that?

Charly: Yeh.

Kinnian: Why?

Charly: Well, so I can be smarter and understand Gimpy and the other guys at the bakery cuz they use a lot of words I don't understand. So I could get a little closer to them.

"Go fight City Hall! You can't tear into *that* one because there's nothing to tear into. By staying away from everything I'd learned about neurosurgery—which was that there still remained more questions than answers—I solved my problem."

Silliphant's other major change is invisible: he moved the story from Charly's first person point of view, which worked in print, to the point of view of an objective third party, which works on screen, including scenes that Charly is not present to observe. He made Kinnian a widow, removed the subplot of Charly's tryst with the neighbor, and cut the book's backstory about how Charly's father landed him a job at a box factory to keep him from being institutionalized. "By staying strictly within the human story and following Charly around," Silliphant explained, "sharing with him both the joy and the anguish of super-intelligence, I followed his arc to its peak, then to its nadir."

Another difficult task was creating scenes that showed Charly's accelerated thinking. Workers at the bakery—Charly no longer works in a box factory—mock his low intelligence by challenging him to operate a complicated bread dough machine. When his mind improves and he effortlessly aces its sequential switches and levers, his "friends" circulate a petition that gets him fired. And he shows that he has surpassed Kinnian when he presents her with an apparently nonsense sentence that she cannot punctuate, but he can.[129] Such tangible, visual moments are what lift *Charly* off the page.

One of the most affecting moments—and arguably the *raison d'être* for the whole piece—occurs in a bar late in the story when a mentally retarded busboy drops a tray of glasses and the customers laugh at him. Charly does not; he leaves his table to help the busboy collect the pieces, and the room grows ashamedly silent watching them. Earlier he had said, "Why is it that people who would never laugh at a blind or crippled man would laugh at a moron?" This wordless scene powerfully underscores that point.

A deeply disturbing note of another kind is struck when Charly, whose paintings reveal his sexual thoughts, forces himself on Kinnian. It not only begs the viewer to ask why such an intelligent man is allowing his libido to trump his brain, it calls for Kinnian to angrily rebuff his advances by calling him a moron. The impact on both of them is so jarring that the film has to digress with a long montage showing Charly's month-long quest through various lifestyles, experiences, and distractions, after which he and Kinnian are seen reconciled. It requires a leap, especially considering the screen's disgraceful history portraying rape, and only Robertson's and Bloom's acting skill pulls it off.

Finally, Silliphant dared to remove the flowers from Algernon's story so he could focus the ending on Charly and Kinnian, right up to the moment when Charly, knowing he is about to return to the shadows of severe retardation, rejects her offer of marriage and asks her simply to leave. "If you will watch the final good-bye scene between Cliff and Claire," Silliphant said, "you will see me in my Pinter period—dialogue so clipped—emotions so restrained—playing against the tragedy of the parting—that the film really ends as Claire goes out the door. We have a coda to close—Charly on the seesaw—and we freeze frame with his silly, moronic expression—at the top of his swing upward—and leave him, childlike, back where he began. *Charly* is one of my favorite films because it is simple and human and unpretentious. And Cliff's performance was deeply moving. As you know, he was given the Academy Award for Best Actor."[130]

Robertson tried repeatedly over the years to produce a sequel to *Charly*, sometimes funding it out of his own pocket, other times raising investment money that always seemed to drop out just before production.[131] He died in 2011 at age eighty-eight, still hoping to revive his signature role of Charly Gordon.

Murphy's War, which Silliphant wrote next and that came and went in 1971, is a war movie that is practically without a war. Exquisitely acted by Peter O'Toole and fearlessly directed by Peter Yates (coming off *Bullitt*, 1968), it's set in the waning days of World War Two and has a British seaman (O'Toole) wreaking revenge on the German U-Boat commander (Horst Janson) who sunk his ship. His obsession infects his relationships with those around him, particularly a kindly Quaker nurse (Sian Phillips) and a colorful salvage operator (Philippe Noiret). Silliphant adapted it from the novel by Max Catto.

"*Murphy's War*, in my opinion, fell through the cracks," Silliphant stated bluntly. "It is a far better film than either the public or most critics ever perceived. Richard Schickel, in his review in *Life* magazine, was one of the few critics who resonated with director Peter Yates and me on the wave-lengths of the film. His review was one of the most laudatory any of my scripts was ever given. It was a curious project; indeed, our purpose was to make a flat-out statement about the absurdity, the meaninglessness, of war. So we went for minimal sound, minimal dialogue, a kind of intense fumbling toward death, toward the showdown between enemies who have no further reason for enmity except the blind stupidity and vengefulness of the Peter O'Toole character. And this is why, at the end, in a high angle shot, director Peter Yates closed out the film with the sub sinking, the barge sinking, and the river surging above both, covering them for all eternity. Over this he shot a ragged flight of jungle birds, wheeling off, the only survivors of this pointless encounter between men and their machines.

"We shot it entirely on location in Venezuela up the Orinoco River, one of the toughest locations any film crew has ever had to cope with. You fall into the river and you don't know what'll get you first—sharks up from the Gulf, barracuda, alligators, piranha or, worst of all, a tiny, tiny catfish, almost invisible to the naked eye, which simply adores swimming up the human urethra—male or female, makes no difference. Once lodged in the kidney it eats away merrily and the invaded dies a lingering and exquisitely painful death.

"The immense silence, the Stone Age people, the awesome expanse of forest, simply took over. It invaded our senses. It dominated us. The silence—the silence of life within death—put a dome over the production and nobody who had experienced the location would ever have countenanced any kind of scoring to accompany the images Peter Yates captured. The script was shot as written. It was, from the outset, a very lean and sparing script and Peter [Yates] elected to use a great number of long shots, once more to distance the people, to set them against an alien landscape, and to emphasize how small they were on the scale of existence."

It was a gamble for its mercurial star. "Peter O'Toole was going through a thing at the time where he wanted to play a character that was totally unexplained, and totally unsympathetic, and totally oblique," Silliphant told interviewer Reed Farrell. "He didn't want to justify or explain anything; he wanted the character to be what it was and not have any explanations. Well, I went along with that to a point, but if you so divorce yourself from your viewing audience that they really don't care, then the whole picture goes out the window. On top of that, he insisted on using a very heavy Irish brogue. And, unless you are an Irishman, and I mean from the same country, it was very hard to understand him. Even having written the dialogue, I couldn't understand a word he said. It could have been a fantastic film. The action was there."[132]

When *Murphy* sank with barely a ripple, Silliphant decided to initiate projects rather than wait for things to come to him. He became a hyphenate. He had used his clout to produce as well as to write *Route 66*, but it was really Bert Leonard and production manager Sam Manners who handled the day-to-day functioning of that series. Now he wanted to be in at the ground floor. He first tried a relationship with the flamboyant independent mogul Joseph E. Levine that produced nothing but emotional distress. Then he found *A Walk in the Spring Rain* (1979). Adapting Rachel Maddux's novel about an academic and his wife whose marriage is challenged by an opportunistic love affair, Silliphant set up Pingree Productions, named after his childhood address. The film's idyllic title belies a tale of violent emotions. Fritz Weaver starred as the professor whose sabbatical takes him and his wife, Ingrid Bergman, to the Smoky Mountain locale where he intends to write his book. Bergman soon draws the attention of a local man, Anthony Quinn, and the two of them have an affair, with horrific fallout. But it was the subplot of their daughter, Katharine Crawford, and her relationship with her mother, that captured Silliphant's interest.

"I was drawn to *A Walk in the Spring Rain* by my disappointment with my daughter,"[133] he confessed. "For reasons I have never been able to resolve with her, once I divorced her mother she kept our relationship in the past, back in her little-girl period. This is what many parents do with their children, feeling disappointment when the child becomes a teenager, intent on his or her own life, but the parent keeps trying to recapture the vanishing childhood and creates friction with the child struggling to emerge into youth. With my daughter, the roles became reversed and she kept trying to relate to me in past terms, rather than in terms of the reality of my now liberated new life. So when I read Rachel's novella, *A Walk in the Spring Rain,* I jumped on it because here was a story of a selfish daughter who expected her mother to assume certain responsibilities simply because she was her mother. It has always struck me that these familial relationships should be based on love and caring and letting go, not on obligation."

Silliphant found his own counterpart in the character played by Weaver, the professor who has to face a blank page, both in the typewriter and in himself (although Silliphant claimed he never suffered from writer's block). However estranged he may have felt from Dayle, by this time his first son, Stirling Garff, had succeeded in reestablishing contact. His first wife, Iris, had married Jim Rasmussen and the boy had taken his stepfather's surname. He had also kept up with Ethel Silliphant in the years after she and Lee had divorced.[134]

"When I was much younger," Stirling Rasmussen recalled, "I did visit Ethel fairly regularly, staying at her and Fred's [Wellershaus] house overnight. I remember a sleeping porch they had on the second floor and the sounds of late night trains moving through Southern California in the area of their house." Iris had never bad-mouthed Silliphant, focusing her disdain on Hollywood, but when Stirling Garff hit twenty-four he felt it was time to seek out his father. They got together several times in the 1960s, and he reported that it was as if no time had passed between them. One visit took place during *A Walk in the Spring Rain.*

"I went on location in Tennessee," Rasmussen said, "with Anthony Quinn and Ingrid Bergman. [Silliphant] had imported a bartender from Trader Vic's and, after shooting, each day, the director and my dad and Anthony Quinn and Ingrid Bergman would do drinks. I remember I walked in—I was pretty decent looking at the time—and I put my arms up and said, 'discover me.' They looked at me and started laughing.

"Another experience was an evening party that Anthony Quinn was giving. A younger (as in my age) actor who was in the film, Tom Fielding, wanted the two of us to head into Gatlinburg for some action. He hadn't been invited to the party, so I thought it was a good plan. My dad made it quite clear to me that my evening would be spent in the company of Quinn and Ingrid Bergman."[135]

When the film was soft at the box office, Silliphant took it personally. "It is disappointing when you know you've succeeded in *your* work," he reported in hindsight. "There were some scripts I had done that had gone to camera where I knew that I hadn't finished my work, where I hadn't licked the script. One of those was a sweet, tender little film, which was totally ignored at the box office called A *Walk in the Spring Rain*. I liked it, but it was never quite what we intended. It just didn't have energy, it didn't take off: the two people weren't quite believable. I felt it was time for a love story between two people who were over forty. Because, when you're past forty, you do still continue to have interest in such matters, although, to see films, you'd never believe it—everybody is nineteen or twenty. I thought I was going to fix that for the world. I was going show how that worked. And I didn't. I just demonstrated again that there are no love stories unless you're nineteen."[136]

Despite this, Silliphant maintained a cordial correspondence with Ingrid Bergman for years following their work together and, of course, his first son was back in his life again. His writer's relationship with himself as producer was more tentative: "I always functioned as producer," he insisted, "thereby cutting down any outside input to its least damaging components—the collaboration between writer-producer and director—a streamlined working partnership, which I enjoyed in almost all of my TV work." But he also expressed his doubts in a *Newsweek* interview once the film's disappointing returns were apparent: "The great frustration of my professional life is that anything I originate never [succeeds]. I understand better than anyone else the failure to achieve power."[137] He would remain of two minds on producing: he recognized the choices it gave him as a writer, but lamented the way it siphoned his time from doing the work he preferred.

The same year that saw A *Walk in the Spring Rain* saw the release of a personal project of another kind, *The Liberation of L.B. Jones*.[138] Not only did it become the final work of the venerable director William Wyler, it began a lifelong friendship with Jesse Hill Ford, the author of the novel on which the film was based. The film was disappointing, the experience was not.[139] Silliphant was paid $200,000 for his adapting duties and co-produced with Ronald Lubin.[140] "Once I had completed my script and Mr. Wyler wanted a writer in residence—something I was unable to do for him because of other commitments—I suggested that Jesse Hill Ford be brought in to cross the Ts and dot the Is for Mr. Wyler. Nor did I have any presence on the location, though Jesse quite faithfully did. Jesse and Willy took to each other instantly, and Jesse hung in throughout the shoot, making the changes Willy requested. As a result, I submitted a request for joint film credit to the Writers Guild, not only because I felt Jesse deserved it but because, with me at his elbow, he did a lot of work during the shoot and added those delicious bits of southern largesse, which I found so fulsome and overly dramatic." Both men are credited.

Unfortunately, Wyler (sixty-seven, but with flagging energy) was not up to the standards he had set in earlier years with *Wuthering Heights* (1939), *The Little Foxes* (1941), *The Best Years of Our Lives* (1946), *and Ben-Hur* (1959). *LBJ* was sluggish and unfocused.

"True, Mr. Wyler was nearing the end of his brilliant career—and the end of his life span—but Willy cared passionately about this film. I guess my passion for [it] is based on the fact that the picture was uncompromising. It offered no solutions, no hope—it simply said this is what happens when two sides hate each other. I value the film because, in the period when it was made, it was decades ahead of all the other 'safe Hollywood black-white themes.' It was far closer to the subtexts in Spike Lee's *Malcolm X*. In short, closer to the truth. We dared to say that racial hatreds run *deep* in America— for that matter, all over the world. We scorned the happy ending—the ray of hope. This is why, to me, *LBJ* is one of the works of which I am the most satisfied. It is sans bullshit.

"Why this personal favoritism? It may, I confess, have to do more with the issues involved than the work itself. When I wrote *The Liberation of L.B. Jones* I was up to my gills with the prevailing wisdom that race relations in the USA were now okay. It was painfully clear to me that this was a dangerous profession of amelioration when, in fact, the only thing that had changed, deep down, in the white hearts of my countrymen, was their delusion that they had at last accepted any person of a different skin color or ethnic background as a fellow human being. So I wrote *LBJ* out of the sense of personal fury I felt about the inhumanity of races, of classes, or religions opposed to each other, out of my anger toward the ideologies toward those burdened with convictions and beliefs and never-to-be-reversed attitudes toward their fellow men, woman and children. For *LBJ*, in its own dark heart, is saying only one thing: fuck all of you, all you white bastards, all you black bastards, fuck you for hating each other, for hating yourselves! The film is unremitting, inexorable, without pity or compromise or solution. It simply states that hatred prevails. Hatred is Boss. Hatred is good. Hatred *works*!

"*LBJ* turned out to be a hard film to watch because the viewer can't really find anybody to identify with—which was my savage intent. Fuck the viewer, I felt. Just tell it as it is—there's no hope, no progress, no advance possible.

"The film caused riots in many theaters where it was shown. It was not a film which whites and blacks could view shoulder to shoulder. It went directly to the heart of human savagery—and offered no solution. Which was exactly my intention."

The violence that Silliphant scripted in *LBJ* came tragically home to roost. On February 12, 1969, his and Ednamarie's eighteen-year-old son, Loren, was shot to death outside the boy's residence at 1764 North Sycamore Avenue in Hollywood, just after midnight. Loren, who had gone through psychological rehab in the east a few years earlier, had just moved into an apartment in Hollywood not far from Grauman's Chinese Theatre. He and his uncle Robert (Lee's son by his third wife, Virginia) were having some friends over when a disturbance broke out in the hallway of the four-story building. A man named Chester Allen Johnson (twenty-two) had pulled someone out of a nearby unit and was beating him with a Lugar, demanding hard drugs.

"Loren was a gutsy guy," recalled Robert's brother, Allan. "He had a lot of self-confidence and he thought he could just convince the guy without kowtowing to him, by not expressing fear of the Lugar: 'Look, we don't have it, we don't know anybody, we can't get it for you any more than anybody else on the street, if you want some pot we'll give you some pot.' That kind of thing." It did no good; Johnson—who later claimed that he was so strung out on pills that he didn't know what happened—shot Loren point blank in the chest.

"My brother [Robert, who also had psychological problems] was the only person that had the balls to go out on a ledge and get around and go for help because Loren was bleeding to death on the floor," Allan said. "So even though he was schizophrenic, he was able to make that choice."[141] Johnson and his girlfriend, Terry Jean Phelps, fled. Loren died at 3:04 a.m. the next morning.

Silliphant was on the road at the time with author Harold Robbins, whose novel, *The Inheritors*, he was adapting for producer Joseph E. Levine. He heard the news, not from the Los Angeles Police Department, but from Robbins's bodyguard, who awakened him in his hotel room and told him to turn on the television. The men sat on the bed and cried as they watched the coverage that began, "The son of Oscar-winning screenwriter Stirling Silliphant was murdered tonight…"

Meanwhile, for three days, Johnson and Phelps hid in a Los Angeles apartment, and then hitchhiked to San Francisco with a hapless Army sergeant, whom they robbed.[142] In Oakland, several days later, they robbed and killed fifty-four-year-old dentist Glen Ivar Olsen. Phelps later testified that Johnson's only comment after he shot Olsen was, "Damn, I got blood on my pants."[143] Stealing Olsen's car, the pair drove to Muskegon, Michigan where they held up a liquor store. When Phelps drove the wrong way down a one-way street making their getaway, she was pulled over by police and the spree ended. Johnson was tried first in Michigan for the robbery and handed thirty-five years, then sent to Oakland for the Olsen murder. Silliphant paid the costs to have him extradited to Los Angeles to face charges for killing Loren, where he was put on trial in late 1969. Phelps testified against him. On December 17, a six-woman, six-man jury in Judge Raymond H. Roberts's courtroom took seven and a half hours to convict him[144] and, on January 7, 1970, Johnson was sentenced to die in the gas chamber. He was next tried in Alameda County for Olsen's murder.[145] His death sentence was later commuted to life imprisonment and, in 1995, he began the long process of seeking clemency.[146] As of this writing he remains incarcerated in the Solano facility in Vacaville, California. He is sixty-six.[147]

"Loren's sister [Dayle] called him 'the little prince,'" Allen remembered fondly, "like in the Saint-*Exupéry* book. He had a band, and he liked to talk like John Lennon. He wanted to be a creative guy. Probably a writer, a songwriter. He was a droll, imaginative kid who was very lovable. A lot of freckles, reddish hair, kind of pale, and a little moustache that a fifteen-year-old boy would have. He had a very funny imagination and he would create characters in his mind that would be, say, the creations of Shel Silverstein. He'd [invent] "'Mary Comworth,' what do you know about her?' Well, he would make her up, and he would attribute all these amazing things. Or some guy who was the longest man in the world. How do you determine who was the longest man in the world? It was almost Lewis Carroll-funny stuff that he would say in his John Lennon accent."

Years later, Silliphant would say of this time, "I suppose, [it was] a period of redefining myself, but I would urge you not to put too much stock in that possibility, because, truthfully, I am redefining myself virtually every day of my life and am continually striving to change events as well as myself. If anything, all these reverses may have impelled me more toward Buddhism and the certainty that everything—I mean everything—is transient and that to arrive at any state of even comparative happiness you have to open your hands and let go of whatever it is you've been clutching—because whether you let it go willingly or are forced to—whatever you're holding is already moving away from you. If you let this certainty trouble you, you have a problem. If you accept it as the basis of all existence you can actually be calmed by the loss of people and things."

Silliphant's embracing of Buddhist precepts was not spontaneous. It came out of his relationship with—and, indeed, his discovery of—one of the most charismatic, influential, and yet misunderstood people whose spirit ever touched the hearts of others: Bruce Lee.

9

Enter, the Dragon

"I OWE MY SPIRITUALITY TO BRUCE LEE," Stirling Silliphant often said—only he said it before everyone else did. It could also be argued that it was Silliphant who made Lee widely known to the western world outside of the martial arts community.

Lee's life and, especially, his 1973 death, have long since entered the realm of exaltation, speculation, adulation, and downright fabrication. The truth alone is the stuff of legend, which, in fact, is what it has become.

Lee Jun-Fan (Lee Xiao Loong) was born in San Francisco on November 27, 1940, to well-connected parents who had come to the States from Hong Kong. His father, Hoi-Chuen Lee, was a stage performer who made occasional films, and his German-Chinese mother, Grace Ho, enjoyed deep family roots. When he was three months old, Bruce (an Americanized name supposedly given to him by a hospital maternity nurse), his parents, and their three other children at the time (a fifth was born after Bruce) returned to Hong Kong. This was not a wise move, as it coincided with the Japanese invasion and World War II.

Family connections led Bruce to appear as a child actor in more than twenty films in Asia. Growing up as a teenager in post-war British-occupied Hong Kong, he was involved in enough gang fights that his father arranged for him to start training in the close-range martial art of Wing Chun. At eighteen, after one too many street brawls (as well as to secure his birthright American citizenship), he was sent back to San Francisco, and then to Seattle where he finished high school, enrolled in college, and began teaching martial arts. Soon he drifted to Oakland, California. Throughout his journeys he networked with such martial arts figures as Jesse Glover, James Yimm Lee,

Taky Kimura, and Ed Parker, Sr., the latter a promoter of the Long Beach International Karate Championships, one of the biggest and most prestigious karate tournaments in the U.S. at the time. It was at Parker's 1964 event that Hollywood hair-stylist Jay Sebring (who was later murdered with Sharon Tate by followers of Charles Manson) witnessed Lee's dazzling demonstration. Sebring mentioned Lee to his client, Hollywood producer William Dozier, who was casting for his new TV series, *The Green Hornet*. Dozier hired Lee for the role of Kato, The Green Hornet's manservant/bodyguard.

This was not necessarily a compliment. Like Blacks and Indians, Asian actors had a painful history of being stereotyped by Hollywood. Whether playing obsequious houseboys, subservient Geishas, inscrutable detectives, or the "Yellow Peril" in wartime propaganda films, Asians were not American movie heroes. Bruce Lee would challenge that.

But it would take a while. After playing Kato from 1966 to 1967 and making crossover appearances on its companion series, *Batman* (1966-1967), Lee was unemployed. It was during this period that he opened the Jun Fan Institute of Gung Fu and developed his freer style of martial arts called *jeet kune do*, reportedly in reaction to the more formal *Jun Fan Gung Fu*. *Jeet kune do's* fluidity suited Lee's physique and flashy personality, and, before long, he was known to the Hollywood cognoscenti, among them Stirling Silliphant.

"I was at one of those instantly-forget-the-name-of-the-host Hollywood parties," Silliphant told writer and martial arts historian John Corcoran, "and I heard someone talking about the fabulous Chinese martial artist named Bruce Lee. The story I heard was that Bruce had been invited to Las Vegas by Vic Damone, the singer." Doubting that anyone could defeat his bodyguards, Damone challenged Lee to do just that. In a dazzling display of speed and agility, Lee knocked Damone's hotel room door off its hinges, put one bodyguard on the floor, and kicked a cigarette from the other's mouth before either had a chance to move. "Whether that story is true or not, I will never know," Silliphant allowed. "But that was the story I heard… [and] it was good enough for me. I decided Bruce was going to be my Main Man – the one I wanted to train with."[148] It took him several months to track Lee down and, when he did, Lee set a high price of $275/hour for private lessons[149] "as a way of showing that the lesson offered has worth – the fee is merely the token of this, not the point of it," explained Silliphant, who became a student first and later a disciple.[150] At times the process was painful:

I often went to his house in Culver City. At this point, we were working out three of four times a week. And no matter how hard I worked, no matter how much I exercised, or how much I sparred or how much I ran, I never stopped aching. I mean, there were times when I would wake up in the morning and wish I was dead,

so overwhelming and total was the pain from every aching mus-
cle. I remember arriving at Bruce's house and being unable to get
out of my car. When I started to move my left leg to get out, pain
exploded throughout my whole body. That's how wracked-up I was
from these workouts. Bruce finally came out and asked, "What are
you sitting there for?" I said, "I can't move, I ache too much." He
pulled the car door open and said, "Get out!" Well, when you're
dealing with a master, you get out – fast. Because you know that
if you don't, he's going to pull you out and that's going to hurt even
more. So, painfully, I pulled myself out of the car. Bruce then said,
"You know, in ten minutes, you're going to feel great. What you're
going to do is like diving into a cold ocean with a wet suit on. There's
that first shock of extreme cold and then it all warms up. The first
minute you test all of your muscles they're going to hurt. After that
you'll feel better." He was right, of course.[151]

"The way I teach it, all type of knowledge ultimately means self-knowl-edge," Lee explained to interviewer Pierre Berton. "So therefore they are com-ing in and asking me to teach them not so much how to defend themselves, rather they want to learn to express themselves through some movement, be it anger, be it determination, or whatsoever. He is paying me to show him, in combative form, the art of expressing the human body."[152]

In addition to technique and discipline, Lee taught Silliphant a kind of spiritualism that helped him address concerns he was beginning to have about his life, career, and the world in general. "I never met another man who was even remotely at his level of consciousness," the writer marveled. "I'll give you just one example. Early on in my workouts with Bruce *in jeet kune do* ('the way of the intercepting fist' in Cantonese), he observed that, while my defensive moves were blindingly fast, my offensive moves were perfunc-tory. I tried to explain to him that, as a member of the three-man foils fencing team at USC for three years and as a West Coast fencing champion in foil, I scored 90 percent of my *touchés* via counter-attacks. An opponent would make a move and I'd counter it while he was still engrossed in having deliv-ered it, and I'd skewer him where he stood. 'Bullshit,' Bruce replied, 'that's a technical rationalization. There's something in *you*, something deep in your psyche, that stops you from attacking. You have to rationalize that the other guy is attacking you, so then it's okay to knock him off. But you don't have the killer instinct; you're not pursuing him. Why?' Well, Bruce and I worked on this for weeks. Finally, I volunteered that my father (pure Anglo) had never once in his life held me in his arms or kissed me. In fact, I had never in my life touched a man or had any body contact with another male. No, I was not homophobic. I just—hadn't—ever—done it.

"I remember that afternoon so vividly. Bruce and I were sweating—we were naked from the waist up, wearing those black Chinese bloomer pajama pants only. Bruce moved in closer.

"'Put your arms around me,' he ordered.

"'Hey, Bruce,' I said, 'you're all sweaty, man.'

"'Do it!' he demanded.

"So I put my arms around him.

"'Pull me closer,' he said.

"'Jesus, Bruce!'

"'Closer!'

"I pulled him closer. I could feel the *chi* in his body—a vibrant force which literally throbbed from his muscles. His vitality passed between us—and it was as though a steel wall had just been blown away. He felt *good*. He felt alive. When I opened my arms and he stepped back, he was studying me. 'You have to love *every*one,' he said, 'not only women, but men as well. You don't have to have sex with a man, but you have to be able to relate to his separate physicality. If you don't, you will never be able to fight him, to drive your fist through his chest, to snap his neck, to gouge out his eyes.'

"Well, this stuff ain't for kids, I'm here to tell you. But over the years I shared as much of my life with Bruce as time permitted us. I had many such lessons. They came from the guy—but they came from higher planes as well—and because of Bruce I opened all my windows."[153]

Lee and Silliphant became each other's protégés as well as mentors. Their exchanged letters are not only complimentary, they are extraordinarily emotional for two men in a world that had not yet evolved the male bonding ethos. Lee was supportive of Silliphant's training, both spiritual and physical, and told him (in graceful, almost feminine handwriting) that he had renewed his interest in working together. Silliphant was even more effusive, telling Lee, in a Christmas exchange in 1967, "I think you know how much of an influence you've been in changing a great number of things in my life for the better. I look forward to a long and meaningful friendship so that some day I can call you 'old friend' in the sense that the years will continue to be wonderful to both of us and our families."[154]

And Silliphant opened something for Lee too: doors. He hired him to play the role of Winslow Wong in *Marlowe* (1969), his adaptation of Raymond Chandler's *The Little Sister*, starring James Garner as the eponymous private detective. In updating the novel twenty years from its 1949 origins, Silliphant simplified the plot—no mean feat—switching events and eliminating characters to focus the action on a fewer number of faces.[155] Despite a fine performance by James Garner, the film achieved its chief notoriety because of Lee's cameo as a mob henchman sent to scare Marlowe off the case.

"By the time of *Marlowe,* I had seen so many parodies of a thin guy with a weasel face and a fat guy with a black suit come into the offices to threaten people that merely seeing such types enter a room would send me into gales of laughter. So I thought, let's send in one of the world's greatest martial artists and have him demolish Marlowe's office. If you see this scene, you will see that I wrote it as a master [long shot] and persuaded director Paul Bogart to shoot it that way, rather than in convenient cuts that would allow the martial artist to catch his breath between kicking out a door or knocking the ceiling fixture from the socket. Since Bruce had the physical capability of doing the whole enchilada in one continuous ballet of directed violence, I didn't want to cut into it. Paul went with this and, of course, I rank this scene as one of the foremost martial arts scenes ever to appear in an American film."[156]

Lee's scene in *Marlowe,* released in October of 1969, created a sensation, but—taken along with his guest appearances in routine TV episodics in the same era—was nowhere near a true career launch. Its importance lay not in the scene's excitement but in the fact that Lee was not playing a stereotypical "Oriental." Silliphant also hired Lee as fight coordinator for *A Walk in the Spring Rain* while angling to give him a more substantial role in a series he was developing for Paramount Television about a blind insurance investigator named Longstreet.

"It's absolutely impossible," Silliphant laughingly told columnist Joyce Haber when Paramount and ABC asked him to write the two-hour Movie of the Week pilot for *Longstreet.* "I'll do it."[157] He was soon regretting his quick consent. "I agreed as part of the contract to write six episodes for the first season," he later confessed, "turning the rest of the scripts over to my producer Joel Rogosin, who is a writer, and letting him run with assignments to freelancers. As it turned out, I had trouble writing even four episodes because, with the concept of a blind detective, how many shows can you write in which, to equalize the odds against sighted opponents, you have to have the lights go out in Act III? I do recall having fun with one such episode, however: the series opener guest-starring Bruce Lee, ('The Way of the Intercepting Fist'[158]) which dramatizes Jimmy Franciscus (Longstreet) learning how, as a blind man, to fight a dock bully he can no longer see."[159]

Lee had a second champion at Paramount: Tom Tannenbaum, another private student, who was the executive in charge of taking *Longstreet* from concept to primetime. Lee's character may have been called Li Tsung, but there was no mistaking where his thoughts originated.

"I think the successful ingredient in it was that I was being Bruce Lee and I could express myself honestly as I expressed myself at that time," Lee said, and gave, as an example, "I said [to Franciscus], 'empty your mind. Be formless. Shapeless. Like water. You put water into a cup, it becomes the cup. You put water into a bottle, it becomes the bottle. You put water into a teapot, it becomes the teapot. Now: water can flow, or it can crash. Be water, my friend.'"[160] Lee's work drew praise from the *New York Times* and, for an instant, both Paramount and Warner Bros. were after him for a series—only it had to be on their terms, not his. They wanted a modern story, Lee wanted a western, reasoning, "How else can you justify all of the punching and kicking and violence except in the period of the west? Nowadays you can't go around punching and kicking people, I don't care how good you are."[161]

Longstreet squeaked through for one twenty-three-episode season. Independently, however, Lee had been devising a television series of his own. It was called *The Warrior* and it was about a Shaolin monk who roams the old west in search of adventure and meaning. He took the project to Warner Bros. and nothing happened. At first. In 1972, however, a series produced by that studio appeared on ABC called *Kung Fu* starring David Carradine as a Shaolin monk who roams the old west in search of adventure and meaning. For years, fans have maintained that the studio stole Lee's pitch and hired a Caucasian for it because they felt American viewers wouldn't watch a Chinese actor.[162] When asked about this, Lee was pragmatic. "That problem has been discussed," he said, diplomatically, "and it's probably why *The Warrior* is not going to be on. Unfortunately, such a thing does exist in this world, you see, a certain part of the country. They think that, business-wise, it's a risk, and I don't blame them. It's like in Hong Kong, if a foreigner came to be a star, if I was the man with the money, I probably would be worried if the acceptance would be there."[163]

It was at this low point that Lee and Silliphant started work on *The Silent Flute*.[164] Lee outlined his vision of *The Silent Flute* in a handwritten, undated eighteen-page document,[165] which Silliphant described as being "About an American who becomes involved in a lengthy search for The Book, which might be compared to the Holy Grail or the impossible dream. Even though he has achieved the pinnacle of success in his chosen field, he is driven to find spiritual peace. Of course, there will be lots of *physical* adventures too, since the hero is an expert in *jeet kune do*... a practice that carries street fighting to the highest scientific level."[166] Set in a future society where martial arts are outlawed and the oppressive government has banned all forms of weaponry, it follows the odyssey of a man named Cord as he learns the way of inner resistance.

Full of hope for their project, they pitched it to another of Lee's private students, Steve McQueen. Lee was expecting McQueen to give him an immediate "yes," even though there was neither script nor financing (McQueen's yes would have assured both). When the mega-star was noncommittal, Silliphant knew it meant "No." Lee, however, felt betrayed. He insisted to Silliphant, "I'll be bigger than any other Hollywood superstar before I'm through," to which Silliphant thought, "Bruce, don't break your heart. How can I tell you that the bottom line is that you are a Chinese in a Caucasian film industry? Warner Bros. wouldn't let you play the lead in *Kung Fu* when you yearned to, when you were perfectly qualified."[167]

Silliphant persevered with *The Silent Flute*, bringing in another of Lee's students, James Coburn, who had become a bankable star with *Our Man Flint* (1966) and had just finished *Duck, You Sucker* (a.k.a. *A Fistful of Dynamite, 1971)* for director Sergio Leone. Busy with paying projects, he hired writer Shelley Burton to start the script, for which he and Coburn fronted $7,500 versus $35,000 if the picture got made. When Burton delivered a script that was "mostly science fiction and screwing," Silliphant fired him in a three-page, single-spaced letter expressing his outrage. "Your script is not about the material we commissioned you to represent," it began. "In your personal apocalypse you appear to have been far more intrigued with sex and computer loopholes and with the martial arts. Martial arts is not an affirmation with the animal, but of the spirit."

Next, Silliphant asked his nephew Mark (his brother Leigh's son, born in 1946) to try, which also didn't work out, although it led to a whole separate gambit.[168] Finally Lee, Silliphant, and Coburn resolved to do it themselves. They met Mondays, Wednesdays, and Fridays from 4 to 6 p.m. and worked the whole film out shot by shot, after which Silliphant took three months to polish it into a treatment-cum-script and sent it to Warner Bros. The studio was interested, but only if it could be shot in India, where they currently had blocked funds.[169] Lee, Coburn, and Silliphant made an excursion to India from January 29 to February 12, 1971, to see for themselves. Tension soon developed among the trio over Lee's penchant for public displays of skill and Coburn's desire for privacy. "Bruce came to me," Silliphant recalled, "and said, '*I'm* the star, not him!' For the first time I realized my guru wasn't just a great martial artist, he was also an actor filled with ego. I didn't respect him any less, I saw him more realistically."[170]

India was a non-starter, even though Coburn wrote production supervisor S.K. Singh in New Deli that they were prepping the film to be shot there, in the end he refused to go.[171] Warner Bros. lost interest and a despondent Lee left for Hong Kong to find work. Silliphant tried to dissuade him, to no avail, saying that *Longstreet* was about to make him an American star. When Lee hit Hong Kong in 1970, he discovered to his delight that his supporting role in *The Green Hornet* had made him famous there. He was signed by producer Raymond Chow of Golden Harvest Films to star in a pair of films that would come to define his screen character: *The Big Boss* (1971) followed by *Fists of Fury* (1972). Both were so outrageously successful that American distributors had no choice but to pay attention, even though they admitted they had no idea what to do with the pictures if they imported them to the States.

The adulation Lee received in Hong Kong supplanted his interest in *The Silent Flute*. He wrote Silliphant on Golden Harvest letterhead in August of 1972, "As you see with the [enclosed] clippings, the 'Super Chinaman' is doing his thing in the Orient. However, my desire is still to sock it to them in the States." He closes with regards for Jim Coburn.[172]

Lee's desire was soon met. Although Chinese martial arts films had been playing in Chinese language cinemas in America for years, they didn't hit mainstream theatres until Warner Bros. licensed the Shaw Brothers' undistinguished 1972 production of *The Five Fingers of Death*. Released in the States on March 21, 1973, it became a monster hit, but only in major cities, and then mainly among Asian, African-American, and Hispanic patrons.

Seeing the bonanza in "chop-socky" films, as the show business trades had dubbed them (*dubbed* being the operative word), National General Pictures—formed in 1967 to distribute films from CBS as well as their own productions—firmed a deal with Raymond Chow to import the two Bruce Lee films. They hurriedly retitled *The Big Boss* as *Fists of Fury* and *Fists of Fury* as *The Chinese Connection* (to leach on the Oscar-winning 1971 *The French Connection*), handily confusing film scholars for the next forty years. Despite poorly matched English dialogue, the addition of cartoon sound effects, and muddy picture quality, these films achieved the breakthrough that *The Five Fingers of Death* missed and captured crossover (read: white) audiences. The reason was Bruce Lee.

Immediately Chow, Warner Bros., and producer Fred Weintraub rushed into production what was to become Lee's only completed English-language film, *Enter the Dragon*. Silliphant and Coburn went to Honk Kong to urge Lee to rejoin *The Silent Flute*, but, by then, he had lost interest. He told them that Dino De Laurentiis had just offered him $1 million to star in his next film after *Enter the Dragon*. *Enter the Dragon* was released in Hong Kong in July of 1973 and in the US on August 17 by Warner Bros., the studio that had rejected him as the lead in, if not also the concept of, *Kung Fu*.

Lee never enjoyed his American stardom; he died in Hong Kong on July 20, 1973.

There has been unending speculation about the nature, suddenness, and timing of Lee's death. The official cause was a cerebral edema, something from which a uniquely fit and healthy man of thirty-two could hardly be expected to endure. Soon it emerged that he had suffered an "episode" during a May 10 dubbing session for *Enter the Dragon* at Golden Harvest Studios. Then the rumors started. They ranged from an ancient curse to a contract put out by the triads he had tangled with as a teenager back in Hong Kong. A forensic scientist blamed it on marijuana—marking the first time that a death had been ascribed to cannabis (he later withdrew his claim). Other findings suggested an allergic reaction to a pain medication that produced brain swelling. In the end, it was termed "death by misadventure," which only increased the mystery. Said Silliphant of such rumors and the cult that has grown over the years, "I find it sad. Where were they when he needed them?"[173]

In 1978, with Lee dead and Coburn developing rheumatoid arthritis, Silliphant and Coburn optioned *The Silent Flute* to producer Elmo Williams at Fox after rewriting it "because, without Bruce in it, we had to make changes."[174] When the budget came in too high (because Fox didn't think a martial arts film sans Lee would be a wide enough success), it was returned to Silliphant and Coburn. But it did not die; instead, it achieved cult status in Hollywood among martial artists, two of whom were actors David Carradine and Jeff Cooper. They prevailed on producer Sandy Howard to purchase the script from Silliphant and Coburn.[175] Howard then made a financing deal with Avco-Embassy Pictures, hired Stanley Mann to rewrite the script, and put the picture into production in Israel. It was shot in Ben Shean and Tel Aviv on an estimated $800,000 budget (some sources have inflated it to $4 million) at a time when Middle East tensions were running so high that the producers had to seduce the completion bond company to issue production insurance by telling them that the Israeli army was standing by, just in case.[176] Howard signed cinematographer Richard Moore to direct, making this his only directing credit.[177]

Following principal photography, it was necessary to shoot inserts at a local Hollywood studio to complete or beef up certain scenes, particularly those involving fights. Martial arts journalist John Corcoran was invited on set the first day of the insert shoot by his friend Joe Lewis, the retired world heavyweight kickboxing champion who was pursuing an acting career. Howard had wanted Lewis to star opposite Carradine in *Flute*, but Carradine insisted on Cooper. Howard later launched Lewis's film career, giving him his first starring role in 1979's *Jaguar Lives*, which Howard produced.

Lewis told Corcoran that Howard was disappointed with the outcome of the original fight scenes shot in Israel. He hired Lewis to double for Cooper in the fight-scene reshoots. Unknown to Carradine, Howard had also hired karate champion Mike Stone to double Carradine in the new fight scenes.

Says Corcoran:

"When David discovered the reason Mike Stone was there, he had a fit and threw Mike off the set. Then he started kicking down the lighting and other equipment. I had just arrived that day and the film's publicist met me at the door to prevent me from entering the set. But I could hear yelling inside and the racket of equipment crashing. I was only permitted to enter after David settled down. That's when Joe Lewis told me what happened.

"When shooting concluded that night, David agreed to my request for a taped interview for a national martial arts magazine. In that interview, he expressly stated without hesitation, 'I'm the world's foremost fighting star,' a comment that drew a lot of criticism from black belts when the interview was published. After all, not only was Chuck Norris's career rapidly rising at that time, but Chuck was a bona fide world karate champion who had won his fighting titles in what is called the 'Blood-n-Guts Era' of American karate.

"Conversely, Carradine's kung fu skills were modest at best. To make him look good on film required a lot of editing cuts."[178]

It was at a pre-release screening of *The Silent Flute* at the Writers Guild West where Corcoran met Stirling Silliphant in person for the first time. At that screening, a publicist announced they were seeking a new title for the film and solicited suggestions from the audience. No one offered any. Later it was retitled *Circle of Iron* and, under that name, it was released on January 19, 1979. The title *The Silent Flute* was restored for home video. A contemplative picture sent into an action/science fiction market, it was not a commercial success or, given its contorted genesis, an artistic one.

There are two scripts for *The Silent Flute*. The first is Silliphant's seventy-page original, dated October 19, 1970, and written in European style, which is more of a narrative than the traditional Hollywood shot-scene-dialogue format. The second is Mann's December 15, 1977, 100-page rewrite carrying both his and Silliphant's names. This is the one that went into production. The first is billed *Pingree-Panpiper Productions*[179] *present a film by James Coburn, Bruce Lee, and Stirling Silliphant* and carries the production note:

> What follows, in spite of the form chosen, is a precisely de-
> signed shooting script worked out shot by shot by its creators,
> that is, by James Coburn, who will direct, coproduce and act
> in it; by Bruce Lee, who will stage and direct all the combat se-
> quences and also appear in the film as Ah Sahm, as the Monkey
> Man, as the Rhythm Man, and as Death, the Panther Man; and
> by Stirling Silliphant, who will coproduce and who has written
> the screenplay. *The Silent Flute* will be shot in three locations—
> Thailand, Japan, and Morocco.

The Coburn/Lee/Silliphant script is written to be read as well as shot. "And so it is with martial arts," it begins with an introduced by Lee that tells a story of three swordsmen who try to provoke a fight with a master at an inn. They flee when the master catches four flies with his chopsticks. "The story illustrates a great difference between Oriental and western thinking… To the westerner the finger jabs, the side kicks, the back fist, etc. are tools of destruction and violence, which is, indeed, one of their functions. But the Oriental believes that the primary function of such tools is revealed when they are self-directed and destroy greed, fear, anger and folly." The bottom line, Lee teaches, is that "true mastery transcends any particular art. It stems from mastery of oneself—the ability, developed through self-discipline, to be calm, fully aware, and completely in tune with oneself and the surroundings. Then, and only then, can a person know himself."[180]

It became the challenge of the script to portray, in the objective medium of film, these subjective and highly ephemeral elements. Watching it now, it becomes painfully obvious why it failed. From a purely cinematic point of view there are simply not enough set-ups (angles) to tell the story. Restricted by budget and time, director Moore couldn't shoot the footage that editor Ernest Walter[181] needed to construct into sequences that could work on a cinematic and emotional level beyond merely telling the story. The martial arts sequences, in particular, are photographed in a disappointingly meat-and-potatoes manner rather than with angles designed to show them off. Fortunately, they are performed without added screams, smacks, and grunts.

The dialogue, which in Silliphant's draft was meant to be spoken in Thai, is translated into English in the Mann script and loses its poetry, sounding like fortune cookies. Subtitles would have been more forgiving. But the death blow is struck by Carradine's expressionless monotone. Where James Coburn could hold the screen with his presence alone (someone noted he has only eleven lines in *The Magnificent Seven*, yet dominates the picture), Carradine exudes an arrogance that undercuts Cord's character.

Circle of Iron fulfilled no one's dream, and, for years, fans yearned for a remake that would do justice to Lee's vision. In 2010, producer Paul Maslansky, who served as one of Howard's producers on *Circle of Iron*, announced that he would bring *The Silent Flute* to the screen as Lee had intended. He acquired the rights from the estate of Sandy Howard, who had died in 2008, and began work. His son, Sasha, who was also his producing partner, would write the new screenplay from Lee's original eighteen-page treatment using neither Silliphant's nor Mann's earlier work.[182]

"It's been an interesting road thus far," he said in 2013, while he was still trying. "I've had so many people that came forward and said they had the financing for it, and then, as so many things are in Hollywood, they turned out to be more illusory than real." Instead of the Spartan fittings given *Circle of Iron*, in 1976, Maslansky planned to mount *The Silent Flute* as a major production. "The ambition we have is a little more expansive," he said, "using state-of-the-art special effects. I'm trying to collaborate with people from the Lee estate so we do it properly to make a large-sized film."[183]

By the time *Circle of Iron* hit theatres in 1978, Silliphant had moved on to other adventures, most significantly one he had begun on July 4, 1974. That was when he married one of Bruce Lee's students—not an established movie star, but one whose career he would encourage while both of their lives were changing. Her name was Du Thi Thanh Nga, but their friends would come to know her by what it sounded like to American ears: Tiana.

10

Tiana

HER NAME—DE THI THANH NGA—means "transparent moon" in South Vietnam and "blue swan" in the North. Her father was Phouc Long Du ("auspicious dragon") and, when he became director of press for the Embassy of the Republic of South Vietnam during the American occupation of his country, he called himself "P. Dulong," then "Patrick Dulong" when he learned that "Phouc" sounded profane in English. Her mother, Hoang Thi Van Anh, was a homemaker and master cook who taught famed restaurateur Joyce Steins about Vietnamese cuisine. "Dad told me about the day he first saw mom," she said in her 1992 autobiographical documentary, *From Hollywood to Hanoi*. "They met on a traditional bamboo swing. Of course, their marriage was arranged, but dad said it was love at first sight." Like her countrymen and women, Tiana grew up knowing only war, and the urge to seek peace and unity would inform the rest of her life and art. "In school we sang songs about a time when our country would be at peace," she said. "I was a kid when the 'saviors' landed. They were huge, they were handsome, they were American boys. They were there to protect us. I was in love."

Tiana has two brothers, Michael and Daniel, who are in law enforcement in Northern California. She also has a younger sister, Marian, and had an older sister, born in 1951, who did not survive. Other details of her life history change with the occasion. "I have two birth certificates," she once explained. "I have a birth certificate from 1951 and a birth certificate from 1961, and I was born somewhere in between. The '51 belonged to my sister, the birth certificate that I came over with, which is on my passport, is my dead sister's birth certificate, which was used to get me over here because I had to be older to join my father, who was getting a scholarship at Georgetown University. My parents say that they got the wrong baby out of the hospital, so there's always been a thing about my age and, also, I always lied about my age to be older so I could work. When I was thirteen, I said I was sixteen so I could work at the May Company department store."[184]

Bright and fiery, with huge dark eyes and a ready, brittle wit, Tiana realized somewhere between Vietnam and America that she wanted to be a performer. Coming from a war-torn country, and living in a family where stability was the byword, however, she knew that she couldn't count on her family for emotional support.

The Dulongs came to America permanently at the end of 1966. "I was four or seven," she said, "depending on the different birth certificates. Now that I'm an actress I'd rather be four; when I was little, I wanted to be older."

Because her father was liaison between press and politicians, Tiana got to accompany him to embassy events. President Kennedy sent her a Chatty Cathy° doll, inspiring her father to call her Catherine, which she didn't like, and which began her habit of changing names several times over the years.[185] Given the highly charged relationship between the governments of the United States and Vietnam, however, stability was not part of Patrick's job description. "Dad had many jobs," Tiana recalled, "and moved us to the U.S.A. via Bangkok, Hawaii and San Francisco. The sounds of the cable car bell and 'Rice-a-Roni, the San Francisco Treat' ditty still swarms in my head. When I was three, he worked in the U.S. Embassy in Washington, DC. Later he was upset that Madame Nhu made him her personal press secretary, which he hated, as his loyalties were to President Ngo Dinh Diem, so he quit."[186]

Deprived of an income and diplomatic immunity, and struggling to survive, the Dulongs settled in Virginia. There her father went to work for the Voice of America and became a night security guard to try to make what he hoped would be a "typical American home." Raised on American movies in Vietnam, Tiana decided in junior high school—where she appeared in a production of *Rebel Without a Cause*—that she wanted to be an actress. At the same time, reality intruded on her childhood, as it did for countless American-born teenagers, who watched the increasingly brutal news reports from Southeast Asia.

"Along with the rest of the nation," she recalled, "we were glued to the six o'clock news. I was scared of the Northerners (NVA); in school, where kids said they hated the gooks, I did too. They were killing our boys. I was ashamed to be Vietnamese."[187]

Her teenage years were stolen from her when her father forced her to take housekeeping work, including a cleaning job at twenty-five cents an hour for an elderly couple, the husband of which would attempt to molest her whenever his wife was out of the room. Attending Thomas Jefferson high school during America's Civil Rights struggle was difficult for an Asian.

"In public schools during desegregation, black kids were really nasty to me because I was more accepted than they were," she said. "I could go to the prom, they couldn't—with a white boy, that is. They'd pull me in the bathroom and threaten to cut me up or to beat me up. That's why I got so tough." Eager to break away as well as to learn how to defend herself, she sought out Washington, DC martial arts master Jhoon Rhee when she was 11, after seeing coverage of his school on local television. "I was the karate princess," she reported, "and I was the demonstrator. I was the girl who showed the guys how high they should kick. I was Jhoon Rhee's performing monkey. What I found out later was that all these performing groups that I was singing and doing Vietnamese hat dances with were probably all CIA."

It was through Jhoon Rhee that Tiana met Bruce Lee. "I read Bruce Lee was coming to town," she said. "He was already legendary as the guy who showed up at Ed Parker's Long Beach tournament and did one-finger push-ups. As Tiana the Karate Princess, I asked Grandmaster Jhoon Rhee to introduce me to Bruce."[188] Her first trip to Hollywood was later financed by Lee and Jhoon, but it led nowhere. "Bruce invited me to the Long Beach tournament and picked me up at the airport in his old Porsche and we made a pact about acting." The pack was to prove both prophetic and historic.

Asians in movies have suffered stereotyping second only to blacks. Even when men wrested roles away from heavily made-up white actors, Asian women had it worse, invariably being cast as geishas while men generally wound up as houseboys or coolies. But not Lee or Tiana. "Bruce Lee and I had a pact," she said, "that I wouldn't play any stereotypical girls and he wouldn't put a braid on—I wouldn't play whores and he wouldn't play a coolie. And we didn't." As they shared their dreams, "he told me I needed an Oscar-winning writer to write for me, and he had just the guy."

Her second trip was more successful but also more traumatizing. "I flew from Washington, DC to Hollywood and who did I fly out with? Jack Valenti. He was taking karate with Jhoon Rhee. I'll never forget this: Jack traveled coach. The two of us were in the back of the plane. And he said he would introduce me to Kirk Douglas and everybody, that everybody would love me, that they were going to make a lot of Vietnam movies. They had made *The Green Berets* (with John Wayne, 1968) and I had all this to offer. I was going to say, 'Hi! I'm Vietnamese!' and they were all going to hire me. It was quite the contrary." Douglas leaned on his agency, CMA (Creative Management Associates, later International Creative Management) to represent Tiana, which they did, but little came of it. "They were so painful, those years," she recalled. "A lot of casting couches. I remember one producer [name deleted]. I had an appointment with him, had my book and all my pictures—it cost a lot of money to put one of these books together, 11x14s, deal with photographers and agents who are all on the make. Then I'm dealing with [him] who is totally on the make."[189]

Tiana found herself in the same position as countless other young women in Hollywood, except that her contacts allowed her to enter at a higher level, which only meant that the compromises came at a higher price. "I had the best," she said. "I had CMA. The best: Ted Ashley. I had the best, and they all just gave me lip service. I've always had the knack to get in to the top but I can't close. I got in to the top, I wowed them, and then I opened my mouth and they said, 'She's trouble.'[190] "Dino De Laurentiis saw me in a film where I played an intelligent career woman, one of the rare roles that an Asian woman was asked to portray. I was very flattered: Dino De Laurentiis, king-maker. But when I went in to see him, he wanted me to do a film called *Tito and the Shark* about a girl who would be romping naked on the beach with a shark. I read the script and I said, 'Dino, is there any way we could get rid of the shark?' and he said, 'No, we get rid of the actress!' So I didn't work for Dino.[191] If I was a blond I would have ended up as Marilyn Monroe: suicide. Thank God I wasn't. But it was really, really hard. There you are, sixteen—they don't give two shits. They'll sell you to anybody, anything. And considering that the day we left Vietnam a woman was trying to sell a baby to my father so that we would take it with us to give that child a better life, I felt like I was being bought and sold in Hollywood. And who was selling Tiana? *Me! I* was driving to the studio, fighting with the guard to get in the gate and meet with [producer] who locked the door and lounged on the couch and said, 'Aren't you going to give me a massage?' I said, 'Why did you lock the door?' There was a window there—I figured I could get out, it was on the first floor of the lot. I could just walk out, don't even have to jump down six stories. But why did I have to think about 'How do I get out of here? How do I escape?' when I should be concentrating on the character, the script. I didn't get it. I hated them."[192]

According to Silliphant, he met Tiana while at a Washington, D.C., martial arts tournament. "Bruce Lee had told me that, when I went east, I must meet his dear friend Jhoon Rhee," Silliphant said. "In 1969, there was a tournament at which Bruce was a judge, Jhoon had sponsored it, and Tiana was Miss International Karate Princess complete with hot pants and a diamond tiara. I met her at the tournament and was instantly smitten by her beauty... . and I have to tell you I was just gone on sight. I figured here was the lady I'd been looking for all these years. But I wasn't really able to get very close to her because, as you know, it's difficult when you first meet an Asian girl if you're Caucasian, just to come breezing up, particularly if she's from a good family, and try to make time. There's just no way."

"SS did embellish from time to time, like meeting me in 1969," Tiana countered. "It was not possible, as I did not meet Bruce until the '70s and had not heard of [Silliphant], although I loved *In the Heat of the Night*. I met SS in Beverly Hills, where I only met Bruce when he invited me to join him for the famed Ed Parker Long Beach tournament.[193] He never did like me at first," she added, "because he said, 'I don't like girls who want to be tough, who want to beat up men.' And I was telling him 'No, I'm doing it for the exercise.' Because truly, it's meditation, and it is very good exercise, and I do dance, ballet and everything, and it all relates."[194]

Despite his infatuation with Tiana, Silliphant was still married to Margot, with whom he desperately wanted to have children. Nevertheless, while *Longstreet* was being shot, he asked Lee to help him find out more about Tiana. Lee related what he had learned from Jhoon: That she was still a teenager fresh out of junior college and wanted to come to Los Angeles to break into movies. Lee made the introduction, and the two started seeing each other.

Silliphant and Margo divorced on September 6, 1973, and it became final on January 16,1974. Stirling and Tiana married on July 4, 1974, at Chasen's, the legendary status-conscious Beverly Hills restaurant. True to form, Silliphant wrote on their wedding day but deferred to the occasion by turning off his Selectric early, delivering a twenty-page, single-spaced treatment of *The Swarm* to Irwin Allen, whom he'd be seeing among the invitees in a few hours anyway. He promised to keep his typewriter in the "off" position for five weeks.[195]

In the Chasen's garden, *Tarzan* Producer Sy Weintraub and his wife, Lindy, acted as best man and maid of honor; Melissa Mayo—Tiana's daughter from her first marriage, to Kent Mayo, had ended on May 3—was flower girl. Both Tiana's father and Abe Lipsey (furrier to the stars) gave her away, and Muriel Lipsey served as witness. The bride's wedding dress was a full red Chinese silk coat embroidered in coral and turquoise over a fitted satin dress designed by Bill Gibbs of London, and she held coral red Abbey roses and baby's breath by Fran Pally of Beverly Hills. Superior Court Judge Larry Rittenband officiated.

Wedding guests dined in the restaurant's Chestnut Room on Squab Montmorency with cherry sauce and (of course) Chasen's chili. Partiers included[196] Gwen and Arthur Hiller, Irwin and Sheila Allen, RJ Wagner and Natalie Wood, Joseph and Dee Wambaugh, Ernest and Tove Borgnine, Andrea Eastman and Doug Cramer, Kirk and Anne Douglas, and the James Aubreys, Irwin Winklers, Robert Chartoffs, David Begelmans, Elliott Silversteins, Joseph Sargents, Sherrill Corwins, Leonard Goldbergs, Gordon Stulbergs, and William Holden. Instead of guns, Asian fire crackers were set off. A rock version of the Lord's Prayer was sung by Shirley Mills backed by the Bernie Richards orchestra, then she segued into the theme from *Shaft* as the newlyweds' wedding dance.

After their ten-day Hawaiian honeymoon, the Silliphants took up residence at 815 Camden Drive in Beverly Hills. He bought her a yellow Rolls-Royce, ordered her custom-made lingerie, and shopped with her at the finest boutiques. Stirling, Tiana, and Melissa made an instant family. "SS loved her like his own daughter," Tiana said. "We lived a dream, each night dressing for a premiere with Sy and the David Begelmans and David Wolper, who brought Alex Haley to the house, and David Brown and Helen who sat me down and said quotable things. I was in hair and makeup at Elizabeth Arden's daily, and he shopped for the gowns for me in London and San Francisco—'nobody' designers he discovered and who became the biggest names. He took me into a Hollywood fairy tale life. We lived at the highest level, especially for a writer in those days. He pitched only to network presidents or chairmen of the board."[197] Often she would accompany him to those meetings.

Silliphant was mindful of Tiana's family and former homeland. "Stirling took me out to Camp Pendleton to meet and greet them," Tiana remembered, "and was very generous helping my family, from both sets of grandparents to nieces. He wrote checks to help them find new beginnings."[198] After the fall/liberation of Saigon in late April of 1975, Silliphant helped Tiana's displaced family regain their bearings. Their Vietnamese citizenship had been taken away by the Communist regime and they were adrift in America. They had moved to South San Francisco, but bad business decisions by Dulong had driven them to San Jose where he became a social worker at the Harold Holden and William James ranches, two adjacent juvenile detention centers in nearby Santa Clara. Respected there and called "Uncle Dee," he also served as a court translator for the area's exploding Vietnamese population.

Her father's social work had lasting effects. His 1997 book *The Dream Shattered: Vietnamese Gangs in America* (written as Patrick Du Phuoc Long, with Laura Ricard) was an early profile of a rising phenomenon, and, says his daughter, "the 'at risk' youths where Dad last worked are finding me online and writing moving e-mails to me about how my father's kindness affected them for the good. Some were gang members and write me that, through my father's kindness and compassion and caring, they turned their lives around. Nice legacy!"

The Hollywood life was fast-moving and offered vast opportunities, but it came at a moral and emotional price. "When it was good, it was so good," Tiana said. "I was a bride of God. It was a company town. At Nate 'n Al's [delicatessen], no credit cards were used, just, 'Yes, Mr. Silliphant.' Items in many colors were sent to our rented homes. We never saw money, nor needed it. Bills went discretely to [their secretary] Lesley Lindstaeder or business manager in never-never land in the Valley and cash was brought by Lesley, who told me they tried to tell him to do the right thing, but he regaled them with stories at business lunch with wine, so they all got back to the office and said, 'What happened?? He didn't sign so and so.'"

The lifestyle was expensive but affordable thanks to Silliphant's agent, Don Kopaloff, who won him the then-extraordinary fee of $350,000 for feature scripts at a time when the WGA minimum was one-tenth that. The offers poured in, and it was tempting for a hot writer to over-commit. Silliphant fell into the trap.

"I would talk to Stirling and he would decide if it's a piece of cake, and he'd do it right away," Kopaloff explained. "Many times I told him to finish writing this and then start writing that, do a segue. Invariably, Stirling was doing rewrites on one script while writing another. It was a juggling job for me. A producer would say, 'What is he doing that for? He hasn't finished my script.' and I'd say, 'He's finished your script, he just hasn't delivered it yet because he needs to polish it.' I said, 'Stirling, you gotta ease up on this stuff, you're gonna get nailed.' He worked well when he was pushed to the wall."[199]

Once married, Silliphant began looking after Tiana's career along with her life. One gambit involved reviving Tiana as "the karate princess" in series of 1987 videos directed by Stanley Dorman titled *Karatecize with Tiana*. Her local profile began to rise, and she had an Oscar-winning screenwriter writing roles for her. "He told all his friends, who were now mine, that I was his fourth and last wife," she said proudly. "He was my college, my guru, my Vietnam teacher, and I was his ward—educating Tiana." An eager student, she acclimated to life in Hollywood, life on the sea, and life as the wife of an A-list Hollywood producer-writer. In turn, he saw her as his protégé and was always looking for ways to put her into the films that he was writing. There was resistance.

"He spent three films trying to give me the role because he believed in me, just as he did Bruce Lee," she said. "But I was harder to sell. Even Bruce had to go to Hong Kong to prove them wrong. Stirling said it was racism when Warner Bros. TV told Bruce that Americans would be offended by a Chinaman in their living room each week [for *Kung Fu*].[200] Stirling went wild furious over this. 'They're wrong, wrong,' he used to say [citing the untapped Chinese market]. 'One person in four speaks Chinese and they will take over and lead the world.'"

The Enforcer, a third Dirty Harry film with Clint Eastwood, detailed elsewhere, presented another casting opportunity. Silliphant had conceived Harry Callahan's new partner, Kate Moore, as not just a woman, but an Asian woman, promising fascinating complexities for the film's proposed Chinese gang subplot. The idea did not get traction.

"Clint and John Calley [head of Warner Bros.] were not amused," said Tiana. "Stirling knew he had a far better story with a Chinatown gang and a gal sidekick. He insisted to Clint and Warner Bros. that my character in a Chinatown tong story with martial arts was good for Dirty Harry. They made him throw it out, made him change it to what Clint wanted. In the end, Stirling was happy I was pregnant so he could say to John and Clint, 'See? She's having a baby. I didn't write for my wife, just see it as a good story!' Guys from studios hated having someone's wife, with assumed no talent, forced on them to ruin movies and careers." Word reached her later that Calley had sighed, "Stirling is in love with his wife too much."[201]

Team Silliphant fared better with the 1978 ABC mini-series *Pearl*, turning it into a showcase for Mrs. Silliphant, who played the key role of Holly Nagata in the sweeping story about the December 7, 1941, attack on Pearl Harbor. But, even there, her casting did not come easily. "ABC and Warner Bros. TV must have resented me. The director, Hy Averback, wanted me, but ABC and Warner Bros. did not want 'the wife.' They went to Hawaii, New York, Los Angeles, San Francisco, and Chicago but no actress could read what Stirling wrote for me. Stirling said throughout, 'Bring me the better actress' and relaxed. 'Tiana is your best actress. I know her and I wrote it for her.' There weren't many Asian women to choose from, but they tried. In the end, they tested me and I still couldn't get an answer. It was very hard on me. I was blamed during filming when Holly had to be cut down, as Stirling wrote me long monologues, more for a movie or a play.

"Filming in Hawaii began. I was taking care of the baby. Stirling always said the bastards would come around. But when costumers had no actress to measure, and filming began, I felt blamed. But Stirling had absolute confidence in me. My husband coached me to go in to the President of ABC, Brandon Stoddard, and say, 'I never did TV because there were no good parts.' Frank Konigsberg—his partner on *Pearl*—said later, 'Tiana, what made you say that?' I said that Stirling gave me the script and I said it. They hated me but it was the biggest hit for them and made a lot of money. Warner Bros. ran an ad to congratulate themselves for 80 million viewers and listed all the actors, but they omitted me."

Away from the studio, times were swinging. There were parties aboard the Tiana II, a seventy-six foot, $1 million Swan yacht built in Finland.[202] Silliphant's to-do logs for this period show that he was a thoughtful host, bringing rare wines and classy meals for cruises with important guests. He was a celebrity, as when he and Tiana spent his birthday on a sailing trip across the South Pacific to Australia and New Zealand in January of 1975.

"We sailed into Sidney Harbor," Tiana reported, "and the press was there. Three cameramen in shorts with three movie cameras boarded the ship, so Stirling followed them around. He asked, 'Who is it you're looking to interview on our boat?' They said, 'Some bloke named Silliphant. His movie's big here, *The Towering Inferno*.' Stirling said, 'I am he!'" He was so surprised. This went on to when Sir Run Run Shaw sent his hunter green Rolls-Royce for us in Hong Kong. Stirling said you could play football in our living room suite at the Peninsula, and Run Me Shaw himself in Singapore hosted us, veddy VIP. We got addicted to five-star this and five-star that."[203]

They moved to Marin County in Northern California around the time that the *Killer Elite* (q.v.) was green-lighted not long after their return. The timing was right; Silliphant had long since tired of Hollywood even though he was not only its beneficiary but one of its leading practitioners. "The move away from Hollywood was a major event in our lives," said Tiana. "This move was crucial for Stirling to see how much he hated the eel pit here. His press attack on the Los Angeles industry and way of life he bought into, and dragged me into, lasted less than a year. But his turning publicly against them, and then our move to Marin and then Thailand, left me with no friends upon his death." Their Marin home on Strawberry Point, overlooking San Francisco Bay, had a swimming pool, sauna, den, and rooms that contained spoils from the couple's extensive world travels. "It's real, but it's eight to ten hours a day, seven days a week at the typewriter," Silliphant told gushing KTUV-TV interviewer Bob MacKenzie in 1989 who visited them there, asking, "Why do you live up here when the action is down there [in Hollywood]?" "Well, that's the trouble," Silliphant answered. "It's Hollywood action, it's not what life is about. I just feel much closer to people up here. See, up here, you have to remember, that the film business is less than the ice cream business. In other words, you can go to an ice cream place and know they do four hundred percent more business a year selling ice cream cones than we do in the movie business. I find it refreshing to be reminded of our place in society, which is vastly overrated. We're not curing cancer, we're just makin' flicks."

One such "flick" was *Catch the Heat* (a.k.a. *Feel the Heat*, 1987). Directed by Joel (Yoel) Silberg, a Palestinian filmmaker whose career began when he worked with Otto Preminger on *Exodus* (1960), it was an avowed action film (written with more flair than the genre requires) designed to showcase Tiana's acting and martial arts abilities. As "Checkers Goldberg," a drug enforcement agent, Tiana goes undercover as a stripper in order to track and trap a ruthless talent agent (Rod Steiger) who is using his young female clients to smuggle drugs into the country. Set in San Francisco and Buenos Aires, it also starred David Dukes and Brian Thompson. Although it follows the numbers plot-wise, Tiana's moves are slick and clearly performed by her.

The Stirling-Tiana marriage lasted twenty-two years. The last two years— 1994 to 1996—were spent largely apart by irreconcilable schedules, not irreconcilable differences. While Silliphant was ensconced in Bangkok writing, Tiana was editing her documentary, *From Hollywood to Hanoi*, in New York. Throughout the project, her biggest booster was her husband, especially after her parents felt that returning to Vietnam—particularly the North—would open old wounds. She persevered, and the film reflects her tenacity.

"It is solely the dream, the hard work, the film of my wife, Tiana, who conceived of it, wrote it, directed it, and has now almost finished her final touches in post-production," he enthused in October of 1992. "She had an initial showing of the film (it's intended for theatrical release as a non-fiction film in the genre of Michael Moore's *Roger and Me*—matter of fact, Michael is one of Tiana's principal backers) at the Telluride Film Festival a month or so ago, then took the film to the Chicago Film Festival, is due in November at the Virginia Film Festival, followed by the Hawaiian Fest, then London. She's hoping to get a nomination for the Academy. It is a remarkable motion picture. She shot more than seventy hours in Vietnam and has edited it into eighty-eight minutes—a truly remarkable work. So maybe after all these years of my efforts in behalf of Vietnam, I've finally succeeded—through Tiana's film."[204]

"It was a film that took great courage to make," he said to Tiana in an interview with Japan's NHK-TV (*NHK Sōgō terebijon*). They sat on the beach, she dressed in Asian colors and he in that white plantation suit. "To go against the wishes of your parents is monumental. You went there and defied all that conventional wisdom about 'you'll be put in prison' and 'the communists will eat you alive.' And you discovered, instead, the truth: a nation has no animus against this country, is trying to forget the war. And we're still caught up in it here. We just can't let go of it. I don't believe it's because we lost, I believe it was a terribly wrenching act of being against everything this country stands for. And it cut the conscience of the American people."

11

Master of Disaster

It's a perverse statement about our media-driven world that, whenever a natural disaster or horrific accident occurs—anything from earthquakes, tsunamis, hurricanes, or tornadoes to 9/11—the first thing terrified witnesses usually say is, "It was just like a movie."

Hollywood is almost entirely responsible for that disaster imagery, and the man who was mostly responsible for Hollywood's disasters was Stirling Silliphant. During the decade of the 1970s, he earned the sobriquet "Master of Disaster," although those who worked on those and other films coyly preferred to call them "group jeopardy" pictures.

"Let me begin," Silliphant said with the wearisome sigh of an oft-repeated response, "by saying that the person most in peril from working on group jeopardy films is the writer." He should know. Between 1971 and 1980 he wrote *The Poseidon Adventure* (1972), *The Towering Inferno* (1974), *The Swarm* (1978), and one that turned out to be an actual disaster, *When Time Ran Out* (1980), all of which were produced and sometimes directed by Irwin Allen. A showman of the old-fashioned school who was as star-struck as any of his audiences, Allen was driven by, and dearly loved, movies and the movie business. Born in 1916 in New York City and trained as a journalist at Columbia University, he entered TV and movies by way of the advertising industry and won his first Oscar in 1953 for the documentary *The Sea Around Us.* Gaining studio access, he produced and directed *The Animal World* (1956), famous for its animated dinosaur sequence, and *The Story of Mankind* (1957), a nutty, cameo-filled version of Henrik Willem van Loon's best-selling one-volume chronicle of the human race. His first real hit was the 1960 remake of *The Lost World*, after which he branched into television and established his legend with *Voyage to the Bottom of the Sea* and *Lost in Space*.

The Poseidon Adventure confirmed a trend that had arguably begun with *Krakatoa, East of Java* (1969) and *Airport* (1970), although the latter successful adaptation of Arthur Hailey's 1968 novel involved a human villain instead of Nature's wrath, as in *Krakatoa* (which, incidentally, is *west* of Java). Others produced during, and inspired by, the Silliphant-Allen canon included *Hurricane* (1974), *Earthquake* (1975), *Hindenburg* (1975), *The Cassandra Crossing* (1976), *Avalanche (1978),* and *Meteor* (1979), as well as sequels to *Poseidon* (*Beyond the Poseidon Adventure*, 1979) and *Airport (1975, 1977* and *1979)*, most of which seemed to star George Kennedy, and some of which were made by Allen sans Silliphant.[205] The trend was so shameless that it even inspired an equally shameless joke: "Did you hear, they're making a double feature out of *Earthquake* and *The Towering Inferno?* They're going to call it *Shake and Bake*." The laughter stopped when the profits started. *Airport*, for example, cost $10 million and grossed over ten times that; *Earthquake* cost $7 million and grossed eight times as much. And *The Poseidon Adventure*, which had to seek partial outside financing because its studio was on the fence about spending $5 million, grossed nearly twenty times its negative cost and returned $42 million in film rentals. And all of these were in the days when a U.S. movie ticket cost around $2.

If anyone had perspective on the genre, it was Silliphant. "I was doing great with the first two," he said, "*Poseidon* and *Towering*. But the downward spiral was my getting involved in those two classic golden turkeys, *The Swarm* and *When Time Ran Out*.[206] I have never been able to bring myself to screen *When Time Ran Out*, so horrendous was the experience of being within a thousand miles of it. What respect my [then] sixteen-year-old son may or may not have got for me has, over the years, been in great jeopardy of fusing out because of my involvement with these final two gasps of the 'GJ genre.'"

Disaster movies were nothing new; the silent cinema offered actual scenes of destruction as early as 1906 with newsreels of the San Francisco earthquake and fire. *The Last Days of Pompeii*, featuring the eruption of Mt. Vesuvius, hit the screens in 1913. But they didn't form a notable genre until American self-esteem was shaken by world events and only the movies, according to Irwin Allen, could offer hope.

"Everybody assumes that, if they had an opportunity, they truly would be heroes," he once explained, "and the disaster films give them an opportunity, within a vicarious moment in time, that they're able to become Errol Flynn."[207]

Silliphant's plunge into the genre was on *The Poseidon Adventure*, drawn from the 1969 book by seasoned novelist Paul Gallico. The project had begun at Avco-Embassy Pictures in 1969, when that company's distinctive president, Joseph E. Levine, acquired the Gallico story and signed Irwin Allen to produce it and three other pictures.[208] In short order, the deal was off, and Allen brought the project to Fox with a $5 million price tag. Fox, which was just climbing back into the ring after a disastrous run of pictures in the late '60s, couldn't afford a tab beyond $2.5 million, so the resourceful Allen prevailed upon exhibitor Sherrill Corwin and distributor Steve Broidy to invest the other half as individuals.[209] Gordon Douglas was announced as director.[210] Almost immediately, Douglas was replaced by Ronald Neame and a January 10, 1972 start date was set for exteriors on the Long Beach, California, dry-docked location of the ocean liner Queen Mary.[211] The first few drafts of the script were written by Wendell Mayes, who couldn't please Irwin Allen, and asked to be released from his contract. That's when Allen postponed the shoot and went to Silliphant in 1971.[212] Silliphant wrote at least four drafts: July 23, 1971, February 10, 1972, February 25, 1972, and the Third Revised Shooting Final, March 24, 1972, which went before the cameras, although there continued to be the usual revisions during production.

It was Silliphant's rewrite that gave *Poseidon* her sailing orders.[213] "*Poseidon* was a straight-out story," he said, "with some—because of Paul Gallico—well-written, flesh-and-blood characters. The narrative line is simple: a passenger liner turns hull up and is sinking by the bow, its time afloat unknown, but hardly more than a matter of hours. A group of survivors has to work its way *up* toward what had previously been the bottom and, if they can achieve that level, attempt to break through the hull before the liner sinks. The group more or less remained intact, despite arguments among them, chiefly a difference of opinion between the Ernie Borgnine character and the Gene Hackman character as to which way is the only way to survival.

"The matter of making the characters empathetic was not a problem because I had a simple and central conflict going between Borgnine and Hackman. In their conflict they exposed their own fears, and therefore their humanity. And as this impacted on the several other characters, we inevitably had to see them as facets of ourselves. And how can you go wrong with an actress of the brilliance of Shelley Winters, whose chubby rump has to be pushed upward—and her face of complaint at such a rude contact—and then, when she has to dive and swim a hazardous course underwater in her bloomers—dies in the arms of her husband before they can get to Israel? Come on, that's really snatching candy from a baby."

Poseidon at once established the genre and transcended it. Stock though its characters may have been, they tagged all the bases and provided one person from every age, gender, and temperament (though not race or ethnicity) for anyone sitting in the audience to identify with. This same trick, incidentally, was used three years later in *Jaws* and became an unspoken casting convention.

With an unexpected smash hit, the race to wreak more havoc on humanity was on. Unfortunately for Silliphant, the disaster wasn't only on the screen, it was also in progress at home. One morning, in October 1972, he kissed Margot goodbye, left their house at 585 Challette Drive in Beverly Hills, and went to work. That afternoon he faxed her to say he wasn't coming home again. His secretary, Nona Joy, typed it for him.

Margot retained famed divorce lawyer Marvin Mitchelson, sued Stirling for $2 million, and took out a restraining order against him. Shortly thereafter, columnist Dorothy Manners linked him with actress France Nuyen, the ex-Mrs. Robert Culp, but that wasn't the case. He had met Tiana and was living with her in a house at 2375 Kimridge Road in Beverly Hills that he had rented from actor James Darren.

Silliphant wanted just three things from the divorce: the stand for his dictionary, his Oscar, and the stamp collection he had been building since he was a teenager. He left Margot the Rolls-Royce, the house, and, carelessly, his credit cards. He was able to retrieve his dictionary stand and his Oscar, but not the stamps or his credit rating. "He showed up here with nothing," Tiana said, "and started all over again."[214] It was nearly a year before the divorce was finalized by Santa Monica Superior Court Commissioner Philip Erbson, who accepted the couple's claim of irreconcilable differences and awarded Margot $500,000 and their Beverly Hills house. The divorce was granted on September 6, 1973.[215]

Meanwhile, the single-minded Irwin Allen was looking for his next film. His first idea, naturally, was a sequel to *Poseidon*, this time having Gene Hackman play his own identical twin brother, and setting the whole thing on a moving train.[216] Not only was Hackman not interested (while shooting *Poseidon*, he had won the Oscar for *The French Connection* and thereafter had his choice of projects), but a far better idea suddenly sparked Allen's mind.

The Towering Inferno came about by coincidence. Two separate books were bought in galley form by two different film companies in 1973: Richard Martin Stern's *The Tower* by Warner Bros. for $390,000, and Thomas N. Scortia and Frank M. Robinson's *The Glass Inferno* by Twentieth Century-Fox for $400,000. Both were about fires in skyscrapers, and both promised to cost a fortune to make. At a time when the average studio film budget was $4 million plus $250,000 for prints and advertising, either of these blockbusters threatened to come in at three times that much just to light up.[217] According to legend, this is what was on the mind of Warner Bros' Chairman Ted Ashley and Fox's chief Gordon Stulberg during a casual tennis game in 1973. By the time it was over (no record of who won), the two men had agreed to co-finance what became known as *The Towering Inferno*. Others say it was the personal project of Frank Wells, the respected President of Warner Bros. Nevertheless, it was Fox that would distribute the film in North America and

Warner Bros. internationally. Because Irwin Allen had just produced Fox's mammoth hit *The Poseidon Adventure*, he was given the reins on *The Towering Inferno*.

Another story has Fox and Warner Bros. in a staring contest over who would shoot first, at which point Allen invited a cadre of Warner executives to his Fox office where he had fabricated a poster, production boards, and a budget even before there was a script. The displays were hidden behind a curtain, and, when Allen dramatically parted the plush panels to reveal his massive preparation, his competitors were so gobsmacked that they stumbled back to Warner Bros. and, in effect, made the studio blink. From then on, Allen called the shots in the partnership which, by the time the film was finished, would have the two companies sharing a $15 million negative cost plus prints and advertising.[218]

Allen had Silliphant write the first of many drafts so the budgeting, scheduling, and, above all, casting processes could commence. Plus the writer had two thick books to read. Or maybe not. "*The Towering Inferno* is, in fact, an original," Silliphant maintained, "although I took elements from two novels, *The Tower* and *The Glass Inferno*, and combined them into my own screenplay working under Irwin Allen's hands-on supervision and with reps from both Fox and Warners since this was, so far as I know, the first major motion picture ever to be co-financed and co-produced and co-released by two major Hollywood studios."[219]

The next trick was surviving the construction process. "It's simple math," Silliphant explained. "Take *The Towering Inferno*. Look at the ads Fox and Warners ran: a strip of star photos with shots of Paul Newman and Steve McQueen and Bill Holden and Faye Dunaway and Fred Astaire and Jennifer Jones and Robert Wagner and O. J. Simpson and Richard Chamberlain, etc. etc., each labeled 'the fireman,' 'the architect,' 'the builder,' 'the contractor,' etc., etc., *actually labeling the stereotype in advance* for the potential viewer. Okay, we had seven major narrative thrusts to fold in—seven major separate personal relationships to be introduced, developed, strained, then resolved—along with their interaction with another group—Holden with Chamberlain, Holden with his daughter, Holden with Newman, Holden with McQueen—seven of the bloody things—and then the eighth character—the *fire* itself (which, while I wrote, I gave a name to—my secret—but my favorite character in the script).[220] I determined to let the fire win—make it the hero—but I always knew that, in the end, the good guys—the Architect and the Fireman—would have to triumph.

"Now you have a script of 130 pages. You have eight major story/character blocks—8 goes into 130 around 16+ times. So you know, going in, that you can only put Holden on 16 pages of the movie in terms of foreground action or any kind of meaningful dialogue, unless you unbalance everything and give him

22 pages and cut Chamberlain to 10, etc., etc., etc. Yes, I call that frustrating because what you are not doing is writing. What you are doing is juggling."

Set in San Francisco (the only major city with a skyline at the time roomy enough to superimpose the world's tallest building) on the night of the skyscraper's dedication, a fire breaks out and all the famous guests must be evacuated. But they can't, because the builder's son, Chamberlain, has cut corners on materials. So the fire chief, McQueen, and the architect, Newman, must work together to save everyone, which they do by exploding huge water tanks on the building's roof that douse the fire—but not before many people die, are redeemed, or otherwise complete their character arcs.

"That's only the beginning of your problems," Silliphant continues. "You have to deal with the logistics of the physical action, and this becomes a matter of charting, not of writing. If something blows up on the 57th floor and, in the scene before that, you had Paul Newman down on the 32nd floor and the elevators can't be used, how are you going to get him up there? Simple, let him use the stairway. What if the stairway collapses on his way up? Okay, we need a scene about that. So before you can get the man up there to do his few pages, you now have to create a new scene out of the mechanical motivations of the action. Jesus, guys, where did we leave Steve McQueen in his last scene before we had to cut away to Fred Astaire looking for Jennifer Jones's cat? What? He was on what floor? How in hell do we get him higher? We can get him lower; Steve loves to rappel down smoking elevator shafts with cowardly young firemen to whom he has to demonstrate unflinching macho so they too can rappel down smoking elevator shafts. We get him up there by chopper, dummy. Yeh, but in a previous scene we had the wind force up there to forty knots and no chopper could land on the roof. How about breeches buoy? Yeh. What in hell is a breeches buoy? See, we get the Coast Guard in and they *shoot* one of the bloody things up."[221]

Steve McQueen was initially offered the role of the architect, but he balked. His keen survival instinct told him that there was something wrong with the role even though it was heroic. Finally he realized what it was, and asked to play the fire chief instead. Cynics remarked that it was just the macho McQueen's yearning for childhood wish-fulfillment. In truth, the savvy McQueen realized that the fire chief was the only character in the whole picture who did not in any way bear guilt for the disaster.[222] With McQueen set, Paul Newman—who had no need to prove himself—was engaged as the architect. Then came the billing squabble.

"The Newman-McQueen thing was, who was first and who was higher," explained David Forbes, who directed *Inferno's* publicity onslaught. "Irwin sat in the middle of the negotiations, and it's not normal—or at least it wasn't then—for the producer to be doing those deals, and he ended up making one actor (McQueen) first so that he would be up on the screen first, and the other actor (Newman) higher, even thought he was on the other side of the screen. So one could say, 'I'm higher' and the other could say 'I'm first.'"

As soon as both McQueen and Newman were in place, Allen called Silliphant, who was on a Caribbean cruise, and summoned him back to rewrite yet again what had to be a Christmas 1974 release. Silliphant immediately realized that the new problems were diplomatic as well as creative.

"The only ego problem I faced from all the actors, he said, "was an occasional (i.e. daily) 'contact' with either Paul Newman or with Steve, or, on blacker days, from both. There was never a problem when they were shooting separate scenes. (Incidentally, I was on the location throughout the filming and therefore, unluckily, in harm's way). Given a scene with Faye Dunaway, Paul Newman was a dream, as he almost always is. It's a pleasure just to be around this guy, he's so bright, so instantaneous, so far ahead of everybody else. But you put Paul in a scene with Steve and we have an entirely different dynamic at work. I was told, privately and separately, by both gentlemen on one occasion or another, 'Don't let Steve (or Paul) "blue-eye" me in this scene!'[223] This meant that if you'd written the scene where the punch line which wraps the scene comes at the end, where the director is likely to cover with a close-up, you'd get Steve socking it across with one of my better lines and laying that cold blue stare right at the camera, and where does that leave Paul? With some kind of vapid reaction shot? No, damn it, Paul needs a last line. He needs that blue-eyed close-up. It wasn't easy. I had a number of calls late at night when I was trying to enjoy a fine dinner in San Francisco at the expense of Fox/Warners about the scene to be shot the next day. I think I handled it decently because I love Paul and I loved Steve, and I just sort of danced around between them and tried to keep all three of us happy.

"Despite this, *The Towering Inferno* did emerge as a powerful and engrossing film, I have to admit, despite all my assaults against having my writing driven by forces beyond my control. I believe this happened because we really took after the shoddy builders, the contractors who gamble with human lives to save a buck, so there was, underneath all the never-ending action, and despite the superficiality of the characters, a deeper dynamic, a humanistic point, which lifted the film an inch or two above its own genre. Naturally, I was astonished when it was nominated for an Academy Award as one of the five best movies of the season. There was no way it could ever win, but at least we all got to put on our tuxedos and eat the standard chicken dinner at one of the big-time hotels."

The Towering Inferno made Hollywood history for a reason other than its twin studio partnership, but few people knew at the time, and even fewer know about now: It was the first film to use modern marketing techniques.

"Between *The Poseidon Adventure* and *The Towering Inferno* there was a period of experimentation where people were trying to figure out how to deal with the changing times," said David Forbes, noting that, in the early 1970s, Hollywood was in a slump. "Up until that point, very little television advertising was used in marketing movies. There was some used, but it was peripheral, it was not scientific or substantial. But everybody in town wanted to understand the value of television. So I did a series of experiments at Fox where I would divide the country into parts and would book a whole bunch of theatres in an area according to ADIs.[224] I probably did that for a year, trying to determine how you got value out of television. It was about selling tickets, but it was also about learning how to use television. That led to a completely different kind of marketing when it came time for *The Towering Inferno*."

In other words, instead of having the sales department book the theatres and then have the advertising department find out what TV stations draw people into those theatres, Forbes got the sales department to book the film only in those theatres that fell under the TV broadcast umbrella. By not wasting advertising dollars, "at the time, that's what helped turn around the industry."[225]

It worked. With a $140 million worldwide gross, *Inferno* set the world on fire, so to speak, and it was inevitable that Allen and Silliphant would be asked to make another disaster movie. They turned out two films that were exactly that: *The Swarm* and *When Time Ran Out*.

"I have little to say about *The Swarm*," Silliphant admits, "because I consider it among my worst credits. I thought it was stiff, boring, ridiculous and absolutely uninvolving for the viewer. My only regret is that I let myself be talked into writing it." Based on the novel by Arthur Herzog about killer bees stinging their way through the country, it was directed by Irwin Allen, demonstrating that his real talent lay in producing. It was followed by one that was even more disappointing, and probably killed the genre: *When Time Ran Out*. From all reports, everyone involved with the picture knew it was going to be a stinker from the first day of shooting. "I believe this film scrapes the bottom layer off a nadir, assuming a nadir has a bottom layer," Silliphant shuddered. "The incredible thing about this bomb is that it was written, in one form or another, by *three*—count 'em—THREE Academy Award-winning screenwriters: Eddie Anhalt (*Becket*), Carl Foreman (*The Bridge on the River Kwai*) and me. Eddie wrote a fine script because he followed the book—written by the team who wrote *Is Paris Burning?*[226]—and told the fascinating story of the eruption of Mt. Pelee in Martinique. Apparently nobody had informed Warners or Irwin Allen that dark-skinned people inhabit Martinique. They may happen to speak French, and Martinique may, as it really is, be an actual state in the French union, but the people kill chickens and do ritualistic dances at full moons and beat drums and are often restless. It is awfully hard to assemble an all-star cast with ladies and gentlemen who remain to this day proud of their African origins. Once this outrageous oddity came to the attention of the proper authorities, namely the guys with the money, skin color had to be changed. Black had to become, well, brown. So Carl Foreman was brought in to switch locales and characters. Martinique now became a mythical South Sea island, as in *South Pacific*. Somehow, brown-skinned girls and guys aren't going to raise hackles in Mississippi. And the next thing you knew, there were white guys and gals in the cast and everything was built around the opening of a new five-star hotel. Unfortunately, the hotel was sited much too close to a volcano, which obligingly has to start acting up as dignitaries arrive for the opening ceremonies.

"At this point, Irwin Allen called me and invited me to lunch with Paul Newman. Irwin had already signed Paul, along with Jacqueline Bisset, Bill Holden, Barbara Carrera, James Franciscus, Red Buttons, and Ernie Borgnine, and had scouted his locations (on the big island of Hawaii) and signed a director (Jimmy Goldstone). What apparently had not been done was to send the script to Paul—only the contract for a great deal of money—enough to tempt any actor to shoot the *Yellow Pages*.

"But Paul did not feel the script was ready to shoot. He asked Irwin if I would come in and do some changes. Since both Eddie Anhalt and Carl Foreman were friends, I was not enchanted. I did agree to read Carl's script and I perceived that Carl had simply done what Irwin had asked him to do. But now—in view of Paul's concern—it wasn't enough. The film was scheduled to start shooting in four weeks. Would I come to Hawaii and rewrite the script?

"In one of those grievous decisions which I so often make, I agreed, but only after driving home one of the most lucrative per-week payments I have ever achieved in my career. It was a *lot* of money, and I was to be given a lavish suite at the hotel with a veranda opening onto the beach, permitted to bring my wife and then-toddler son, handed three first-class round-trip airline tickets, and told that I could sign for room service, etc, etc. up to an unlimited amount of credit.

"Arriving in Hawaii, I discovered tension between Irwin and his director and a cast who, after the first run-through reading of the script I demanded so that I could then spot weaknesses and try to get ideas from the actors, was totally confused by the material and unhappy about their scenes. The only character *not* complaining was the goddamned volcano. I saw that the only way we could all live through this experience was for me go to work directly with the actors without either the producer or the director present. And believe it or not, Irwin—who disliked surrendering power or control as much as Napoleon—agreed. I started with Paul and Jackie—the three of us locked in a room taking the 'worst' of their scenes first—and trying to improvise a new circumstance and fresh dialogue. There was, for example, a love scene on the beach. We felt we'd seen it before, possibly in *From Here to Eternity*. What could we do to create an absolutely one-of-a-kind *new* love scene in the sand between two consenting adults? I wish now I had taped those sessions. They were worth the price of admission. Paul and Jackie were simply great. I felt I'd discovered a new way to write a movie. Then, when we were finished, I went on and worked with other combinations of actors and in one way or another put it all together by the time it came to roll.

"What we all failed to perceive was that, while here and there, we had come up with some stuff that didn't sound too embarrassing, it seemed to lack unity, perspective, a single point-of-view. And no mater how we arranged the furniture, the room still looked shabby because of that volcano out there which had to kill some of our people and cause others to trek to the far side of the island where, we hope, rescue ships would be waiting in the bay as dawn comes on. Ghastly! So what can the writer do when he's caught in the production juggernaut and you know your best efforts have failed? Smile, exhibit grace, blame nobody—especially yourself for taking the money—and try—in the future—to never fucking get into the same situation again."

When time ran out for *When Time Ran Out*, it ran out for Irwin Allen too. He never made another feature, although he did produce a number of television shows, including a series, *Code Red*, about his beloved fire fighters. He kept producing through 1986 and died in 1991.

"Irwin liked everyone to think that he ran everything, that he was boss man in charge," said Ronald Neame for a 2003 documentary. "He was also a frustrated director. He liked every shot on a storyboard, and he put the drawings all around the wall. When people came to visit him he'd say, 'You see, we plan everything ahead.' Now, I fought Irwin on that; I don't like storyboards. I don't use them, and I won't. But I didn't completely win because, the next day, when we had the rushes on the screen, he would send his sketch artists into the theatre and they would draw my shots and put them 'round his wall because he had such an ego that he couldn't bear the idea that he wasn't in charge of everything."[227]

"He was, in some respects, like a bull in a china shop," said Silliphant's agent, Don Kopaloff. "He was Hollywood all the way. Everywhere he went, he had to be first class. There were limos everywhere. And to a lot of the younger executives in Hollywood, and to a lot of the young people who were just starting to come forward—don't forget, this was the time when the old guard was on its way out and the new guard was coming in—they didn't take him seriously."

Said David Forbes, "He was always driven by being bigger and better. He was truly old-time Hollywood in the sense that the show was everything."

The Allen-Silliphant association worked to both men's benefits. From Allen, Silliphant won a place as one of Hollywood's highest-paid writers, but it came at the cost of leaving behind most of the perceptive, character-based projects that had first distinguished him. From Silliphant, Allen gained the respectability of having an Oscar-winning screenwriter working for him.

"Irwin Allen gave Stirling as much credit as he ever gave anybody," said Don Kopaloff. "Irwin always considered him as a ticket into the society of successful producers and directors, by way of Stirling's material."[228]

"He was one of a kind," Silliphant appraised. "He was a dear friend. He was often irascible, but never toward me. He was endlessly demanding. He was a perfectionist. He knew filmmaking. He was, for a writer, a superb producer because he made available to you any and every tool money could buy or imagination could create. He had his designers bring models of buildings and rooms and elevator shafts and upside-down ship compartments into my office so that I could write to the specifics of each location. He was available for meetings and conference. He was never late. He worked longer hours than anyone else on his productions. But, yes, he was vain. He could be arrogant because he knew what he wanted, even if what he wanted was sometimes not the best choice. He lacked, I tend to say with regret, the kind of sophisticated taste which would have let him produce a film like *Chariots of Fire*. But then, who knows, he *might* have been able to do that had he chosen. But he was a showman. He loved the circus. He loved prancing horses and gyrating clowns. But be stayed too long at the Fair. He should have gone onward and upward after *The Towering Inferno*—sought new directions."

Silliphant did seek new directions after dwelling in the fantasy world of disasters. For years he'd been saying that he thought his best writing had been for *Naked City*. Throughout the 1970s, he returned to the gritty realm of police stories, only now that he was an acclaimed Hollywood writer, he was expected to burnish the genre into gems that would shine on the big screen. The results were mixed, but his efforts were not.

Silliphant produced *The Joe Louis Story*, a job that convinced him to become a writer.

Stirling and Margot Gohlke Silliphant at the June, 1970 premiere of *A Walk in the Spring Rain*. Stirling Rasmussen, nee Silliphant, stands at right.

Top: Hollywood's most successful screenwriter (circa 1970).

Left: Tiana and her sister, Marian, are flanked by parents Anne (Hoang Thi Van Anh) and Patrick (Phouc Long Du).

Stirling and Tiana aboard the Royal Star liner in January of 1973. He was still married to Margot.

Stirling and Tiana apply for their marriage license in June, 1974.

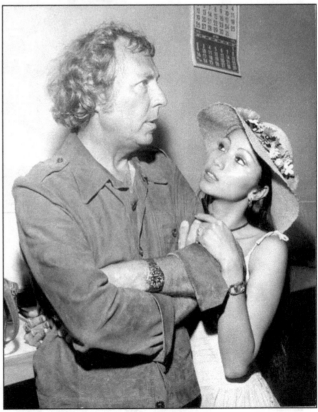

Mr. and Mrs. Stirling Silliphant,
July 4, 1974.

Tiana Alexandra resume photo.

L-R: Silliphant, Rod Steiger, Sidney Poitier, and producer Walter Mirisch
backstage after the Oscars®, April 10, 1968
©Academy of Motion Picture Arts and Sciences

Stirling and young Stirling Linh, circa 1978.

Stirling and his son, Stirling Linh, have a musical
Christmas, 1986.

Stirling poses in his and Tiana's
home gymnasium.

Tiana brought Stirling to post-war Vietnam. The journey affirmed his belief in Buddhism, the wrongness of the war, and his doubts about America's role in it.

Stirling Silliphant faces San Francisco Bay, the view from his home office in the mid-1970s in Marin County, Northern California.

Silliphant and writer David Morrell, who started as a fan and became a collaborator. Malibu, California, 1985.

The Silliphants visit General Vo Nguyen Giap and his family. The General led North Vietnam's strategy and command during the war, and inspired Tiana's later film, "Me & the General."

Silliphant and Le Duc Tho, the North Vietnamese negotiatior to the Paris Peace Talks. When Tho and U.S. negotiator Henry Kissinger were awarded the Nobel Peace Prize in 1973, he famously rejected it on the grounds that Kissinger had violated the peace.

Tiana, Stirling Lien, and two others at Silliphant's Vietnamese gravesite, located after considerable difficulty.

12

Police Stories

AFRICAN-AMERICANS HAD APPEARED IN FILMS long before Melvin van Peebles made the revolutionary *Sweet Sweetback's Baadasssss Song* in 1971, but his story of an angry fugitive putting it to The Man (white society) for a lifetime of degradation was the spark that ignited a screen revolution. The history was not complimentary. At the beginning, movie blacks were generally the butt of racist humor or condescension, usually cast as comic relief, servants, or, at best, "a credit to their race." Unless they appeared in the productions of Oscar Micheaux or other visionary filmmakers on what was then known as the "Negro Circuit," blacks in fully realized characterizations were the exception rather than the rule. Even when a new generation of actors of color emerged in the 1950s and '60s—Harry Belafonte, Sidney Poitier, Beah Richards, Diahann Carroll, Ossie Davis, Ruby Dee, Ethel Waters, or Diana Sands—they struggled for meaningful roles.[229]

As shown earlier, when Sidney Poitier's Virgil Tibbs returned a slap to Larry Gates's George Endicott in *In the Heat of the Night*, American movies began to catch up with where the Civil Rights struggle was heading. The April 23, 1971, release of *Sweet Sweetback* kicked it up several notches. Advertised as "rated X by an all-white jury" (the MPAA), van Peebles's kinetic, incendiary movie ably served as wish fulfillment for millions of black filmgoers who embraced its revolutionary style and vengeful message. Its $15 million gross on a $500,000 investment goaded every Hollywood studio to look around for movies that could star black actors and actresses, although most of them wound up being made by white directors and producers. The "blaxploitation" cycle had begun. Produced cheaply because film companies figured only "urban" (read: black and brown) audiences would buy tickets, and distributed

133

primarily to cities where the "urbans" lived, they provided limited entrée into the largely segregated Hollywood industry for many black filmmakers.

Shaft, released on June 25, 1971, was an event as notable as *Sweetback,* for it was directed by Gordon Parks, the award-winning photojournalist for *Life* magazine, who had made 1969's *The Learning Tree.* More to the point, it was from MGM, a major Hollywood studio whose sales department was able to secure prime theatrical runs, turning it into a crossover smash.[230] "It was fantastic, a very special project," recalled the film's seasoned producer, Joel Freeman. "It was the beginning of a whole other era toward black films. It was a quality production and the studio was behind it."[231]

Parks's street cred made the film authentic to uptown audiences who flocked to see it, and it gave other audiences, especially in big cities other than New York, a taste of Harlem life. The throbbing title song by Isaac Hayes didn't hurt either.[232] What the screen credits don't reflect, however, is that Silliphant and his producing partner Roger Lewis were the pair that made the film happen.

"Ernest Tidyman wrote a book called *Shaft,*" Silliphant told filmmakers Carol Munday and Robert N. Zagone in 1984. "The manuscript was sent to me, I took it to MGM, MGM said, 'let's go.' It was not difficult."[233] Actually, *Shaft* had been in the works at MGM for some time. Tidyman's 1970 novel was about a black detective, John Shaft (Richard Roundtree), who plays the black Mafia and black nationals against the white Mafia to solve a kidnapping. Silliphant and Lewis bought the book after other studios (including MGM) wouldn't commit; it was their involvement that brought MGM's James Aubrey to the table. Silliphant, Lewis, and Tidyman formed a joint venture to produce *Shaft,* and Tidyman wrote the script.[234] They split $50,000 producer fee, another $50,000 deferred, and 33 1/3 percent of net profits, which would be cut to twenty-five percent if other profit participants were brought on board.[235] Once Tidyman turned in his draft, dated August 19, 1970, Parks took writer John D. F. Black with him to New York to show him around the locations (which Parks knew intimately) and then worked with Black to rewrite and shape Tidyman's script. Shooting began on January 11, 1971, dangerously close to a planned July 21, 1971, release on a $1.24 million negative cost coming in $200,000 under MGM's already tight budget.

Even before *Shaft* racked up huge grosses—$2 million on only 105 screens was just a start—MGM put a sequel, *The Big Bamboo,* into the works. Silliphant and Lewis signed writer B.B. Johnson to write it[236] but, by the end of the year, he had been replaced by Tidyman.[237] With its title changed to *Shaft's Big Score,* the picture opened on June 8, 1972.

There has long been speculation that Silliphant did rewrites on one or both films. This may arise from knowledge of his facility and speed as well as his producing experience on *The Joe Louis Story.* Nothing can be found in his files that supports such a claim. What does emerge is his bona fide interest in African-American cinema.

"I'm neither ashamed nor proud of having been a part of that movement," he continued to Munday and Zagone, whose 1984 documentary was subtitled *The Erosion of Black Images in the Media.* "It simply struck me that it was time to amuse people in the theatres and that what the black people needed, and maybe the white people need to see, was some black heroes. It was all part of the 'black is beautiful' movement of, when was that, the sixties, whenever it started. If black was beautiful, therefore black should be heroic, and we all know about the beautiful muscular structure of young black men, so why not show a guy who's that way, who's good with the ladies, who's good with a gun? It struck me as a very simple thing to have an important black hero."[238]

Inevitably, a third *Shaft* was ordered, and, this time, Silliphant decided to write it himself. When it came out on June 14, 1973, he realized that the film was "one of my great miscalculations. I felt that black Americans might have, deep within their psyches, some basic and lasting connection with their antecedents, their ancestry—as was ultimately demonstrated by the success of David L. Wolper's mini-series, *Roots* (1977)."

In fact, *Roots* was never far from Silliphant's mind. In 1976, its author, Alex Haley, had personally come to the Silliphant home on Benedict Canyon, handed him his manuscript pre-publication, and asked him to script it. "Stirling wept when he read it," Tiana recalled, "and he asked Haley, 'Why did you bring it to me? You want a black man to write it.' Said Haley, 'I don't want a black man to blacken my script. I want a professional writer. I want you.' When Warner Bros. wouldn't let Silliphant out of his commitment to write *The Enforcer* for Clint Eastwood, he was heartbroken to have to turn Haley down. Scripted by Haley and James Lee, *Roots* redefined television as well as America's view of race.[239]

There were some bumps getting to *Shaft #3* when Tidyman submitted a screenplay pitch titled *A Carnival of Killers* to Lewis, then went behind Lewis's and Silliphant's backs to Dan Melnick, by then chief of production at MGM, to set up the sequel on his own. This was a breach of his joint venture agreement with Lewis and Silliphant, whose attorney wasted no time informing Tidyman's attorney of this in a letter that alludes to an exchange of verbal abuse on a phone call that preceded it.[240]

The third sequel was always Silliphant's call, according to the original agreement dated April 7, 1970. "I persuaded Jim Aubrey, at the time heading up production at MGM, to let me write and produce a story dramatizing the slave trade in Africa," he said. "Incidentally, this sort of thing still goes on. I was convinced that black America would flock to see Shaft 'stick it to 'em' in Africa and single-handedly throw a wrench into this miserable traffic in human beings. We shot in Ethiopia and in Paris and we made a slick, Hollywood product (lacking all the raw street vigor and honesty of the first *Shaft*). The film is a disaster. I was wrong about black America. They avoided the movie by the millions. At that time the connection with Africa was not yet in fashion. This was before all the African historical revisionism and the now-trendy African thing, right up to this week's fashions out of Paris, definitely showing an African style influence."[241]

As to what a white writer was doing making a black story, Silliphant became prickly: "I am not in the cheering section for African-American cinema, although I certainly would do everything to encourage it, only because I dream of a time when Spike Lee, should he choose to, could direct *Star Wars* or *Home Alone* or *Basic Instinct*. Or that Ron Howard could direct *Malcolm X*. I am agin' this apportioning of rights to any individual based on his race or religion. When a white writer can write a better 'black' novel than James Baldwin and a black man can write a better novel than Proust—*then*, I say, we're finally getting somewhere.

"Yes, I have devoted much of my writing to this matter of human (I do *not* say 'race') relationships because, like war, inter-racial strife is just too fucking stupid for words. It is simply the extension of ignorance, of primitive fears, of Neolithic attitudes. And so I have written many stories and characters about this. But in no way do I see myself as a trail-blazer. Others have written more tellingly about this subject than I could ever hope to. And have I been criticized or obstructed from within the TV or film industries? Not if the writing is good enough, the story powerful enough. Hollywood will make *any*thing if it promises to return a profit. Any failure I may have had in this regard is a failure of my writing, not of the bankers."

The previous year, Silliphant had adapted for the screen, and for Richard Fleischer to direct, one of the more realistic and fatalistic police novels: Joseph Wambaugh's 1971 *The New Centurions*. Wambaugh, a former Los Angeles policeman with a bittersweet relationship toward the force,[242] wrote a moody, episodic book that fell to Silliphant to stitch into a drama with a clear narrative through-line. The multi-character piece involves policemen Andy Kilvinski (George C. Scott), Roy Fehler (Stacy Keach), Gus Plebesly (Scott Wilson), Sergio Duran (Erik Estrada), Roy's wife, Dorothy (Jane Alexander), and a nurse, Lorrie Hunt (Rosalind Cash). In the course of a one-year time span, Roy is shot but recovers thanks to Lorrie; Roy's marriage to Dorothy hits the skids because of his obsession with police work; Andy sinks into depression and kills himself; and, to seal everyone's fate at the end, Roy is killed when he answers a policeman's most dangerous call, a domestic disturbance.

The middle 1970s were a time when, to paraphrase producer Robert Evans, you had to call your psychiatrist to understand the movie you'd just seen. Realism was the ticket, and filmmakers reveled in finally being able to show life as it was rather than the way Hollywood wanted it to be (the phase lasted about seven years until *Star Wars*).

By that measure, *The New Centurions* did not disappoint; in fact, it retains its power thanks to Silliphant's ability to combine characters and situations as he had done with *In the Heat of the Night* so that viewers, as opposed to readers, could follow with their hearts as well as their brains.

One scene is especially instructive in displaying his craft. The book *shows* an incident in which Kilvinsky goes into a woman's house to talk an intruder into leaving, later revealing to his befuddled partner that there was no intruder—the woman had the DTs. As written, it's an example of an experienced cop's ability to judge human nature. In the film, Kilvinsky *tells* that story in his valedictory phone call to Fehler before killing himself. Then, at the end of the film, Silliphant keeps a scene from the novel between Fehler and a woman (Anne Ramsey) in a similar incident, only this time the intruder is real and Fehler is killed. By alertly planting the anecdote and paying it off with the act, he creates irony and closure in the film where neither existed in the book.

"I'm pleased [about] that coupling of incidents," Silliphant said. "It was quite deliberate because I was looking for a linkage between Kilvinsky's death and Fehler's death. And it seemed to me that *seeing* him go into the house and playing out the intruder-who-wasn't-there scene was not as dramatic—since the intruder *wasn't* there—as letting Kilvinsky *tell* it out of a wistful final moment of recalling the past as he is about to terminate for all time his future.

"Joe Wambaugh's dialogue in *The New Centurions* is so excellent, so real in terms of its coming out of his experience in the LAPD, that I quite simply combed through it searching for bits which, in turn, suggested scenes. I found this a most rewarding search. As to the mechanics involved in recognizing moments which may illuminate the story or its characters, I have no way of explicating that process. It comes solely from having done it for so many years that my trial-and-error sensors have become acute, and, because of my own life experiences, I seem to make instantaneous choices from any number of options. In a way it's the same process as the ancient Polynesian navigators used: years of remembering the scent of drifting flowers, observing the stars, watching and feeling the currents and waves, [and how they] gave them the feeling of where in the pacific they were—without sextants, compasses, or sat-nav."

Wambaugh draws his characters quickly and deeply. In a film, the cast, particularly if they're stars, do half the lifting. But it demands writing skill to keep them from becoming "types." Silliphant used "nothing more than dialogue—the character's dialogue—and his line of action and reaction. Both what he says (or doesn't say) and what he does define him as an individual. No matter how much spin you put on him or how you hype him up, if you do not keep his dialogue and action line pure—once you know your character—he will evade you and confuse the viewer. Or, if you slap the labels on too early or too conspicuously, you will overstate him and push him straight into the stereotype."

An example: "If a guy comes down the steps of a Baltimore town house and steps on the tail of a sleeping cat—and the cat screams holy hell—you now have to decide how this guy reacts to what he's just done. Is he pissed off at the cat? At his own clumsiness? Does he feel any guilt? Or does he wish he'd stepped on the [cat's] head? If some kid has seen it happen and stares at him as though he's a Martian, what does he say to the kid? It's all a matter of choices. Every moment in a drama, one character impacts on another—or his environment impacts on him—or he simply impacts on himself. What's driving him? What are the ghosts in his closet? Where is he going right now? Or doesn't he have anywhere to go? So you follow this and see where it takes you and you hold back and hold back and try not to reveal more than a momentary bit of information about the character. If a guy is sitting on a step and a great looking bimbo in a mini-skirt sways by and the guy just keeps looking straight ahead and pays no attention to the girl passing, what's *his* problem?

"I always try to find the unexpected when I introduce a character. For example, if a guy who's behind in his rent has to get back into his West Side tenement and the landlord is out front, hosing the sidewalk—and waiting—what does our guy say as he breezes in? Assume the landlord says, 'hey, Eddie, you forgot what today is?' (meaning the goddamn rent is due *right now*), what does Eddie say as he continues into the tenement? Well, if it's one kind of character, he might say, 'Yes, isn't it the 926th anniversary of the Battle of Hastings?' Jesus, we have to say, who is *this* guy? He looks like a bum, but what's this shit about the Battle of Hastings?"

The action in *The New Centurions* is set against the 1965 riots in the Watts area of Los Angeles, a tinderbox neighborhood that went up August 11-17 when police officers tried to arrest a resident on a DUI and the whole place erupted in long-simmering resentment against the LAPD. But by the time *The New Centurions* was released in 1972, the timeliness of the riots had passed. In addition, the LAPD was staring to clean up their act.[243]

Silliphant explained: "I had a wonderful producer, Bob Chartoff, who permitted me to work closely with Dick Fleischer. We were able to arrive at a mutual concept. We decided to do a nonlinear script, a sort of pastiche, a great number of short scenes with impact, constantly hitting at you, so that the structure of the story, which covers a five-year period, seems to be formless, yet its form is within the changing aspects of the characters, and the multitude of experiences they undergo, which you, the audience, undergo with them. And, at the end, when one of the characters is killed, you've got the end of the story. You could figure out twenty-five different approaches to the book. We chose this nonlinear structure in order to give us a large canvas covering a great deal of time."[244]

"The decision to stay away from the Watts riots was a joint one made by Bob Chartoff, Dick Fleischer, and myself," Silliphant continued, "We felt it would date the picture and, frankly, I didn't want to exacerbate that unhappy time by re-staging it and possibly rekindling it. Also, I felt that switching it over into the Hispanic street gangs was somewhat fresher and more contemporary of the period at the time we were shooting the film."[245]

By the time *The New Centurions* was in production, Silliphant was in Hawaii. After writing fourteen drafts for producers Chartoff and Irwin Winkler, he refused to do any more, and Robert Towne was brought in.[246]

Not long after *The New Centurions*, Silliphant was asked to write a *Dirty Harry* sequel. When the original *Dirty Harry* came out in 1971, director Don Siegel's forceful police drama was criticized by liberals, such as *The New Yorker*'s Pauline Kael, as a fascist treatise on law enforcement. Its first sequel, 1973's *Magnum Force*, offered a seeming rebuttal as Clint Eastwood's Harry Callahan goes after, not a psychotic killer, but vigilante cops.[247] Its firm box office assured a third outing for Clint Eastwood's iconic Detective Callahan.

In 1975, Eastwood had received a spec submission called *Moving Target* from two Oakland High School students, Gail Morgan Hickman and S. W. Schurr, who somehow got their script over the star's transom. The story brought Harry into conflict with a revolutionary group something like the Symbionese Liberation Army who had kidnapped Patty Hearst in February of 1974 and robbed the Hibernia Bank in San Francisco two months later.[248] Perhaps it was because Silliphant lived in Marin County, Northern California, and was close to Eastwood's home in Carmel, or perhaps it was Silliphant's rich association with Don Siegel, but, one day, the star picked up the phone and dialed.

"I had a call from Clint Eastwood," Silliphant said. "I mean, from Clint himself. No lackeys, no executive secretary, no 'Can you fly down to Hollywood, Mr. Silliphant?' None of that classic shit. It was Clint over to you, Stirling. 'Hello,' he said, 'This is Clint Eastwood.' (You always have to, at moments like this, hold back your impulse to say, 'And this is Mary Poppins.') 'I'm thinking about doing a third Dirty Harry,' he said. 'You any notions?' 'Matter of fact,' I said, 'I do.' Because I actually did. 'Okay,' he said, 'I'll fly up and we'll meet. Tomorrow, okay?' 'Tomorrow's fine,' I said. 'Where?' I asked. 'You decide,' he said. 'Okay, you know that little restaurant over in Tiberon, by Seal Rock, hangs out over the water, you look across at Angel Island?' 'Twelve thirty,' he said.

"I loved the guy the instant I met him. We had lunch and I told him he needed a new partner for his third movie—one of the world's primary underclass—forget African-Americans, Hispanics, and Asians. 'What does that leave us?' he grinned. 'A woman,' I said slyly. 'The female of the species. Can you imagine the absolute horror—it's truly Conradian—of Dirty Harry being saddled with a *woman* as a partner?'

"His eyes began to dance as he played with the concept. Finally, he said he liked it. But what was the story? Unimportant, I said. 'We'll come up with some basic caper line—like the French do—but in this third *Dirty Harry* the emphasis is on the character relationship—the slowly evolving relationship of trust which develops between you and your female partner—how it opens you up as a human being and you begin to shed all the sexist shit human beings are burdened with—and in the end she gets blown away and you go fucking rampage crazy—big shoot-out at the end—and Dirty Harry's a different man than he was at the top of the show.'"

In what he called "one of the most enjoyable experiences of my career," Silliphant rejected *Moving Target* and constructed *The Enforcer,* although some of the ideas in the spec script survive, and Hickman and Schurr get story credit. After creating carnage while thwarting a crime by members of the People's Revolutionary Strike Force, Harry is reassigned out of the homicide division. When his partner (John Mitchum) is killed as he and Harry try to stop another PRSF robbery, Kate Moore (Tyne Daly) becomes his replacement. She slowly earns Harry's respect but is herself killed during an explosive climax on Alcatraz Island between Harry and the PRSF, who have kidnapped the glory-seeking Mayor (Bradford Dillman).

"So I was hired and wrote the script and Clint liked it—*almost*. He felt it still needed more narrative drive, that maybe I'd put too much into the relationship and not enough into the bread and butter stuff that would pull in Clint Eastwood fans. So he took [*Moving Target*] and, with a writer [Dean Riesner] with whom he had worked before, folded it into my own script." Tyne Daly, later of TV's *Cagney and Lacy,* was cast as Harry's partner.[249]

"I wasn't happy about this, but I liked Clint so much and have so much respect for his sense of what works for him that I put aside my unhappiness.[250] Yet, to this day, I wish we could have persevered with the original concept arrived at that day as we watched the seals in Raccoon Strait and the ketches tacking toward Angel Island. It might have been a memorable film."

Despite the revolutionary political possibilities in the story, not to mention Eastwood's and Silliphant's political affinity, it's intriguing that the film avoids pretty much every philosophical conflict except the age-old battle of the sexes. "No political thought crossed my mind when I gave Clint my idea for *The Enforcer* and his female partner," Silliphant confirmed. "My entire thought process was concentrated solely upon the humanistic elements such a combination of all-male and tentative-new-cop-female-gender thrown into the crucible of street crime in San Francisco and having to face the challenges together—and how this would affect each of them—from within and from without. And my take on Eastwood? I'd write a film for him any day or night of the week were he to invite me to do so. I can't remember a single second of stress or dissension or temperament or authority or arrogance or any manifestation or anything except a kind of self-confident sense of what he was after. But no sniffing-dog stuff, no shark-under-the-surface. Open, forthright, but always with a sense of humor and what we call in Thailand the most important of human attitudes: *sanuk* (fun)."

The one thing the writer declined to give the star, however, was a catch-phrase. It's no accident that there is no "I know what you're thinkin'" or "make my day" in *The Enforcer*. "As a dialogue writer I've never been apt at such sound bites," he said. "I leave that catchphrase stuff to ad writers or spin doctors. I am too involved with the human voice. People tend to speak more in the way Paddy Chayefsky wrote them—especially in *Marty*—than they do in the ping-pong, smart-ass, attempting-to-be-trendy style of most of today's scripts. You take a flick like most of those made by Arnold Schwarzenegger and you get such magnificent dialogue as—when he has just stabbed a Bad Guy into a door and leaves him hanging there—'Stick around.' I got weary enough during the barrage of James Bond flicks with Richard Maibaum's one-liners (*e.g.* Bond to Bad Guy he's just heaved into a moat of piranhas, '*Bon appetit*"). There is *no way*, even in my dullest moment, I would allow my brain cells to clot in that direction."

As *The Enforcer* rolled, so did Stirling's and Tiana's lives. On July 10, 1976, she gave birth to a baby boy who, after some discussion, they named Stirling.[251] "The discussion was important," Tiana said, "because he wanted a son named Stirling. I said, 'don't you already have a son named Stirling?' He said, 'Yes, but he got adopted, so he's not my son. The mother remarried a man named Rasmussen.' Stirling declared that our son was 'from the stars. His birth was life-changing for him, to right the wrongs as a man and father. Stirling wept for joy that our son was born at 3:04 a.m., the same time [seven years earlier] that Loren had died. He enjoyed being a father and took lots of time off to be a parent, which hurt Dayle, of course, as he never did that with any of his children from his other marriages."[252]

Living at 915 Benedict Canyon Drive in Beverly Hills, little Stirling gave his father perspective on where he had been and where he was headed. It was a time to change yet again, and for the country too. Having come out of a deadly, costly, and soul-scarring war in Southeast Asia, America was moving from an age of rebellion into an age of forgetting, and this rankled Silliphant. For years he had wanted to shape the next generation of writers, to imbue them with his sensibilities and discipline. This mission led him into projects that brought as much heartache as elation. To see where this led him, it will be necessary to see where he had been.

13

The Agony and the Agony

WHEN SILLIPHANT WAS HOT, he was blazing hot, and in 1966 he got an idea to spread the wealth of his industry access to up-and-coming writers. He established Pingree Productions, not just as a personal loan-out company for his own work but as a place to nurture young scripters. By 1970 his plans were set to roll.

"I had this idea of getting together some younger writers and directors and trying to find projects and raise the funding to let them make the kinds of films I wished I had made before I got parachuted into the Hollywood mainstream," he explained. "I acquired the rights to Carlos Castanada's *The Teachings of Don Juan: A Yaqui Way of Learning* and made a [handshake] deal with [Avco-Embassy Pictures'] Joe Levine by which Joe was to give me $500,000 for my 'guys' to develop and to shoot *The Teachings of Don Juan* in 16mm for distribution in college towns only, four-wall deals where I planned to rent the theatres and to keep anyone out of the theatre who was any older than twenty-three. Can you believe the arrogance of that?"[253]

In an era when police rioted against hippies on the Sunset Strip, rednecks beat up flower children, and Ohio National Guardsmen shot protesters, Silliphant's embracing of America's growing youth culture seemed strange to entrenched industry types. Unlike many Hollywood veterans, however, Silliphant did not view youths as competition but, rather, as a resource. Calling them "the most exciting aspect of the medium today" he saw video, rather than film, as a looming breakthrough. "Filmmakers will become overnight pop artists and millionaires," he predicted in a guest column for Joyce Haber. "The variety of video programming will be expanded a thousand-fold and our library shelves will be more crammed with more film cassettes than with books. There will still be room for theatrical super-screen films and broad-casted (sic) television, but the over-all utility of visual media will have need multiplied for the benefit of both artist and audience."[254]

Pingree's first announced project, however, was the stock television series, *Maya*, for which Silliphant served as Executive Story Consultant, based on the 1966 MGM film about a boy and his elephant. The Castaneda project was assigned to a Pingree subsidiary called Yaqui Film Company. Mark Silliphant, his nephew, who had attended UCLA's filmmaking program, was deeply involved in this gambit, which veered into another direction that Castaneda scholars continue to debate. On January 23, 1977, Mark Wood Silliphant, then thirty, married Patricia Lee Partin, a nineteen-year-old waitress. Partin was also known as "The Blue Scout," a woman both embraced and reviled as the spiritual gatekeeper to Castaneda's inner circle. Although Mark had already passed the entry test, he and Partin separated after nineteen days and filed for divorce two weeks later—it became final in 1978. Some sources say that she then took up with Castaneda himself, to whom Mark had introduced her the year before. Meanwhile, Mark changed his name to Richard Rollo Whittaker (he had briefly used Mark Austin before that).[255] Needless to say, the film was never made.

There have been whispers over the years that Pingree, beyond its business purpose, was also a boiler room where young writers anonymously turned out first drafts of Silliphant's lesser assignments that he would then edit and polish before turning them in under his own name. Nothing else, skeptics insist, could account for his immense output from year to year. In the 1930s and '40s, the equally prolific Ben Hecht was rumored to maintain such a cottage industry, and some big-name film composers today are indeed known for employing elves to take up their slack. No evidence of this has been uncovered at Pingree of such a scheme.

While that was going on, Silliphant practiced his craft, did research as needed, toured the lecture circuit, and built his bankability through publicity and hob-nobbing, rare for a writer, but essential for what today would be called "branding." A Silliphant script came in on time, was read by top people, was eminently shootable, and was distinguished by character relationships, not glibness, that attracted major talent.

"I am always, always conscious of language and attitude in order to avoid using words which either had lost their significance or not yet gained it," he insisted. "For example, in now writing *Flying Aces*,[256] having to write dialogue for people in 1914, I found myself stuck in my tracks yesterday by the use of the word *guy*. Did anybody say *guy* in 1914 in reference to another bloke? A check of *Patrice's Dictionary of Slang Usage* informed me that the word in that sense came into use in 1896, so I was okay for 1914—but you can see I just don't toss off a phrase such as, 'Cool, man' or 'no way!' in a non-contemporary window of time. But I do make an effort to use the common language of the film's period. Another example: I would hardly consider referring to somebody being a 'spin doctor' in 1914. But in 1992 [the date of this interview] it's already a cliché.

"As to TV permitting better social criticism than features because it's more timely, in theory that perception makes sense. In practice, it doesn't. Because the networks, the programmers and 99 percent of Hollywood TV writers deal with social issues in the most superficial, viewer-slanted sense. Life, as you well know, is hardly ever solved in fifty minutes. TV, unlike theatrical films, leaps to its hardcore points, losing mood and texture and depth in its skip-dancing." [This has changed since these interviews. – NS]

One of the most disappointing experiences Silliphant faced was the 1981 TV movie that was to serve as a pilot for a series about Vietnam, a subject—indeed, a passion—to which he devoted the last half of his life. *Fly Away Home* was designed to be, in his words, "a television *War and Peace* about Vietnam" that he alone would write to the tune of twenty-two hours broadcast over the course of a single year. As early as 1962, he had addressed the difficulties of returning Vietnam veterans in a *Route 66* episode, also called "Fly Away Home," with Glenn Corbett. Silliphant stressed that his series would be not just about one battle, but an overview. Unlike *The Deer Hunter*, which he didn't like because it used Koreans as Vietnamese, or *Apocalypse Now*, which he liked even though they used Filipinos as Vietnamese, *Fly Away Home* would hire real Vietnamese performers, including Tiana, who would play the surgeon daughter of a Saigon politician. It would go, he promised, "from the Tet offensive in 1968 until the fall of Saigon in 1975 when the last of the invaders butted out. ABC let us make the two-hour pilot,[257] but whatever flicker of courage had caused the network to authorize me to develop such a bold and daring show suddenly was extinguished. I suspect that New York [ABC's headquarters) shot it down. The sales people probably said to the West Coast, 'You fucking idiots, what are you guys doing? What corporation is going to sponsor *this* thing?'

"I can't even begin to tell you what a crushing blow it was to have this mini-series aborted in the way it was. It sent me into weeks of destructive behavior. I went public. I announced—imagine, I, a lone writer without resources or power—that never again would I work for ABC until certain executives were fired. And I named them. Well, three years later I was back at ABC. All the guilty had been expunged; vengeance would have been sweet had their dismissals come as a result of my pissing in the wind. But, no, simple attrition did them in. They're gone—and I'm still producing—so possibly there and there only can one isolate the triumph, meaningless as it may be. But the bitter bottom line is that what might have been a major contribution to the American psyche—airing the issues of the U.S. involvement in

Indochina—never came to being.

"I think the thing that haunted me the most was the fact that, for once in all my years of writing, I had actually written the last line of dialogue for a script which would have run 1,320 pages and covered a period of seven tumultuous years cross-cut between Vietnam and the States—and never got to use it. The line was to be spoken by the news cameraman, the part played by Bruce Boxleitner, as, remaining behind after the Americans abandoned Saigon, he is photographing the first NVA tank breaking through the fence at the Presidential Palace. He looks at the faces of South Vietnamese—faces without expression—a series of cameos which tell you nothing—and everything. And he says, more to himself than to anybody, 'Won't anybody say we're sorry?'

"Over and out. I never got to use the line. And to this moment nobody—no American I have ever heard, certainly nobody in either our government or in our military hierarchy—has ever spoken those absolving words: 'WE'RE SORRY!'"

Networks were not Silliphant's only *bête noir*. On occasion, a star could assume the position, as a big one did on *Over the Top*. "As warming as was my experience with Clint Eastwood," Silliphant said, "my experience with Sylvester Stallone represents everything I detest about Hollywood. Stallone has one talent: that is to have soaked up all the bullshit which has accumulated in La La Land over the years, coated it with an ersatz patina of culture and love of fine art, and created from his boot-straps a genuine, authentic Monster."

Over the Top (1987) is about a divorced trucker who wins his estranged son's love by entering an arm-wrestling contest. "I have managed to expunge from my memory the where and how of my getting involved in this disastrous project," Silliphant added, "but no matter how many sponges I pass over the blackboard, I can't erase the underlying chalk which spells *my own fucking fault*. It was to be a quick rewrite of an existing script and the money was good and I was about ready to buy a new BMW in Munich—or some such nonsense—so I went along with the producer to the brick-walled house in which at the time Stallone was serving time. I was tempted to ask where are the Dobermans, but I didn't. When I met Stallone, I was surprised to see how small he looked. But of course I am a person, not a special camera lens. I will tell you that I found him at this first meeting charming, respectful, and intelligent. I dismissed at once everything I had heard about him that had been negative. He told me a few ideas which he had which he thought might help in the rewrite, then encouraged me by saying, 'It's your ball, Stirling. I don't have to tell *you* what to write. But if at any time you get stuck or want to bounce ideas around, call me.'

"A few days into the rewrite, I did find a need to talk to Stallone. I was seeking his reaction to some Indian stuff I was adding to the mix. I called him. I found myself in a Kafka novel. There was *no* way I could get through. The entourage had closed in around their deity. What did I wish to talk to Mr. Stallone about? It's about making him part-Indian, I explained; you see, before he goes to Vegas he needs to renew his strength—his soul. It's much like the sun-dance performed by the Lakotah. But in this case I'm inventing a really weird sort of Apache ritual involving a lot of rattlesnakes. *Click!* Why is he calling our Sly about *rattlesnakes*? I persisted, however. I called the producer, I called a few art galleries where the rumors were he might be showing up, I called the restaurants he's known to haunt (if that is the proper verb). No Stallone. So I went ahead on my own. Goddamn rattlesnakes and all. I finished the rewrite in short order, turned it in. The producer loved it. I got my money. But never a word from Stallone. Until a while later I get a letter from the WGA about writing credit and I discover that the screenplay is by Sylvester Stallone *and* Stirling Silliphant, based on a story by a couple of honest and innocent other writers.[258]

"The term *going ballistic* came into being at that moment. I prepared an appropriate letter of protest to the WGA Arbitration Committee and sent along the supporting materials, story notes, research and finished script, and shortly thereafter Rocky was knocked out of the ring. He not only was not granted first position, he was granted *no* position. I was given sole screenplay credit." (Not exactly; keep reading.)

"Now here we have a case of winning the battle and losing the war, because the finished film was about as embarrassing as most Stallone films— except that in this instance I stood clearly delineated as the dumb sonofabitch who had written it. I can't possibly explain to you the hundreds of little cuts and jabs that were performed upon the screenplay I turned in. All the Indian stuff was out. Rattlesnakes? Forget it. The relationship between the truck driver and his estranged and dying wife had been turned into a comic strip. The 'love' scenes between father and son somehow were trivialized. Much of my dialogue was changed, not so much in its narrative sense as in its literary sense. Wherever I might have written a piece of dialogue which had at its center some kind of feeling or concept, it seemed to have suffered a sex-change. Or maybe it's just that Stallone can't get too far beyond 'Yo.' I'm simply at a loss to explain how it ended up so badly. Even if I just came right out and said, hey, I wrote a bad script, it still wouldn't explain the depths to which the film ultimately descended.

"My vehemence and distaste for Stallone is not personal, strangely enough. In person he can be, I understand, a warm and delightful friend. I believe my abhorrence is based rather on the fact that he has let himself become the ultimate example of Hollywood excess. It's the stretched limo, the need for the number one table at the trendiest restaurant in Venice, the private jet, the expectation that this is the best suite in the hotel—all the trappings which have nothing to do with the World. Only with the business and all the thousands of remora who swarm around the sharks they create."

When informed that the film credits bear Stallone's name *following* his, Silliphant responded, "The only explanation for my obviously having got the facts wrong here is that in winning the Guild reversal of Stallone's attempt to grab credit, I was so pleased that I must have 'rewritten' the actual events. I doubt that I would have become quite so determined to seek a reversal of the producer's credit claim if the submitted credit had read 'Screenplay by Sylvester Stallone and Stirling Silliphant.' What difference really does it make if the other guy puts his name ahead of yours when he's the bloody star of the movie? Could it have been (I frankly don't remember) that the submitted credit only listed one name as the screenwriter: *his* name? That would have launched me on Jupiter orbit. Then, if the Guild not only restored my name, but put me in first position, that would have signified the triumph. At least, now that we both know Stallone has his name on this garbage, I am no longer quite mystified about that happened to my script as I was when I was going around under the illusion I was solely responsible for it. So your news, dear friend, is good news."

One other train wreck presented itself on Silliphant's track: Sam Peckinpah and *The Killer Elite* (1975), a spy thriller written by Marc Norman in which an Asian politician is spirited out of America for counter-revolutionary purposes in his homeland. James Caan played a CIA agent whose best friend turns on him in the course of the mission and he has to go after him. The picture also starred Robert Duvall, Arthur Hill, and Bo Hopkins, and was shot throughout Northern California during 1974, under conditions that were as dramatic as the story itself. Peckinpah had hit worse skids than usual following the failure of 1974's *Bring Me the Head of Alfredo Garcia* and figured that an action picture would restore his clout. But he was incapable of hiding his disgust, and he took it out on everyone, starting with himself.

"Yeh, Sam was into the Scotch malts at the time," Silliphant confirmed. "His heart wasn't in *The Killer Elite* because he had a script of his own he wanted to shoot instead, but he was alone in this desire, and so was forced to do *The Killer Elite*. He had little input on my rewrite because I didn't accept any and, since we had reached the point where I refused to come on the set, there was no need for either of us to be too polite to each other, nor for me—since I was working for the producer Marty Baum and fuck the director—to be even courteous. My changes in Marc Norman's draft were to change London to San Francisco and an African political figure into an Asian political figure. It was basically a location rewrite. I added the martial arts stuff. I was able to obtain employment for most of my karate buddies by bringing ninja into play."

He also masterminded the casting of Tiana in the key role of Tommie, the politician's daughter, but he kept his machinations to himself and let the System run its course. "I'm happy to report," he told writer John Corcoran, "that Sam and Marty tested Tiana for the lead opposite James Caan and hired her for the part *before* either knew she was married to me. With Tiana in the film and Sam directing, I saw a chance to write the definitive martial arts film. Originally, when I rewrote, I wrote Tiana's part as the daughter of an important tong leader in San Francisco, a female Billy the Kid, a great martial artist, an absolute killer, and a tough little Chinese cookie who was appointed to be one of the bodyguards for this politician and to work with some snappy ex-CIA guys... . What happened was that Sam simply didn't like what I did with the script. But United Artists did, so he accepted the script. When we got up to San Francisco, everyone started changing everything. I got so disgusted by the changes and the direction everything was taking, I walked off the film and refused to have anything to do with it... . They totally changed Tiana's part, then cut out everything that she did." Added Tiana, "The Sam Peckinpah experience still counts deeply in my battered psyche. It was my dream to act. First there were no parts for me, then I got an Oscar-winner to create them, but no acceptance!"

According to Silliphant, he not only wanted to give Tiana a plum role he wanted to take a stand for her people. "I had taken the assignment because essentially it gave me a chance to say something about Asian points of view," Silliphant later elaborated to a panel at the 1983 Manila International Film Festival. "And, as they got to the shoot, they began to change it around to kid Asians and make all kinds of racial slurs. I felt the film had become very racist. I was absolutely embittered about it and wouldn't go to rehearsals and began to yell and scream. I tried to get my name off, and I couldn't. Before you accept a contract, you specify that in the event the film is changed and dissatisfies you, you have a pseudonym that you can substitute, then it can be done. But when the studio hires you, they're really hiring you too, for your name, and if you then say to the public, 'I hate this picture,' you're damaging the film and they have a cause against you,. So it becomes a very interesting legal issue. The only way you can protect yourself is, in front, you say, 'I have reservations about this. If it doesn't work out, then I have the right to use a pseudonym." I didn't know that at the time."[259]

Despite strife on the picture, the Silliphants were so taken with the Northern California setting that they bought a house and moved there after the film wrapped. It was a bad choice; the house, purchased from real estate developer and philanthropist Mark Taper, was built on a land appendage overlooking the Bay called Strawberry Point. It turned out that it had been erected in violation of local environmental ordinances, and the Silliphants spent the next seven years in legal battles over zoning, access to water, the unhealthful condition of the house, and the sale itself. Eventually they sold it at a loss and moved back to Beverly Hills.

The rewriting of *The Killer Elite*, perfunctory or not, rekindles the question of why Silliphant was offered so many novel-to-screen adaptations in his prime years when his reputation had been built by writing over one hundred television originals. He constantly pondered this, particularly whenever he had to tackle massive, big-budget mini-series projects *Pearl* (1978, three hours), *The Brotherhood of the Rose* (1989, four hours); like *Mussolini: The Untold Story* (1985, seven hours); and *Space* (1985, thirteen hours).

"If it's based on somebody else's novel," he told TV host Mike Douglas in March of 1975, "you read it, you absorb it, you try to find his intent. As you know, writing a novel and writing a film are two separate things. A novel has introspective passages, it has flashbacks when the guy was two years old that you can't have in a film. So you have to extract from the book that central part of it which you think is the film that you and the producer want to make. If it's an original, he doesn't have to read anything, it comes out of himself. It's much easier. Writing adaptations is the most difficult thing to do."[260]

As the '70s yielded to the '80s, the politics of TV mini-series—all of them inspired by the immense success of *Roots*—got to be as screwy as features, yet Silliphant mastered it. Novelist David Morrell, who had written him the *Route 66* fan letter, recalled reconnecting with him by phone after *Rambo* had become a hit. "He said, 'What are you working on?' I said, 'Brotherhood of the Rose.' He said, 'I'm going to go over to NBC' and then next thing I know, I had a deal there." Morrell wrote three drafts of the script from his novel, then Silliphant wrote one, and then Guy Waldron did the one that was shot and aired in 1989 as a two-part mini-series. "It was the only mini-series ever to be broadcast after a Super Bowl," Morrell said, "making it another television 'first' with which Stirling was associated. The ratings were huge." Nevertheless, both he and Silliphant were disappointed with the results. "They develop and develop until they exhaust themselves and the material," he added, "but they've spent so much money by then that they film the last one they have. Stirling said, 'They've spent so much that if they don't make it, they'll lose their jobs.'"

The shift from originals to adaptations continued to gnaw at him. "In television, I'm guessing, I had a high rate of success with originals because, except for mini-series and an occasional MOW [Movie of the Week], networks seldom buy source material as the basis for their scripts When he started, best-sellers were gobbled up for movies, not TV. "For one thing, TV couldn't afford it. For another—and far closer to the truth—it is my theory that few people at networks have the capability of reading, let along making a judgment call on, something they may have been forced to read. These are not literary folk. Hence the 'original' works, because the writer pitches a story concept and, since these stories are all the same story, just reworked, the buyer is familiar with the product and, feeling comfortable, he green-lights the freshly regurgitated pap.

"I can recall no writing assignment which took more out of me than adapting James A. Michener's massive body of research, disguised and presented to the American public as a novel, the work called *Space*. The screenwriter is forced to plow through pages of space data, NASA reports, virtually everything except computer print-outs to seek the central storyline and to find the human beings. The characters all seem to have been invented out of their service to the research. Say you need a rocket scientist in order to expound the thousands of words in the book on rocketry—okay, coming up— one rocket scientist. Does he have prostate trouble? Does he tremble at the sound of thunder? What are his fears? His fetishes? Can he satisfy a woman? Can he satisfy himself? What kind of a child was he? What has he read? Did he throw the shot-put in high school? All the trillions of things one must know about a character before you can have him say 'Hello,' I found missing in *Space*. Or at least badly obfuscated by all the data.

"How much easier would it have been had Dick Berg, the producer— and a very talented writer—simply decided to write a thirteen-hour original for CBS based on the idea of covering the period between the first rockets fired against Britain at the end of World War II up until Man's landing on the moon, creating his own characters, told his own story.[261] Or let me do the same thing without having to spend weeks trying to digest Mr. Michener's elaborate and massive account and then to find the sparse thread of humanity buried within the print-outs. Of course, we all know that a Dick Berg or a Stirling Silliphant original wouldn't have got CBS to put up the millions they paid out for this prestigious novel and its transfer to the electronic medium. I do not decry this favoritism. It is totally justified. It is the way the system works. Neither Dick nor I have achieved the international reputation achieved by Mr. Michener and in no way do I, by this example, mean to denigrate either his success or his ability to build up a book through research so that it bristles with facts for all one thousand or more of its pages. I am simply trying to show how much *easier* it would have been for Dick and me to have started on our own, from scratch, and do probably a more powerful, personal and memorable mini-series than we ended up doing having to follow the pre-set and pre-determined course laid down by Mr. Michener's book. And so—lest I exceed the thousand page count myself—I rest my case in the matter of 'originals' versus adaptations. For me, give me always and until the last day of my life, the writing of the original."

Silliphant had the chance to do just that with *Pearl*, an alternate view of the events surrounding Japan's December 7, 1941, attack on Pearl Harbor, that drew from the same well as James Jones's *From Here to Eternity*, only told with a greater emphasis on the civilians than the military. It was the first project of Silliphant-Konigsberg Productions, a partnership brokered by agent Don Kopaloff between Silliphant and former agent Frank Konigsberg, and set up at Warner Bros. Prepared as a six-hour drama with intertwining plots that come together during the dawn attack, it starred Angie Dickinson, Dennis Weaver, Robert Wagner, Tiana (as Tiana Alexandra), Leslie Ann Warren, and a huge supporting cast; it used stock footage of the dawn attack from Twentieth Century-Fox's *Tora! Tora! Tora!* (1970); and it was equal parts dramatic invention and history.

Its own history is unusual. Produced at Warner Bros. and bought by ABC as an "event," the studio balked when producers Konigsberg and Silliphant insisted on shooting it on location in Hawaii instead of at Warner's Burbank facility. The producers also removed the original director, Alexander Singer, early on and replaced him with TV veteran Hy Averback. According to Konigsberg, the network also tried to fire him as producer, but Silliphant fought for him and he prevailed.[262] Aired on November 16, 17 and 19, 1978, *Pearl* was a significant network success and has remained so in international sales. It has also developed a cult following despite only a limited exposure on home video (at this writing it has become quietly available as a burn-on-demand title from Warner Archive).

Future Silliphant-Konigsberg projects never took hold. Silliphant wrote, and Konigsberg solo produced, a 1981 pilot for a detective series titled *Hardcase*, but it didn't sell. They also considered doing for D-Day what they had done for Pearl Harbor but Twentieth Century-Fox, which had been eager to license footage from *Tora! Tora! Tora* for *Pearl*, declined to let *The Longest Day* out of its vaults, so the idea fizzled.[263] Silliphant's move to Thailand in 1988 pulled the plug on Silliphant-Konigsberg Productions.

If the 1960s were Silliphant's transition from TV to movies, and the 1970s were his heyday of disaster films and mini-series, the 1980s saw the networks' entrenchment. Cable was starting to sap their dominance, the studios were youthening, and America was Reaganizing—all of these bringing a decaying sensibility that Silliphant saw but could not buck. Once again it was time for him to change.

14

A Novel Solution

SPEAKING IN 1994 TO AN ASSEMBLY of admiring Vietnamese film-makers, Silliphant was asked to describe the role of a screenwriter in motion pictures. "When I write, every shot is there," he began. "I see in my eye the film before I write it. If I don't see it, I don't write it." But then he said, "Last year I made a film and everybody on the crew changed the script. Everybody! The only person who didn't change the script was the generator operator, the one who runs the machine. I went out and bought him a gift. I took it to him and I said, 'I'm very grateful. You were the only man who liked my work.' And he said, 'I never read it. If I would have read it, I would have made changes too!'" Once the laughter stopped, he added, "To be a writer, because we are treated so badly, the only thing you have is your ego. Now, they take that away from you, and you have nothing, You have no talent. You are just a rug."[264]

After thirty years in the business, Silliphant got tired of being walked on, even if he was well paid. Scuff marks came with the territory, but now there were too many heels. He knew the world was round, and he structured his so he could dodge conflict, except when he was in full charge of it on the page. Confident, even domineering, in pitch meetings, he was often the opposite in his personal dealings, preferring to delegate personnel matters to proxies or through missives. He became a specialist in a passive-aggressive Hollywood technique known as "the non-No 'No,'" in which you refuse work by setting your price so high that the other guy backs down, thereby making it look like the deal fell apart because of him, not you. At other times he could let proposed projects die on the vine by ignoring them. In addition to faxing himself out of an unhappy marriage with Margot, taking swings at ABC in an interview, and berating the *Silent Flute* writer with angry coverage, he fired his longtime agent, Don Kopaloff, by leaving him a dismissal letter that tried to make it sound as if it was for Kopaloff's own good. "I'm writing it so you'll have time to absorb it without having to look either brave or cheerful or understanding—or what-ever," he wrote, "and then when you're ready we can talk about it."[265]

Kopaloff was devastated. "He was one of the few people that I represented without having had them sign management agreements," he recalled. "I trusted him. Next thing I know, I get a letter on my desk—it wasn't even mailed—that sounded like he was crying, he felt so bad. We had been together for a lot of years. I must say I was absolutely furious with him."[266]

Most surprisingly, especially for someone who was so forward-thinking in terms of racial equality and in opposing the war in Vietnam, he was a Republican. "He was a classic Hollywood liberal who voted Republican," his son, Stirling Linh, reported. "My father was pretty conservative. One time during the Bush years, Mom said, 'Oh, your father was outraged by the war in Vietnam and he would have been outraged by what's happening in Afghanistan today' and I thought, 'No he wouldn't; he would have totally supported it.' He would have seen this as fighting the good fight just like he supported the first Gulf War. He would have had the same subtext of fighting the forces of religious fundamentalism and fascism."[267]

Such conundrums add to Silliphant's complexity, particularly in his functional use of violence in drama but not in reality. "I've never been aggressive by nature," he told writer John Corcoran, perhaps explaining this trait. "It's the reason why I could never have been able to compete [in martial arts]. I simply do not enjoy getting out there and beating the shit out of some guy. I don't feel I have the right to harm another person."[268] He could be even harder on himself, even reckless. Although he was paid handsomely, he spent profligately, assured that the work would never stop. After all, with his fame, his skill, and the summit of Hollywood at which he thrived, who could conclude otherwise?

By the early 1980s, however, he was in a financial crunch. The man who had challenged himself to earn $60,000 when he was staring out in 1956 had, by 1984, set a goal of $600,000 to $750,000[269] and was being politely dunned by the banks.[270] His response was reminding them that screenwriting is an uneven business. Nevertheless, his activities during this period show that he was trying to grab as many assignments as possible to get ahead. His appointment books reveal how determined he was, and begs the question of whether he needed inspiration to write or had developed the skill to just sit down and crank it out. During, for example, April of 1982, in addition to writing the novel *Bronze Bell* for 1983 publication, he was dubbing the TV pilot *Welcome to Paradise*; writing the six-part mini-series *Mussolini*; picking up Krugerrands for bank deposit; finishing *Space, Episode 1*; going to Bora-Bora while continuing to write *Mussolini*; and having meals and meetings with Stan Lee, Irwin and Sheila Allen, and Brandon Stoddard; trying to set up *Forbidden Diary* at Disney with actress/producer Nancy Malone; meeting with Marty Baum on an unspecified Sidney Poitier project; and writing letters to friends and colleagues. And most of it got done (see filmography).

These same years saw the kind of upheavals that the film industry hadn't felt since TV shook its financial base in the early 1950s. The tremors begun by the blockbusters *Jaws* (1975), *Star Wars* (1977), and *Alien* (1979) rearranged the Hollywood landscape. Now all anybody wanted to make were youth-oriented action films, a decision that left the people who wrote character-driven scripts, such as Silliphant, striving to reinvent themselves.

Silliphant chose a novel solution. Literally, a novel. "When I undertook the John Locke series of paperback novels, I announced in advance of publication that none of them would ever be available in terms of its motion picture rights," he stated unequivocally. "I further buttressed that position by writing each of the three novels so far for this series in a style which would make it virtually impossible for any living screenwriter to be able to fashion a script from the work. In short, I determined to be totally out of the reach of studio group-think and to write books I damn well wanted to write for *myself.*" He offered a more cynical reason for this decision by explaining, during a 1983 promo appearance for *Steel Tiger* on LA's *The Sunday Show*, "It's the first of a series of twelve books based on the same character. Imagine what would happen if I were to sell it and they were to make a bad film? What happens to the other eleven books? No one would want to read them." When asked by the host, "What happens if they make a good film," he replied wearily, "The chances are ninety percent that they wouldn't."[271]

There was pragmatism in his move to Bangkok five years later in July of 1988. Before Skype, international phone calls cost a bundle, and e-mail didn't become a factor until the World Wide Web kicked off in 1991. So the cheapest and fastest way to reach people in other countries was fax. The advantage of faxes, Silliphant explained, was that, when producers were forced to put their promises in writing, they were less prone to bullshit. Perhaps because of this, the screen offers dwindled, and Silliphant focused on novels. He extolled them to the *L.A. Times*'s Charles Champlin in 1985, saying, "If I could find a producer who would do for me in 1989 what Cubby Broccoli did for [James] Bond, well, now."[272] Published by Ballantine, the first, *Steel Tiger*, came out in 1983; then *Bronze Bell* in 1985; and *Silver Star* in 1986. A fourth, *Iron Kiss*, was never begun, and the series ended after three titles.

Silliphant took a hit in his income to start writing them, but he felt it was something he had to do.[273] John Locke is a Vietnam vet, a former San Francisco narcotics and vice officer, the son of a poet, and a sailor-of-fortune who lives aboard a forty-foot ketch, the Steel Tiger, out of San Diego, but can more often be found on the high seas. His voice—which is to say, Silliphant's—is equal parts narrative and commentary, rich in detail and monologue. Although Locke has left 'Nam, 'Nam hasn't left him, and he is drawn back into the intrigues for which, in an existential sense, he shares moral responsibility. Locke is named after one of the Enlightenment's most important thinkers, John Locke (1632-1704), whose writings were key in defining the idea of consciousness, much as Descartes postulated, "I think, therefore I am." For Silliphant's Locke, it became, "I am, therefore I'd better think fast." Part of him is Silliphant and part is a Norwegian sailor with whom he formed a disastrous charter boat company called Oceanic Enterprises in St. Croix that magically made money for everyone except him.

Although he had dabbled in novels at the very beginning of his writing career and novelized occasional scripts, those forays had been more utilitarian than literary and were driven by residuals and the need to control his properties. The Locke books were a way to get out of that trap and write what he wanted to write. They allowed him to ponder two subjects for which he held a vast ocean of emotion: Southeast Asia and sailing.

The seafaring worm, picked up as a seven-year-old in San Diego, bored deeply into his soul. Over the years he had owned a succession of vessels: racing daysailer, Laser, Montgomery, 470, Sansare, then a Hobie Cat. He sailed out of Marina del Rey in an Islander 36 (the Tiana I) that slept seven and of which he was so proud that he said, "the first night aboard, I slept in every bunk." Later he admitted that it slept seven only "if the seven have just come from an orgy and don't mind the close contact."[274] One of the reasons he eventually sold it was that the five-man crew he hired to staff the boat got to thinking that they owned it; he'd come aboard and find women's underwear and the residue of parties that neither he nor Tiana had thrown. He got rid of it.[275]

Now he could focus on writing. For *Silver Star*, John Locke learns he has a half-Vietnamese son living in Hanoi whom he must rescue from the slave state that has devoured the postwar nation. The title refers to the medal for gallantry that Locke received, and which he entrusted to Doan Thi, the woman he loved, and who, when she died, passed the talisman to their little boy.

Facing a comparatively forgiving publishing deadline, he could allow ideas to simmer until they were ready to hit paper, and then type furiously as they poured out. Like an athlete unable to explain the ineffable, he allowed his instinct to guide him. But he also stored notes, sometimes as scribbles on the backs of restaurant tabs, sometimes as neatly typed musings on blue, white, or yellow pages—whatever was handy when the spirit struck—or, if he was in one place, in loose-leaf notebooks. One such tan, padded binder is labeled "scenes" and is filled with an inch of disgorged thoughts for Locke novels, chiefly *Silver Star*. His notes stockpile research from the broad to the narrow. On the mundane side, there are pages of synonyms for words such as *danger, dissent, thought*, and *disregard*. A more detailed set of pages lists possible character names by nationality (Arab, French, Thai, and Vietnamese) and by first and last names that he can mix and match. He wrote page upon page of possible scenes:

- One way for Locke to get into Vietnam is aboard a Thai trawler. These trawlers leave from ports along the southeast coast and carry textiles, medicines, and a broad range of consumer goods to Rach Gia and other points in South Vietnam.

- A worker's basic wage hovers around $1 a month at the black market exchange rate; about $25 at the inflated official rate.

- To protect themselves from the enemy arrows and bullets, the Vietnamese made bed-sized shields of water-soaked straw mats, each carried by 20 strong men. These shields served as armor in modern war.

- You could still get a good bowl of Pho soup from the mobile vendors' carts.

- The Armson O.E.G. [gunsight] is a single-point type scope, made for use with both eyes open.

- The war in Vietnam was a signal that national governments could no longer get away with such things.

- The [Silver Star] medal is hidden within the frame of a photograph of Doan Thi—along with a note in English—which his father will read to him if he ever finds him—and translate to him. THIS HAS TO BE A BIG, BIG SCENE IN THE STORY.

- For scene with prisoner: truth-inducing drugs.

- Scenes: [Locke] has to choose between Thanh Hoa and Dasima. He chooses Thanh Hoa—but she is killed. When Doan Thi dies—and he realizes he would have taken her to America with his son, then to France to meet his mother—he knows that his love for Dasima is not conclusive enough. He will call her from somewhere and tell her not to wait.

- When Clotaire II, King of France (615 A.D.), was at Sens in Burgundy he heard a bell in the church of St. Stephen, which pleased him so much that he ordered it to be taken to Paris. The bell was so distressed at being carried away from home that it turned dumb on the road and lost all its sound. When the king heard of this, he was much concerned. A few years before, the French army had been frightened away by the ringing of the bells in St. Stephen's church, and now the king was perhaps no less frightened by the silence of this one. He commanded that the bell should be carried back to Sens. No sooner did the bell approach the town than it recovered its voice, and rang so loudly that it was heard at Sens while it was yet seven miles away.[276]

15

Sunset In the East

THE LONGING FOR SOUTHEAST ASIA started in 1971. Asked to adapt *The Khaki Mafia*, the explosive Robin Moore/June Collins expose of graft in the U.S. Army in Vietnam under General William Westmoreland, Silliphant visited Saigon with director Jules Dassin and producer Hannah Weinstein to research the project. "Understandably," he reported, "we were not warmly received at MACV (Military Assistance Command, Vietnam).[277] The financing was supposed to come from [Edgar] Bronfman and all his booze money, but the final important money never came our way. The production funding stayed locked up in Toronto, Jules went back to Athens, Hanna to her apartment in New York, and my twenty-two-year love affair with Southeast Asia kicked in, ultimately causing me to write and write and write about Vietnam, but without much success (*The Fall of Saigon, Fly Away Home*, are two primary examples). Ultimately, as you know, I moved to Southeast Asia in July of 1988, but that 1971 trip solidified my knowing that I belonged over here, not in Hollywood." It also reminded him of his roots as a novelist. "It took me 17 years after *The Khaki Mafia* to make the move I should have made when I was still in my twenties and wanting to write only novels and poetry," he said. "Ah, Graham Greene, Andre Malraux, Joseph Conrad, Somerset Maugham—how I envy those guys."[278]

The moving process began at the beginning of 1988, in January, when he had finally had enough of Hollywood. Holding what he sarcastically called "a Beverly Hills garage sale," at the Camden Drive house, he and Tiana sold (directly or metaphorically) two houses, six cars, and a yacht, and put the rest in storage. For the next six months, with little Stirling in tow and Melissa in a relationship in Montana, Silliphant settled in Thailand while Tiana took off for Vietnam to begin work on her autobiographical 1992 documentary, *From Hollywood to Hanoi*. When they needed to return to Los Angeles to wrap up

159

business, they accepted the largesse of Abe and Muriel Lipsey, who lent them one of their spare Beverly Hills homes. By July they had made the final break.

"I think I was born on the wrong continent and into the wrong race," he would come to say of this move. "I cannot explain it. I have always been fascinated with Asia, with its history. I know far more about Asian history, including the history of Indonesia, the history of Burma, than I do about the history of Germany or France. I have never been that interested in Europe, but have always been fascinated by Asia. I am happier in Asia aesthetically and emotionally. I feel somehow safer."[279]

Silliphant settled into a lordly residence atop Bangkok's Natural Park Apartments. When asked, he said he made the move so he and his family could further their study of Buddhism. He also mentioned starting a film school for Thai filmmakers and had written a script about an adventurer, that, according to fellow novelist Christopher Moore, he hoped would do for Thailand what *Hawaii Five-O* and *Magnum P.I.* had done for Hawaii.[280] To those who knew him better, he added that it was the credits flap surrounding *Over the Top* that was the final insult. To those who knew him much, much better, he admitted that it was for tax reasons: "He told me he owed a million dollars in taxes," said one friend, "because business people had put him in tax shelters that didn't work. So he got out of the country."

"I didn't come here on a fling," Silliphant maintained to Los Angeles *Times* writer Daniel Cerone, who tracked him down for an interview in 1994, "but to change my whole existence, my personality, my understanding of life, and to leave what I call the eel pit of Hollywood behind. And it feels so good to be part of the human stream and not some Hollywood big shot who worries about what table he gets at Jimmy's and won't let the parking attendant touch his $80,000 Mercedes. That seems so far away now. That's not the way we're supposed to live."[281]

The Hollywood lifestyle may cost less in Bangkok, but it still costs. No longer able to be the romantic expatriate who could make do on a paltry book advance in Cuba in 1954, Silliphant—in his early seventies when he moved to Thailand—was disappointed when the job offers slowed down. The young people he embraced in the *Yaqui* days had by now taken over the industry and forgot who he was. He was even told by his new agent, "For God's sake, don't take in a list of everything you've written, nobody will believe it."

One project did come through. In 1992, he adapted Truman Capote's 1951 *The Grass Harp* for Charlie Matthau, Walter's son, to direct. The rights had been obtained by Matthau's colorful mother, Carol, who had been a close friend of Capote (and was believed to have been the model for Capote's eccentric *Breakfast at Tiffany's* heroine, Holly Golightly). The picture would not be released until 1995, and it became Silliphant's last produced script, but it would be one of his favorites.

"I couldn't pay Stirling to do a first draft based on what he would normally make, or even, for that matter, WGA scale," Matthau said. "I was a big fan of Stirling's and really liked him when I met him, but I figured nothing was going to come of it because I didn't have a paycheck for him. He called me a few days later and said, 'You know, I have a really good feeling about the project and you. I'll write it on spec.' I worked with him for about a year on it." The two men communicated by fax.

The Grass Harp is a picaresque story of a young boy, Collin Fenwick (Edward Furlong), who comes to live with his two aunts—the straightlaced Verena Talbo (Sissy Spacek) and her free spirited sister, Dolly (Piper Laurie)—when his parents die. Its incidents range from the poetic to the outlandish, yet remain rooted in Capote's strong notion of character. Set in 1930s Alabama, partly in a tree house, the script attracted a cast befitting its pedigree: Nell Carter, Charles Durning, Jack Lemmon, Mary Steenburgen, Scott Wilson, and Charlie's father, Walter.

"Stirling had a great sense of story and he was great viscerally," Matthau continued. "He knew what would work well on screen. Of course, he was delightful to work with—I had a great time with him—a gentleman. He was also very intelligent. He could 'get' these things that were ephemeral and abstract and could relate them to a story that was being told visually, and not lose the audience, and also keep the spirit and the idea that were the reasons that you fell in love with the material to begin with."

Silliphant, in turn, expressed his confidence in young Matthau's talent and abilities. "I must tell you," he wrote, "that, of all the directors with whom I've worked over some thirty-plus years, you, without any question, have shown me the keenest story and construction sense."[282]

While the project was still in development, Matthau asked Kirk Ellis, his classmate from the University of Southern California Cinema-Television school, to do a rewrite. "[Kirk] was working for me at the time as a story analyst," Matthau continued. "He had some coverage of the draft that Stirling wrote and he had some good notes on it, and I said, 'Well, why don't you just take a crack at it?' I think it was a nice mesh of all of their sensibilities, mostly Capote's, but I thought Stirling was great because he's a wonderful craftsman. He was able to make sure that there was a real story and that it didn't just drift off into being poetic. It was an instinctual thing and sometimes when you're developing stuff, especially from books, you can be dead wrong or dead right, and in this case it worked out."[283] The move was enough to finance the $8 million picture, but it also meant that, in accordance with industry standards, Silliphant's deferred writing fee would be shared with Ellis so that, instead of $600,000, he received half.[284]

Throughout this, the dream of starting a Thai-centric film industry never left his mind. He tried to make films there with Robert Ginty, a heavily credentialed theatre actor who became better known as a TV and movie action star. The two men decided to shoot an adventure film in their country in 1992. They didn't exactly use Silliphant's John Locke novels, the ones he had declared unfilmable. Instead, *Day of Reckoning* grew from his proposed Thailand-boosting TV series whose main character, "Jack O'Brien," is an American Special Forces captain who served in 'Nam and then moved to Thailand, became a Buddhist, and opened a travel business. All Silliphant and Ginty needed was THB 38 million (USD $1.5 million)[285], the Thai baht being the crucial part because they wanted to shoot the movie in Thailand with a Thai crew and evocative locations that revealed the sensibilities of the country and didn't just serve as picturesque backgrounds. When they had no luck raising the money after a year of trying ("Most Thai investors would still rather fill a swamp and put up buildings than back a film," Silliphant said bitterly), Ginty—Silliphant insisted it was without his knowledge—sold the property to Paramount and NBC where Fred Dryer, fresh from the success of his *Hunter* TV series, was looking for another project. Dryer and Victor Schiro were executive producers, and Ginty and Silliphant wrote the teleplay with Dryer's input (via fax). When Dryer arrived in Thailand to shoot the picture, however, the script, said Silliphant, was vastly different from his own.

"There really was no story there before," Dryer told Daniel Cerone. "It was about a guy who lived out on a rice barge in front of the hotel. He had a travel agency, with these slow-turning fans, and a lot of women taking care of him. He was a typical American expatriate who lives in Asia for specific womanizing reasons, and he was very sexist. It was very deprecating to the Thais. I brought in a guy who's there because he has found a place in the world that fits him."

Silliphant disagreed with the accusations and charged that Dryer "slashed and burned" his work: "I saw all the grace notes and textures of the writing and characterizations vanish one by one—the dialogue reduced to easy banality or to strong, silent looks; the story line pounded into an A-B-C linear form. There may still be two scenes left in the entire two-hour movie in which some hint, some faint luster of the original writing, may be sensed."

The final picture, which cost $4 million, aired on NBC on March 7, 1994. It did not inspire a series, as was hoped. "Obviously, no word from NBC, Paramount, Dryer, et al," Silliphant wrote after the movie aired and the Cerone article broke. "It is as though a massive non-event has just occurred, something you thought might be as disastrous as the earth abruptly becoming a black hole but which turned out to be as unnoticed as a silent (but non-deadly) fart. Only in Hollywood do people destroy each other during a fractious production, waste four million dollars and months in post-production hassling, then all on a Monday night the boil breaks. And—nothing. Well, not that it matters. Here in Bangkok, infants slept soundly in their beds. Nobody knew about *Day of Reckoning* and, had they, they couldn't have given a fuck less, so why should I?"[286]

The experience massively reinforced Silliphant's image of Hollywood as an "eel pit" and stiffened his desire to establish an indigenous Thai film industry. To that end, he announced plans to write a screenplay called *Forever* that would be directed by the Thai director Prince Chatrichalerm Yugala. The next year, in fact, he co-wrote with, and Yugala directed, the Thai-based action picture *Gunman II*.

What troubled him the most, he told Cerone, was "the American insular point of view. Our refusal to learn languages. Our refusal to really look around and see this is one big world.... We are so absolutely insulated—and Hollywood, in particular. We're like in a shell. We're like the crab. We scuttle around on the rocks but we can't break out of the shell to realize this is a huge world. And there are wonderful films to be made." [287]

Life in Bangkok wasn't just movies. As a famous ex-pat, Silliphant lived well, courtesy of "raids" that he would make to Los Angeles. He would fly there without announcing visit, make a script-doctoring deal, and flee back with money in his pocket that he never told Uncle Sam about. He downsized from his penthouse and he moved into a house, throwing parties for visiting Hollywood friends. Writer Jerry Hopkins noted one such affair where he asked several of his ex-pat friends to bring their Thai girlfriends so his Thai girlfriend would have someone to talk to. Once the women realized that they all came from different social classes, however, they refused to mingle and silence enveloped the festivities.

In Thai culture, a mistress is called a *mia noi* (minor wife), and Silliphant had two of them. By then, Tiana was in Vietnam shooting *From Hollywood to Hanoi* and editing it at DuArt in New York. She and Stirling remained married while inhabiting separate worlds. "It was a difficult time for her," the son knew, "because she was, on the one hand, being pushed away by a husband who wanted to live his own life however he wanted to live it, and then, on the other hand, he was very much into the idea of them being husband and wife. He refused to consider a divorce, not that she pushed for it, but that she was getting, as any woman would, just kind of wondering what was up and where it was going."[288]

Friends also reported that, despite proclaiming the spiritual, Silliphant reverted to the sybaritic life he had known in Hollywood, the one he insisted he'd left behind. To his new friends he was a king. To his old, he was distant. "He and I had plans that I would come out and visit," recalled writer and protégé David Morrell. "The schedules were always a little strange. I sent him a letter and I got a letter back and I know Stirling's stuff, and I swear he did not write it. It was full of all these Britishisms, and I'm sure somebody else wrote it, telling me that it wasn't going to happen. It wasn't in character for him, as I knew the guy."

Explained Tiana, "He was seriously studying the Joseph Campbell documentaries. He got into Joseph Campbell. I believed he was on a spiritual quest. He said he was going to Buddhist retreats. I was editing my film in New York. He said, 'you will heal America and Vietnam, and I am doing the Ho [Chi Minh], story. Maybe you will direct it and it will be the biggest thing in my career and I've got to find my spiritual side for this.'" She takes a long pause before saying, almost in a whisper, "He was preparing to die."

It was after the 1992 Telluride festival, where her film was honored, that Tiana met playwright Christopher Hampton. Hampton, who had received a Tony nomination for his 1987 play *Les Liaisons Dangereuses* and the Oscar for its screenplay (as *Dangerous Liaisons,* 1989), was as politically savvy and as passionate about Southeast Asia as were the Silliphants. (He later adapted Graham Greene's *The Quiet American* [2002], which is set in Vietnam.) Tiana introduced him to her husband in Los Angeles in 1993, where Hampton's musical adaptation of *Sunset Boulevard* was in rehearsal. It was their only meeting, but it made an impression on the younger writer, who would go on to win Tonys for *Sunset Boulevard* (1995) and for his adaptations of *Art* (1997), and *God of Carnage* (2009).[289]

Prostate cancer is not a quick or easy death, but it is highly detectable and usually treatable if it is discovered early enough. Silliphant's first presented as an enlarged prostate around 1976 when Tiana noticed he was getting out of bed several times a night to go to the bathroom, with no results. "We were in the house on Benedict Canyon," she said. "He said that his brother had prostate cancer and got reamed out (was catheterized), and his father, but you never pay attention to that—an eighty-year-old guy dying of prostate. Stirling said, 'I don't have prostate, I'm never going for a checkup.' I said, 'You've got to.'

"We got him the best—Abe and Muriel Lipsey knew every doctor—and they got us the best urologist, a woman doctor. He went in. She said we need a biopsy. He said no. I talked him into it. Well, they did a biopsy. Then she called and said they need another one, we're not sure. He went ballistic. He said, 'You cut into me!'"

Before the doctor could report her findings to the Silliphants, according to Tiana, she died, and apparently left no one to take over, or even unravel, the practice. Whatever the reason, from this point on, Silliphant's mind was closed. "After that he fled the scene and never went back to doctors again," Tiana said. "We all went into denial. He began to hide his symptoms. He didn't want me to know. He would sleep always turned away and said he was discovering his female side. That's when he plotted moving to Bangkok. We had already been to Bangkok. He said the American medical system is killing me. Look at American medicine, then look at all these geezers living in Asia. He let it grow fifteen years. Stirling insisted it was bronchitis because he coughed a lot. Well, all older men cough a lot."

It's highly likely that he opted not to have his prostate removed because doing so would have resulted in incontinence and sexual dysfunction. He covered this by insisting that he considered this existence to be merely a transition from a past life to a future one, often telling friends, "I have come to believe that I was Thai in a previous life."

When the pain was such that he was suffering twenty-four hours a day, he had Tiana take him to a traditional clinic in Hanoi where she translated and he received massage, acupressure, and incense. "I feel like I'm 125 years old," he reported. "I feel feeble. I have no strength. I can't even hold a chopstick properly. And my back is in terrible pain...what medical people call constricture[290] I had to roll out of bed, onto the floor, get onto my knees, and then do a push-up on my feet. I went to the hospital and she said I had to relax my muscles and she gave me Valium, which I took for two weeks and, when the muscles finally relaxed, it too me ten days at the end of the course of Valium to recover any kind of clarity of mind or focus of eyes. Really totally disoriented by a drug. That's when I determined I was going to try Eastern medicine and herbal medicine and stop taking pills coming out of the United States, Belgium, and the United Kingdom."[291]

During the ordeal, he did not tell his son that he was sick. "Like most things that were secrets of his, I heard from Mom," young Stirling said. "I graduated high school in 1994 and started college the same year. In December of '94 I went to Bangkok for Christmas holiday. His health had deteriorated and my Mom was there and she was really concerned. Pretty much made him go to get x-rays or see an oncologist—it was the first time he had been to a medical doctor. He had been trying all these holistic therapies, thinking that the problem was somewhere else and diagnosing himself with his *Grey's Anatomy*. She finally forced him to go in and not only was he diagnosed with cancer, but late stage cancer. The pain that he's complaining about, the back pain, that was actually the cancer that, by that point, had eaten the cartilage away, so his spine was just grinding against each other. He was living with it because he didn't want to—I don't think he was keeping a secret from us. I think he was keeping a secret from himself. He genuinely believed he did not have cancer up until that time."

Young Stirling was attending the University of California, Santa Cruz, but quickly put his life on hold to join his father in Bangkok. "He just kind of completely went into denial. He was pissed off. He felt he was a guinea pig of the medical establishment. He always had this kind of rebellious punk rock attitude towards the institutions and whatnot. He felt like the medical institution was corrupt and incapable of telling the truth and he felt he was guinea pig and had been de-balled by them, as he put it, and he was not going to let another gloved finger near his ass or get his balls fondled again. He refused to go onto any kind of testing or screening after that."[292]

"You can get killed in a hospital," Silliphant insisted. Like most of his deeply held opinions, this one was the result of research for a script, in this case a 1977 Screen Gems pilot called *A Small Step Forward*. "The third largest cause of death in America is doctors. It's true. There's cancer, heart, and doctors." The show was to be the medical profession's version of *Police Story*, the then-current series that brought new realism to cop dramas. "Doctors are human. They make mistakes; they also have been known to do things like the rest of us; they don't know all the answers."[293] The show was never produced, but Silliphant's steeping himself in statistics may have been enough to put him off treatment.

Having refused prostate removal, his only remaining options were chemistry, radiation, and blood augmentation. He chose them all, but, by late 1995, it was clear that the disease was terminal. "The cancer never, never lets you forget it's in there doing its thing," Silliphant wrote from Bangkok. "I wake up one morning and test for pain. I roll over slowly and sit up in bed. Jesus, not dizzy this morning! Great! Then I get up and I feel a stab in the rib at the 10th. level. No, ho, ho, old friend, I say, there you are! Another morning—no pain. I'm planning on going back in next month and taking some more radiation, once more at that 10th. level where the initial damage was the worst, and also in the femur and lower spine. This is a kind of holding action. It doesn't cure anything, but it does help relieve the pain."[294]

"With this disease there is no such thing as a 'speedy recovery,'" he added in a letter to Tom Brown, a friend from both Thailand and the USA. "With mutating cells within one's body, one simply fights a holding action, a delaying action, pushing back the inevitable as long as possible with every means possible—in my case a double hormonal approach. Median survival rates under this treatment appear to be currently running around thirty-six to sixth months, with some blue ribbon contenders actually logging ten years. Since I will be seventy-eight in January, these ratings are meaningless." He advised friends to be patient, for it was his problem, not theirs. "My life as I have now ordered it is perfect for the time, the place, and my condition," he wrote. "I do not need anything additional because I would simply not have the capacity to absorb or accept it. Please try to explain this to all concerned in a loving way. This is not rejection—this is a simple statement of the actuality of things."[295]

However pragmatically he might have been facing another life, he was not eager to put his current one in order, including rapprochement with his daughter. "I get really sad when I think of the story about Dayle," reported Stirling Linh. "[Tiana] pushed for reconciliation because, being Asian, the mom is always more of the family bridge-builder. He wasn't interested. And I don't know if [Dayle] had gotten wind that he was sick or it was just coincidence, but it was four or five months before Dad died that she sent him a long letter, which he refused to read. I opened it and said, 'Well, if you won't read it, let me read it to you.' It said, at the very least, if I can't see you again, I'd like to know what I did to make you cut off contact with me. And he actually wept for about thirty seconds, and then promptly dried his tears and put himself back together and said, 'Well…'"

A similar incident involved his murdered son, Loren. Novelist David Morrell recalls an evening he and his wife spent at the Silliphant home in 1988. "We had just lost our son to cancer the year before and we were still shaken by it," Morrell recalled, "and, as we had dinner, Stirling began talking to me about his son having been shot—which I now realize was nearly twenty years earlier—and he began to weep. He was sobbing, and tears were falling into his plate. That was the last time I saw him." [296]

And yet Dayle was different. "He had a funny thing with women," Stirling Linh continued. "I wouldn't call him a retro-sexist, but he really surprised me a few times. I think it was really hard for him to have a daughter. He was never able to deal with that. The things he was going through at the time—the divorce, the death of Loren—I think poor Dayle was just at the wrong place at the wrong time. I don't know why he took it out on her so hard."[297]

With Tiana traveling the festival circuit in 1996 with her film and young Stirling enrolled at the University of California in Santa Cruz, Silliphant, his health rapidly declining, fell under the care of a series of house retainers and hangers-on, including lawyers who, Tiana said, had him sign a one-page power of attorney, which was actually the last of a forty-page document that he never saw.

One day, Silliphant summoned Stirling Linh. When the boy saw his father's condition, he called Tiana. "He said, 'Mom you better come home.' He put his father on the line who said, 'Darling, I have to check into the hospital.' He went to the hospital and they washed his blood and he felt great and had energy. But in the end it had gone to the bone. We had to find out the hard way in these three weeks of tests and he hated me again because I was the responsible wife who made him face the truth. He didn't want to know."

Silliphant died on April 26, 1996. He was cremated following a service in a Buddhist temple in Thailand and his ashes were given to Tiana. But he did not go gently into his final resting place. Before she left Bangkok, Tiana had asked her hotel to ship a suitcase packed with video equipment to a cinematographer she had met. It was a gift. Silliphant's ashes were packed in a similar-looking suitcase, which she intended to take home. But the hotel sent both of them to the cinematographer. When Tiana discovered the mistake, she asked the cinematographer to return the ashes. He refused, said he had buried them in a grave in North Vietnam under a name and location he would not reveal, and demanded an excessive "reimbursement" for the information. Tiana traveled to Vietnam, turned detective, and made inquiries of local residents, using the blackmail photograph of the gravesite to identify the cemetery. At first, she encountered resistance from some of the peasants who believed that she was a counter-revolutionary, until she produced the extortion letters that proved her legitimacy. By 2009, Tiana and young Stirling had tracked down the fake grave (marked with the name Nguyen Van Ich), broke into the sepulcher, retrieved the urn, and held a proper Buddhist ceremony. They scattered his ashes into the waters of the world, the seas that he loved to sail, the oceans that did not know borders.

"I not only think about him as my dad and as a teacher but as one of the best friends I ever had," young Stirling said. "In some ways it wasn't as hard as I thought it would be coping with everything because I was rehearsing that scenario my whole life. He was so much older than I was. When I was at El Rodeo school, I remember being conscious of other kids asking me if that was my grandfather, because he was as old as their grandparents were at the time. I was very conscious of his mortality. I didn't think it was going to come as soon as it did. But I don't think kids think that way."[298]

There was continuing discord between the Estate and the Thai lawyers who had glommed onto it. People whose connection with Silliphant had been ephemeral, at best, came forward claiming that they had been in his employ. A grieving Tiana leveled charges of malfeasance ranging from taking payroll money away from the servants to stealing Silliphant's *In the Heat of the Night* Oscar. When she threatened to hold a public press conference to level charges at those who were supposed to be administering the Estate, the statuette was returned, along with vague threats of defamation, and were ignored.

Now Tiana found herself, for all intents and purposes, homeless. She returned to America in 1997 and stayed with Silliphant's old military buddy, Raymond Katz, who had become a successful manager/producer. Although all the recent widow wanted was a place to stay until she could settle matters in Bangkok and rebuild her career in America, Katz had other, more personal desires, and the arrangement quickly became untenable. When she was able to gather the resources, she rented a Spartan apartment in Hollywood while her son finished college in Santa Cruz. Over time she was able to gather funding and favors from friends, find a house, and retrieve the family's possessions from storage.

Ethel Noaker Silliphant Wellershaus died in 1996, a few months after her older son, who had been supporting her in a Sun City rest home. Tiana was one of the last family members to visit.

There had been no memorial service at the Writers Guild. Such a commemoration would have been *de rigeur* for as prolific and successful a writer as Silliphant. But he had not just burned bridges when he left Hollywood, he'd blown them to smithereens, and much of his good will along with it. Referring to the town as an "eel pit" in print or telling the San Francisco Sunday *Examiner* that "Television has reached the bottom of the barrel, yet it constantly finds fresh, new depths,"[299] were not endearing deeds. Rather than risk a sparse house, the family and their advisors opted for a private remembrance. Tiana held an intimate service for friends (including the author) in a garden beside the Bergamot Station art gallery in Santa Monica where she was exhibiting photographs from Vietnam. Incense, flowers, candles, his picture, and the recovered Oscar were accompanied by chants and tears.

16

The Measure of a Man

STIRLING SILLIPHANT'S LEGACY IS DIVERSE. Most of his scripts were works-for-hire under a controversial provision imposed by U.S. Copyright law (alone in the world) that deems the employer to be the author of a registered work, not the person who actually creates it. Thus his estate has no control over remakes or assignment of rights by their corporate "author" other than to receive residuals, where applicable. Tiana and her son Stirling have spent considerable time and resources pursuing their rights.

As for the speculative writing into which he poured so much of his soul and his rare free time, most of these properties remain in narrative treatment form awaiting expansion into screenplays—as if anyone but Stirling Silliphant could ever write a Stirling Silliphant script. When he was interviewed by William Froug in 1972 for *The Screenwriter Looks At the Screenwriter*, Silliphant impressed Froug with his efficiency as well as his achievements. "A conversation with Stirling can leave you both stimulated as well as exhausted," Froug wrote. "His mind races ahead seizing new ideas and articulating them with the ease of a trapeze artist who knows precisely when to leap." Speaking with Silliphant at the Pingree headquarters at Paramount Pictures—one of six offices he kept all over town including one on the Sunset Strip—he noted that the writer drove around in a white Rolls-Royce, had a personal income of $500,000 a year, and "is neither Glick nor Gandhi" but is "a brilliant, determined, ambitious man moving at all deliberate speed toward his own private destination."[300]

Froug reported that Silliphant went through the 100-page transcript of their interview the afternoon he received it, made notes and changes on every page, and gave it to his secretary to retype while phoning Froug to discuss the changes, then had it back in Froug's hands that very evening.

In other words, a writer writes, but a good writer *rewrites*. This begins to explain his literary legacy.

"I suppose at the beginning of my screenwriting," Silliphant recalled of his evolution as a writer, "I still had one foot in the old bear-trap—still unable to escape from the constant reminders all writers get all the way back to Greek theater—about act one, act two and act three. It was not until I wrote more and learned from my mistakes, and until I lived more and learned from life itself that every moment is a lifetime, and that matters seldom have a remembered beginning or a conscious end. When life ends, we are, fortunately, not aware of the exact split-second of our passing. So that we are constantly having to deal with the existing moment in time, and this present-time moment has always fascinated me at the expense of past and future. So, when I write, I let the characters drive the story. If there are expositional or connective elements to be dealt with, I keep trying to push them back, deeper and deeper into the film, right to the very end—and, at that point, to avoid the Agatha Christie summary/round-up scene where all the suspects are called into the parlor and we learn the butler did *not* do it, I try to end my story *without* the explanation, that is, without the factual explanation, hoping that the emotional truth of what has happened to the a characters will be resolution enough. I must concede that if you're doing a typical piece of Hollywood shit where nobody can leave the theater until the good guy has blown the bad guy away, you have serious problems with my way of handling a story. My answer—for me, at least—is not to get involved writing the kind of film in which I have to solve a plot problem. Just a simple choice of material!"

He had an even stronger feeling about plot: "I *detest* that word *plot*. I never, never think of plot. I think only and solely of character. Give me the characters, I'll tell you a story. Maybe a thousand stories. The interaction between and among human beings is the only story worth telling." He had similar disdain for writers who try to direct the film from the page, that is, add camera angles and movement (even though he had done both) and parentheticals to show what the actors should be feeling. "I fucking detest it," he fulminated. "I spit in the milk of the brothers of the bastards who do it. It is so inexperienced of such writers. It reveals instantly their lack of knowledge of the hard process of filmmaking. First of all, the director isn't even going to read such nonsense. And any actor who's not on his first gig and who has never before held a real-life-by-God-script in his trembling hand is going to black out all those 'instructions' in his copy."

"He was attracted to the kind of simplicity that could happen at any moment when there was conflict and contact between people," noted his son, Stirling Linh, who is also a writer. "One thing he would coach me on is how to make a scene between two people talking or arguing even better, and that was to bring in an unexpected third element, which could be something as simple as a janitor dropping a mop and one of the participants in the conversation stopping the conversation and walking over and picking up the mop for the janitor. He was detail oriented in that those little things mattered to him. Signature aspects of his writing are its leanness and its simplicity. He felt the same way about filmmaking. He was always saying that if the camera isn't from someone's perspective then it shouldn't be there. And the John Locke novels were sort of the Bourne before Bourne, that sort of thinking man's mercenary."[301]

Though he lived well into the computer age, Silliphant refused to use one. "I tried, really gave it my best shot, but it never connected for me," he insisted. "I felt too much separation between me and the [computer] screen; somehow the words up there lacked immediacy. I could not relate to them." His weapon of choice was not exactly a steam-powered Royal manual model, though. "I find that I am faster on the IBM Wheelwriter than any computer instructor I've ever known is on the computer. Believe it or not, I've held contests with the doubters and every time creamed them. Also, the painful process of retyping, as opposed to the instantaneous capability of the computer to change and revise, makes me deal with what I've written in a constantly intimate sense, so that, by the time I'm through with a script, every page has been revised, polished and rewritten a dozen or more times. If I were to make this process computer-easy, I would divorce myself from the hard work of facing up to every word as though for the first time."

His writing method was similarly precise: "I type on plain white paper with three holes punched into the left side of the sheet so I can place the finished pages into a loose-leaf notebook and move them around if I decide to change my continuity or if I want to replace the scenes already written. Also, I never write a script in continuity. I always write my favorite scene first. I always ask myself, 'What is the single most important, most moving, most dramatic scene in the film, the single scene people will still be talking about a week later?' I write that scene first, no matter where it might play in the finished script. And I put it into the notebook. Then I write my next-most-favorite scene and put it into what may end up being its appropriate position. And so on and so on until I have to start connecting those fragments. The last thing I write are these connections and I spend hours thinking of them in terms of images and locations."

"Stirling was a brilliant writer who could turn a blank page into fantastic material by just dropping that paper in the typewriter (no computer in those days)," said Charles W. "Chuck" Fries, for whom he and Bert Leonard had developed *Route 66* at CBS.[302]

"Once he started his work day, he never left the office," his son recalled. "We barely saw him unless he had to go pee or make coffee. I don't know if he took lunches, which is funny, because he was such a big food person. I'd do my homework in his office, on the carpet. He was totally in another world and didn't even notice my presence. I was also not making any noise." In addition to wearing the green eyeshade, he would act out the scenes at his desk, gyrating, bouncing, and rocking back and forth at the keyboard, sometimes speaking his dialogue aloud, and other times reacting to it. He would play music on headphones. There were sometimes complaints from neighbors who could hear him typing into the night. Only a writer who has been "in the zone" can appreciate what it's like when a character takes hold. Where Silliphant was using many of his characters as surrogates, his identification with them could be doubly profound.

His concentration was legendary. "One day I went to his office to see him," David Morrell said. "He'd just had his wisdom teeth out that morning and, by god, that afternoon he was writing. He's sitting there at his typewriter with his cheeks all puffed out with cotton like a chipmunk, and he's writing."

Just as William Goldman had no idea what a script looked like the first time he was hired to write one, Silliphant refused to be confined by formats that made it easier for studio budget wonks to do their jobs but harder for writers to do theirs. "I have no self-imposed criteria for 'how a script should look.' Or all the rest of the incantations which the guys who write the 'How To' books recommend. All that stuff tends to be trendy and to drop by the wayside as time drums relentlessly by. Every script is different. Laying these 'rules' in is like coaching a guy on foreplay. Scripts cannot be ground out by guidelines. To me, a script should be seamless: one complete piece, with nothing that can be added and nothing that can be taken away. You can only arrive at that totality from within a script, not by waxing and buffing."

What is seldom, if ever, brought up is Silliphant's chameleonic ability to write for an astonishing number of ongoing television series, sometimes only one or two episodes, and yet pick up on the characters, their speaking rhythms, and their interpersonal dynamics. Today it is common for a freelancer to slave over a script, endure network and producer notes, turn in a final draft, and then have the executive producer or show runner do a final pass, sometimes for credit. Silliphant's scripts were seldom molested.

Moreover, his impressive—no, incalculable—output of over 200 *produced* credits in his forty-five-year career (Appendix A) begs the question of whether he has ever been blocked. Surprisingly, the answer is 'no,' but that's because the question was wrong, and the explanation is as good a writing lesson as one is ever going to hear. "Never in the sense most writers think," he said. "It doesn't hover out there like some dour incubus. I have never felt it was going to get me. Simply because the act of writing is a professional exercise. You assemble words to express a point of view. I can see no reason, short of being drunk, drugged, or physically incapacitated in some other way, why a professional cannot just do the work at hand. The only writer's block I have ever experienced is the sense that what I may be writing is below my hopes for what I may be trying to write at any given time. Sometimes you simply can't get it right. It eludes you. I have learned in these cases to let it go. Don't chase bad writing. Replace it with good writing—and start all over again.

"The writing is the easiest part of it,"[303] he said, then corrected, "the trying period is the period of conceptualization, followed by research. This pre-writing time can take anywhere from six months to ten years. But once I know everything there is to know about my story's milieu, once I have taken the separate pills of their characters, then the actual writing of the script switches to automatic pilot. It makes no difference whether the script is for TV or a feature, the writing period is the same: five pages a day, seven days a week. That's it. Nothing mystical. You just sit there and keep typing. When you've got your five pages, you're the hell out of there and off to explore life away from the IBM. So, okay, that's 35 pages a week. If you're talking about a one-hour TV show, you should finish in two weeks. Less, since these scripts should run between 50 and 60 pages, depending on their content. A two-hour MOW takes me three weeks since these end up anywhere from 105 to 110 pages in length. A script for a feature, using this measurement, should take no more than four weeks, at the max. But here, in consideration of the fact that you can elevate the quality of dialogue and the visualization of the scenes themselves, their staging, their mood, their texture, given the fact that a director is going to have more money and can spend more time in shooting a feature than a TV chunk of sausage, I cut down my page count per day to three pages rather than maintain the five-page-a-day pace. I round this out at 20 pages a week and allow myself between six and eight weeks for the first draft. If a writer takes more time than that he is bullshitting you. Of course, if you want to calculate working time from sitting down without the faintest idea of what you intend to write—until you finish whatever that thing may be—you could spend a lifetime and produce nothing."

"What is this mystique when people say, 'I spent all year working on a script?,'" he added to interviewer Bill Collins. "I say they spent all year at the beach, goofing off, avoiding the responsibility of trying to solve their scene. They didn't sit down, as a producer or director must, and work at the film. My 'inspiration' comes by sitting there. If I don't write anything that day, the next day I have to write ten pages. Another thing I find, if I'm really blocked, when I go to bed at night, I will feed it into my head before I go to bed and do a thirty-minute self-hypnosis in the dark, and it has never yet failed me. I don't do it too often; I'm afraid of using it up. You wake up the next morning and wonder what the problem was. You don't die when you sleep, so why not let your brain work?"[304]

"I feel that the screenwriter must isolate himself from the established ignorance of the people he's writing for—the producer, the director, the actors (with some exceptions), the studio executives—and write for himself, that he must invest his script with a visionary energy which not only describes a particular scene but communicates his own unique and utterly subjective apprehension of what the scene feels like to him at that moment. I don't believe one can do that by simply having your coffee, rubbing your eyes and sitting down at some machine and writing your scene off the top of your head. Hence, my belief in an almost mythic or spiritual hype before starting work each day.

"What I am saying here is that, once you've done all your spade work—got your locations in mind, have dressed the sets, selected the wardrobe, decided on the weather, cast your characters and know more about them than the average guy ever knows about his wife—at that point, if you take more than two or three months to write a script, I don't ever wanta have lunch with that writer. Too fucking depressing to consider.

"Let me sum it up by saying that it shouldn't take the writer any longer to write his script than it takes the director to shoot it or the actors to get it right."

Stirling Silliphant "got it right" more often than not, and more often than most. He was both a craftsman and a businessman, someone who just did the damn job, sometimes because he wanted to, and sometimes because he had to, but he did it. When the source was inspired—when he found a way to make it touch his own life, as with *Route 66* or *Charly* or *In the Heat of the Night* or *The Grass Harp* or *The New Centurions* or *The Silent Flute*—the results were personal, revealing, and moving. Even with pictures that turned out to be worth less than the paper they were typed on, he found ways to invest himself in the characters and tried to engage the audience to do the same.

Not all screenwriters' lives are the Hollywood tragedy the wags gripe about. Billy Wilder said that of the oppressors that "theirs may be the kingdom, but ours is the power and the glory." Stirling Silliphant had the gift of writing scripts that could be taken straight to the soundstage and, when the director did his job right, the results went straight to the heart.

"Stirling could do anything with both hands tied behind his back," said Charles Matthau. "He was so able, so instinctually smart and emotionally intelligent. He was a great storyteller and he could 'get' something that was cerebral or something that was not on the nose and he could distill that quality while moving the story along. When you combine that kind of a brilliant mind with the great craft he had, and instinct about what not to write, that is, skipping over the boring parts, you get that he's one in a million."

John Corcoran, whose long interview with Silliphant about the martial arts developed into a mentor-protégé relationship, got a call from him six months after the series had run, "and [he] said that a *Variety* staffer asked him to do an interview about his martial arts involvement. He said he told her that she should talk to me since I had already done the quintessential interview with him on the subject. He told her he had nothing left to say about the subject. I never heard from her, and I got the clear impression that SS didn't want to grant the interview. But I felt his endorsement of me and my work to an important media professional was a wonderful compliment."

Michael Ventura touched on the downside of Silliphant's literary fecundity. "He had a marvelous gift, and he sold it out," he lamented. "I'd written a piece (in 1986) for *LA Weekly* titled 'A Swastika in the Snow' in which I quoted Stirling and *Route 66*. I wrote another piece for *LA Weekly* around that time, directly about *Route 66*, in which I called Stirling's writing 'jukebox existentialism.' He liked that a lot and quoted it back to me. In any case, after I wrote those pieces, he wanted to meet me. I hadn't expected that—I simply wanted to meet and thank the writer who'd meant so much to me at such a crucial period of life. Stirling spoke to me without hypocrisy and almost without self-pity. He justified nothing and blamed no one. Stirling enjoyed calling himself a whore... As he'd written long ago: 'Every criminal acquits himself before he's judged. Every violator considers himself excused by circumstances. Don't you acquit him, don't you excuse him.'[305] Well, I hadn't come for hero worship. I'd come to say, 'Thank you.' I believed it. I did it. Stirling was right. What he knew didn't save him but maybe it saved me. What could he have been, had he believed in the integrity he helped teach me? I am grateful I said my thanks to that damaged man, eye to eye. He saw in me evidence that his best work mattered. It was all I could give him."[306]

Stirling Silliphant's legacy is larger than he could have known, even if it isn't all he may have wished. In a business where everybody blames the director for the good stuff and the writer for the bad (if they give him any credit at all), Silliphant is an anomaly. Whether he was writing from the heart or for the wallet, an incomparable percentage of his scripts actually got made, even if many of those he wanted to get made, didn't. Their sheer number assures him an impressive percentage of hits versus an expected number of flops. Beyond that, his moral and philosophical beliefs found kinship with the public, and his technical skills were of such caliber as to persuade money people to risk a trip off the fence to invest. As a man, he was an acute judge of character, both on the page and in real life, yet learned to expect from others no more than they were able to deliver. This is the refuge of the writer: when life hands you lemons, don't make lemonade right away, save them for when you're thirsty.

More importantly, Stirling Silliphant was the first screenwriter of the modern age to create and ply a public persona. In an era when a best-selling novelist might, at best, land a quickie guest appearance in the last ten minutes on *The Tonight Show*, Silliphant was a frequent interview subject on any number of talk shows, newspapers, magazines, panels, lectures, and even TV game shows. He made the public aware that, as the WGA would say in a publicity campaign, years later, "somebody wrote that."

Back in 1953, when he quit his well-paid publicity job at Fox, it was because, "it was time either to write or be unhappy for the rest of my life." He spent the next forty-three years proving he'd made the right decision.

Appendix A

Credits

AS COMPILED BY THE WRITERS GUILD OF AMERICA in 1992 and cross-referenced with the Internet Movie Database (http://pro.imdb.com/name/nm0798103/), this is a list of Silliphant's registered credits. Most dates reflect when Silliphant did the actual work rather than when the project was released. Feature films are shown in CAPS:

1953   THE JOE LOUIS STORY (producer; uncredited contribution) (UA)

1955   *Mickey Mouse Club* (Disney/ABC-TV)(various episodes)
           5 AGAINST THE HOUSE (also producer)(Columbia)

1956   *Alfred Hitchcock Presents* (Revue TV)
           "A Bottle of Wine"
           "The Manacle"
           "Jonathan"
           "Never Again"
          Zane Grey Theatre (Dick Powell/CBS-TV)
           "No Man Living"
           "The Three Graves"
          Ford Theatre (NBC-TV)
           "The Idea Man"
          Studio 57 (Dumont TV)
           "Mr. Cinderella"
          General Electric Theatre (CBS-TV)
           "Never Turn Back"

HUK! (UA)(script from own novel)
Stage 7 (CBS-TV)
   "The Warriors"
NIGHTFALL (Columbia)
Jane Wyman Fireside (NBC-TV)
   "The Thread"

1957   *Suspicion* (NBC-TV)
   "Meeting in Paris"
MARACAIBO (UA)(novel)
THE LINE-UP (Columbia)
Chicago Manhunt (TV)
   "Neighborhood Killer"
DAMN CITIZEN (Universal-International)
Alfred Hitchcock Presents (Revue TV)
   "The Perfect Crime"
   "The Glass Eye"
Perry Mason (CBS-TV)
   "The Case of the Nervous Accomplice"
   "The Case of the Fan Dancer's Horse"
West Point Story (CBS-TV)
   "Ambush"
M-Squad (NBC-TV)
   "Neighborhood Killer"

1958   *Naked City* (ABC-TV)
   "Goodbye, My Lady Love"
   "The Shield"
   "Even Crows Sing Good"
   "Burst of Passion"
   "And a Merry Christmas to the Force on Patrol"
   "Ladybug, Ladybug"
   "The Manhole"
   "Ticker Tape"
   "Susquehanna 4-7598"
   "Stakeout"
   "The Canvas Bullet"
   "The Bird Guard"
   "Line of Duty"
   "Welfare Island" (possibly never filmed)
   "Sidewalk Fisherman"
   "Nickel Ride"

"The Other Face of Goodness"
"Meridian"
"Violent Circle"
Alfred Hitchcock Presents (Revue TV)
    "The Canary Sedan"
    "Little White Frock"
    "Return of the Hero"
Suspicion (CBS-TV)
    "Voice in the Night"
    "The Woman Turned to Salt"
Rescue 8 (Screen Gems)(syndicated)
    "102 to Bakersfield" (as "Loren Dayle")
    "The Ferris Wheel" (as "Loren Dayle")

1959   *Naked City* (ABC-TV)
    "The Canvas Bullet"
    "A Wood of Thorns"
    "The Bloodhounds"
    "The Scorpion's Sting"
    "A Piece of the Action"
    "Baker's Dozen"
    "Four Sweet Corners"
    "The Rebirth"
    "A Running of Bulls"
    "Turn of Events"
    "Beyond Truth"
    "The Bumper"
    "Hey, Teach!"
    "Fire Island"
Alfred Hitchcock Presents (Revue TV)
    "Graduating Class"
    "The Crystal Trench"
Markham (CBS-TV)
    "Image of Love"
    "The Altar"
    "Mutation"
    "The Seamark"
    "The Nephews"
    "The Dual"
Tightrope (CBS-TV)
    "Appointment in Jericho"
    "Stand on Velvet"

Man from Blackhawk (ABC-TV)
"Biggest Legend"
"The Trouble with Toliver"
Alcoa-Goodyear Theatre (NBC-TV)
"Medals for Harry"
"Corporal Hardy"
"The Silent Kill" (story only)
Adventure Showcase (CBS-TV)
"Brock Callahan"

1960   VILLAGE OF THE DAMNED (MGM)(coscript)
Route 66 (CBS-TV)
"Black November"
"Sheba"
"The Quick and the Dead"
"Play it Glissando"
"A Fury Slinging Flame"
"Lay Out at Glen Canyon"
"Legacy for Lucia"
"Three Sides of a Coin"
"The Strengthening Angels"
"Man on the Monkey Board"
"Swan Bed"
"A Lance of Straw"
Naked City (ABC-TV)
"A Death of Princes"
"Pedigree Sheet"
"A Succession of Heartbeats"
General Electric Theatre (CBS-TV)
"Learn to Say Goodbye"
Checkmate (CBS-TV)
"The Cyanide Touch"
Brothers Brannagan (CBS-TV)
"Equinox"
Mr. Lucky (CBS-TV)
"Hair of the Dog"
June Allyson Show (Dupont/Four Star/CBS-TV)
"So Dim the Light"

1961   *Route 66* (CBS-TV)
"A Long Piece of Mischief"
"And the Cat Jumped Over the Moon"

"Some of the People, Some of the Time"
"Burning for Burning"
"Birdcage on My Foot"
"The Mud Nest"
"Mon Petite Chou"
"A Month of Sundays"
"Blue Murder"
"Incident on a Bridge"
"The Opponent"
"The Trap at Angie's Corner" (possibly never filmed)
"The Newborn"
"Most Vanquished, Most Victorious"
"Don't Count the Stars"
"An Absence of Tears"
"Effigy in Snow"
"Sleep On Four Pillows"
"Fly Away Home" I and II
THE SINS OF RACHEL CADE (coscript)(Warner Bros.)

1962   *Route 66* (CBS-TV)
"...Shall Forfeit His Dog and Ten Shillings to the King"
"Give the Old Cat a Tender Mouse"
"A Bunch of Lonely Pagliaccis"
"Only by Gunning Glimpses"
"Hey, Moth, Come Eat the Flame"
"Lizard's Egg and Owlet's Wing"
"From an Enchantress Fleeing"
"Hell is Empty, All the Devils Are Here"
"Between Hello and Goodbye"
"Love is a Skinny Kid"
"Kiss the Maiden, All Forlorn"
"There I Am, There I Always Am"
"Go Read the River"
"You Never Had It So Good"
"Aren't You Surprised to See Me"
"How Much a Pound is Albatross"
"One Tiger to a Hill"
"Ever Ride the Waves in Oklahoma?"
"Across Walnuts & Wine"
Naked City (ABC-TV)
"Prime of Life"
"Five Cranks for Winter....Ten Cranks for Spring"
"Torment Him Much and Hold Him Long"

1963 *Route 66* (CBS-TV)
     "Child of Night"
     "Like This It Means Father...Like This Bitter...This Tiger"
     " A Long Way From St. Louie"
     "I'm Here to Kill a King"
     "Come Out, Come Out Wherever You Are"
     "Same Picture, Different Frame"
     "Where Are the Sounds of Celli Brahms?"
     "The Stone Guest"
     "A Cage in Search of a Bird"
     "Two Strangers & an Old Enemy"
     "But What Do You Do in March?"
     "Peace, Pity, Pardon"
     "The Cruelest Sea of All"
     "In the Closing of a Trunk"
     "Somehow It Gets to Be Tomorrow"
     "Fifty Miles From Home"
     "Suppose I Said I Was the Queen of Spain?"

1964 *Rawhide* (CBS-TV)
     "Marshlight"
    Chrysler Theatre (Hope Enterprises/NBC-TV)
     "The Shattered Glass"
     "Murder in the First"
     "The Sojourner"
    Route 66 (CBS-TV)
     "This is Going to Hurt Me More Than It Hurts You"
     "Where There's a Will There's a Way" (I and II)

1965 *Chrysler Theatre* (Hope Enterprises/NBC-TV)
     "The Highest Fall of All"
    THE SLENDER THREAD (Paramount)

1966 *Wings of Fire* (NBC-TV)(MOW)

1967 *Maya* (MGM TV)
     "Caper of the Golden Roe"
     "Blood of the Tiger"
    IN THE HEAT OF THE NIGHT (UA)
    Wings of Fire (NBC-TV/Universal)

| 1968 | MARLOWE (MGM) |
| | CHARLY (Cinerama Releasing) |

1969   A WALK IN THE SPRING RAIN (also producer)(Columbia)
THE LIBERATION OF L.B. JONES (coscript)(Columbia)

1971   *Longstreet* (also producer)(ABC-TV)(MOW)
Longstreet (TV series; also producer)
    "Please Leave the Wreck for Others to Enjoy"
    "The Shape of Nightmares"
    "The Way of the Intercepting Fist"
    "A World of Perfect Complicity"
MURPHY'S WAR (Paramount)
SHAFT (exec. producer only)(MGM)

1972   *A World of Love* (two TV pilots)(Paramount)
THE POSEIDON ADVENTURE (coscript)(Twentieth Century-Fox)
The New Healers (Paramount)(pilot)
Movin' On (TV pilot)(Screen Gems)
THE NEW CENTURIONS (Columbia)
SHAFT'S BIG SCORE (exec. producer only)(MGM)

1973   SHAFT IN AFRICA (also Exec. Prod.)(MGM)
A Time for Love (also Prod)(ABC-Paramount)(MOW)

1974   THE TOWERING INFERNO (Fox/WB)

1975   *The First 36 Hours of Dr. Durant* (pilot; also producer) (Columbia TV)
Rodriguez (TV pilot)(RSO Films)
THE KILLER ELITE (UA)(coscript)
WHEN TIME RAN OUT (Warner Bros.)(coscript)
Death Scream (Robert Stigwood)

1976   THE ENFORCER (Warner Bros.)(coscript)

1977   TELEFON (UA)(coscript)
THE SWARM (Warner Bros.)

1978   CIRCLE OF IRON" (Avco-Embassy)(coscript)
Pearl I-II-III (also producer)(ABC-Warner Bros.)(mini-series)

1979   *Salem's Lot* (exec. producer only)(CBS-Warner Bros.)

1980   *Hardcase* (NBC-TV)(pilot)
        Golden Gate (ABC-TV)(MOW)

1981   *Fly Away Home* (also exec. producer)(ABC-TV) (MOW/pilot)

1982   *Travis McGee* (ABC-TV pilot)

1984   *Welcome to Paradise* (also producer)(CBS-TV)(pilot)

1985   *Space* (CBS-TV)(five episodes of mini-series)
        Mussolini: The Untold Story (also exec. prod.)(NBC-TV)
        (mini-series)

1986   OVER THE TOP (Warner Bros.)(coscript)

1987   CATCH THE HEAT (Trans-World Entertainment)
        The Three Kings (also producer)(ABC)(MOW)
        Harry's Hong Kong (Aaron Spelling)(Supervising Producer)

1989   *The Brotherhood of the Rose* (exec. prod. only)(NBC-TV)(MOW)

1992   *Sidney Sheldon's 'The Stranger in the Mirror'* (ABC)(MOW)
        The Flying Aces (Showtime)(mini-series)
        THE GRASS HARP (Fine Line Features)(released 1995)

1993   GUNMAN II (a.k.a. *Salween*)(distributor unknown)

1994   *Day of Reckoning* (NBC-TV) (novel)

Appendix B

Unrealized Projects

"**I HAVE TWO CAREERS,**" Stirling Silliphant said. "I write for the studio and for the shelf. I have at least fifteen scripts on the shelf that will probably never be made into films."[307] All screenwriters endure the heartbreak of working on projects that they can't sell. The difference in Silliphant's case is that the scripts he wrote for producers or studios were paid jobs. It was tempting to go for the money, especially in the lush days when it was offered to him so freely. Sometimes he was given seductive sums to polish another writer's work or add flair to an existing script in order to attract a particular star. Sometimes a Silliphant polish was what turned a "close but no sale" script into a go project. When he was really hot, in the early 1960s, producers or networks would pay him upwards of $1,000 just to pitch them an idea, and thousands more if they wanted him to write it. (Today, everyone, including Writers Guild members, are expected not only to pitch for free but, often, to write on spec after pitching and even do free rewrites).

Following is a list of unrealized or aborted projects that were discovered among the Stirling Silliphant papers at UCLA and in his family's personal files. If he commented on any of them, his remarks are included. Dates and remarks are given where they are known.

2 Plus 2 (Fries Productions,1985). Silliphant was announced to make his directing debut with this drama about the marriages of two couples who live together and whose relationships reflected the morals of the day.[308] Six years earlier, he had said, "I would consider directing a demotion, and it would take time away from my writing."[309] And thirteen years before that, just prior to making *The Slender Thread*, he had said, "I consider producing a demotion for a writer."[310] The show never happened. Fries: "Sometimes people plant stories just to try to generate interest in their career and maybe Stirling did want to direct it and he thought that story would attract other directing opportunities."[311] Silliphant never directed.

Adieu, Saigon (ABC-TV, 1988). Four-hour mini-series made with Warner Bros., television.

All the Emperor's Horses (Avco-Embassy, 1969). True account of a young American scholar who goes to China, falls in love with the daughter of one of China's richest families, and then comes the Revolution. Drawn from articles in *The New Yorker*. "I ached to write the movie, but [producer] Joe [Levine] opted not to go ahead with it. I was probably paid off, I don't remember, but I never wrote the script."[312]

America the Beautiful (Avco-Embassy, 1969). A satire on sex, security and the soft buck from essays by David White. Written for Joseph E. Levine's company. "I don't regard it as a successful script. It never quite jelled beyond the fact that it seemed merely a collection of the essays on which I based the screenplay. Today I would do it as a non-fiction film." Silliphant wound up bringing legal action against Avco-Embassy through the Writers Guild for his unpaid $15,000 fee.

Angel's Twenty (1956). Independent film set in Korea about the attack carrier U.S.S. Princeton. 117-page spec script.

The Artful Dodger (undated). For director John Sturges and Mirisch Productions, United Artists. "What happened here is that Walter Mirisch, pleased with my contribution to *In the Heat of the Night*, called me in and assigned me to write a what-might-have-happened-after *The Great Escape* (1963). It was an original and John Sturges, who had directed *The Great Escape*, was signed to direct this new follow-up of what happened to the few people who escaped in the original. My script was originally designated *The Artful Dodger*, but I soon enough changed it to *The Yards at Essendorf*. I focused on the thousands of French prisoners the Nazis put into forced labor in the main railroad yards because John wanted to shoot trains and locomotives—much as John Frankenheimer did later on in his film about the French and trains (*The Train*, 1964). I thought it turned out to be a powerful script, but John kept, as I accused him of, moving the piano from one part of the living room to another, while at the same time he was spending moist of his thought in getting a yacht either designed, outfitted, or some goddamn diverting thing, so after about six or seven more rewrites, I simply divorced myself from any further obligation to the project and it died on Walter Mirisch's shelf.[313]

Atlas Shrugged (NBC, 1979). Treatment, 1,240 pages. "It broke down into ten hours. Not only is it formidable, but Miss Rand is a little formidable. She has absolute total creative control over the project; that was the only way she would make her deal with the network. That means she has to initial every page. She's quite a taskmaster, a brilliant writer, and a lady who won't let you change very much. For instance, let's say there's a line of dialogue, '*I think I'll go upstairs.*' She'll say, 'Why did you write that line of dialogue?' I say, 'Miss Rand, it's from the book on page 452 if you will look.' She said, 'I don't have to look. I would never have written that line of dialogue for the character of Dagny.' I say, 'I'll show you.' Now I open the book and the dialogue is not *I think I will go upstairs*, but *I will go upstairs*. I added the two words, *I think*. She will say, 'Why did you do that?' 'Well,' I said, 'because I wanted to suggest that she wasn't too sure whether she would or wouldn't.' [Rand] said, 'That's wrong. Dagny is a character who always knows what she's going to do, what she has done, what she will do. She would never qualify it with *I think* or *possibly* or *perhaps*.' She said, 'on top of that, her dialogue is written in iambic pentameter and when you add *I think*, aside from destroying the character I've created, you are destroying the rhythm of the sentence.' That is how precise she is. As a writer, I learned craft from this lady. Suddenly you realize you've been writing dreck all these years. I worked for a year on this one only to have it destroyed *in utero* the first weekend NBC changed management, ousting the execs who had ordered it and replacing them with that shining genius of the tube, Fred Silverman." (*Atlas Shrugged* was produced and released in two parts in 2011 and 2012 by independent producer Harman Kaslow's Strike Productions. Silliphant's material was not involved.).

Battle. 162-page script dated January 3, 1975. No producing information.

The Bitter and the Sweet (Universal, 1985). Proposed daytime drama (soap opera) with Dick Irving Highland for Universal City Studios. Silliphant felt that daily daytime television would have less censorship than prime time television because its viewing audience is mostly mature women as opposed to the mixed audiences who watch at night.[314] Fifty-one-page script dated May 24, 1965.

The Burma Horsemen. Written for Raymond Chow, Golden Harvest Productions. No further information.

Captain James Cook project (1990, United National Pictures). UNP sued Silliphant for reneging on a verbal commitment to write a six-hour mini-series on Captain James Cook even though they say he deposited their $50,000 advance check.[315] He agreed to write the show bible on the condition that he write all of the scripts, and UNP said they'd make "best efforts" for him to do it, but they did not or could not, and, explained Silliphant, "in short, a $425,000 deal now suddenly was cut back to $125,000. I stopped my work and kept the $50,000 [start-up fee]. This has resulted in their suing me and I suing them. It's in the hands of attorneys and I spend about one hundredth of a second every six months thinking about it."[316] (Alternate title: *The Magnificent Invader.*)

Chasing the Dragon. First draft screenplay, March 30, 1990. No further information.

Cinderella and the Pilot (Summerton Productions, LA and London). Outline written by Irina Summerton based on a story by Stirling Silliphant).

A Circle in Water. Notes for a novel. No further information.

Cleaning Up (1983). Mr. T (*nee* Lawrence Tero) is a Chicago garbage man who not only cleans up the trash, he cleans up the streets. "I went off with Mr. T to Chicago and to the neighborhood where he grew up and I'm here to tell you I never felt so white in my life. I saw things I'd never seen before; Mr. T took me into his world more deeply than Joe Louis ever did into his. Mr. T's Chicago was a place where you could lose your ass in a fraction of a second. Menace dripped from every doorway. Eyes looked into mine with expressions I had never seen before and would elect never to see again. And I was supposed to be writing a *comedy*. But after the first few days I began to go with the flow and turn myself inside out and let the black of me surface and put the white of me away somewhere and suddenly all the booby traps became disarmed and I felt and shared and went with the sense of humor that exists out there in the street because without humor there's no fucking way you would want to live until tomorrow. Then watching some kid being chased by three other kids with baseball bats became hysterically amusing. 'Hey, T, what they gonna do to the bro'?' I'd ask. 'Oh,' T grinned, 'Gonna kill him.' '*Kill?*' I played back. 'Yeh,' he said. 'Looks like it to me.' And we keep driving in his Mercedes. Ha, ha!"

The Color of Deceit (1992). Dramatized outline for a story set in Hong Kong involving stock traders and romantic intrigue.

Daredevil (Warner Bros, TV,1982). Based on the Marvel Comics character created by Stan Lee and Bill Everett. Silliphant owed Warner Bros. a third script on an overall deal, but his agent renegotiated that his commitment would be satisfied if *Daredevil* did not go to pilot but his other script, *Travis McGee,* did. This came to pass.[317]

Dial 116 (Wilbert Productions, 1958). Silliphant wrote three scripts ("102 to Bakersfield," "The Ammonia Trap," and "Ferris Wheel") for this series, which Bert Leonard wanted to produce. When the series didn't happen, Leonard re-purposed the scripts, changing the title of "120 to Bakersfield" to "Dial 116" and selling it to CBS for *The Lineup*, and using "The Ammonia Trap" and "Ferris Wheel" on his own 1958 CBS Screen Gems series, *Rescue 8*. The name "Wilbert" combines Willeta and Herbert Leonard, who were married at the time. Silliphant used the pseudonym "Loren Dayle" after his two children by Ednamarie.

The Dilly Road (Paramount, 1966). Set near Antofagasta, Chile, in the American mines and smelting plants. Dilly roads are the roads leading out of the mines in this escape drama. "I never wrote this because I never found the time to zip on down to Antofagasta. Since I seldom write anything without first researching the place and people, I couldn't proceed without that first vital location trip. And anyway, I always thought of *The Dilly Road* (a title, incidentally, which I continue to love) more as a novel than as a film. I had this fantasy I'd write an even better book than the superb *Under the Volcano*. It never happened—and sadly never will—that book I didn't write—that title I never used.

Dreamstreet (1985, NBC). Mini-series about a group of young people who come to LA seeking fame and fortune in rock, film, communications, etc. A morality play.[318] "This was a final effort on my part to get something about young people going. I set this script on LA's Melrose Avenue and I changed the characters to become the trendy kids who brought that street to life in the early '80s. I've never seen Aaron Spelling's *Melrose Place* (Fox-TV) but I suspect I may have preceded him by a decade with this subject."

East-West, Ltd. Pilot (1986). script for a one-hour TV series. Revised draft January 10, 1986.

Embargo (undated). Silliphant and best-selling European novelist Gerard deVilliers were signed to simultaneously write an original motion picture *and* a novel, which indie producer Doug Netter planned to develop in tandem for publishing and screen.[319] "It was one of those high-action, realism-based stories about Middle East bad guys striking back at the U.S.A. by planning to stage a series of raids on American refineries, thus bringing the country to its knees, since this lack of fossil fuel, coupled with a simultaneous Arab embargo, would permit political extortion of Washington. Gerard and I cooked up the story together, working both in Paris and in Hollywood, and set the primary action in Houston, Texas, where our research revealed that most of the American refineries, certainly the ones in Houston, had lousy security.

Determined Campfire Girls could easily knock out the cracking facilities and take the refinery off-stream for months.

"I wrote the script (I believe Gerard also wrote the novel), but Doug was never quite able to put the deal together. I seem to remember—but only vaguely—that Doug indicated he might be able to put some kind of a deal if I were to back off from the terms of my original contract and surrender profit points. I, of course, refused, and have the sense that somehow, when the smoke cleared, I got blamed by Doug and Gerard for being a spoil-sport and the wrench in the machine. For my part, I thought they had one hell of a nerve asking *me* to give up *my* points. Why didn't *they* give up theirs? It was something like that, but it's way back into the past and trying to remember exactly what went wrong here is like trying to remember what you ate for dinner three months ago."

Face-Off. Screenplay, May 25, 1973. No further information.

The Falcon of Siam. Treatment by Axel Aylwen and Stirling Silliphant from Aylwen's novel set in Siam (Thailand) in the late seventeenth century about an English trade merchant rising to power in his adopted and beloved country. Dated April, 1995.

Fall of Saigon (1987, announced 1989). 266-page treatment for six-hour mini-series for producer David L. Wolper (*Roots*) and Warner Bros. drawn from the photojournalistic accounts of David Butler. Combining actual historical people with fictional characters as they are caught in the last gasp of the American war and the helter-skelter evacuation.[320] "This script was and always will be one of my favorites—a really outstanding piece of work if I alone say it—but we got caught in three changes of long-form bosses at ABC over the course of our developing and my writing this—and there we were— too many cooks. Pity!"

Forbidden Diary (Lilac Productions, 1982). eighty-one-page original screenplay/teleplay set in the Philippines in 1941 following the Crouter family during the Japanese occupation. His producing partner was *Naked City* actress Nancy Malone.

Forbidden Planet (1992). Scripted a proposed remake of the 1956 science fiction classic, which itself was based on Shakespeare's *The Tempest*. For producer Lindsay Parsons.

Great Smoky River Marathon, The. First draft screenplay, January 29, 1982.

Groundswell (July 6, 1965 treatment). A Viet Cong group comes to the United States, kidnaps the Chairman of the Joint Chiefs of Staff, hides out on Fire Island and, using satellite communication, puts the General on trial for the Vietnam war citing the tenets of the Nuremburg trial on genocide. Silliphant wrote it for producer Herbert Brodkin well before the emergence of America's anti-war movement, but Brodkin (producer of TV's *The Defenders*) said it would be a tough sell because it was "soapboxing." "I was alarmed by Washington's attitude toward the Vietnamese as far back as 1954 when the brass seriously considered nuking the Viets to save the French colonial regime there. A decade later I had become so disturbed by our replacing the French in Indochina that I had to write something. Every studio in Hollywood turned this one down within forty-eight hours. I was widely accused of being a Communist for even daring to write it." Silliphant had furtive discussions with Frank Sinatra based on Sinatra's earlier success with *The Manchurian Candidate*, but it never came about.[321] In 1968, Brodkin tried reviving it but, by then, Silliphant said he didn't have the time to rewrite it.

Hanta Yo. Six-hour adaptation of Ruth Beebe Hill's novel following three generations of two families of the Mahto band of the Teton Sioux. Hill spent thirty years researching and writing the mammoth novel that was said to do for Indians what *Roots* did for blacks. Stan Margulies was to produce for David L. Wolper, and Silliphant did a huge (434 page) treatment and step outline. "In the language of the Lakota Indian, which we call the Sioux, it means 'clear the way.' It's a battle cry. It's Wolper's Indian *Roots* for ABC. I went to the San Juan Islands to live for the three months it took me to write this one so I could be close to the novelist and have daily access to her Sioux companion/adviser. Ultimately ABC discarded my script, which faithfully followed the novel, and opted instead to bring in another writer to take only a fraction of the novel and dramatize it into the ill-fated four-hour mini ABC called *The Mystic Warrior.*"

Haven't I Seen You Somewhere Before? (1966). Proposed half-hour TV series cowritten by Silliphant and Richard Collins, who collaborated on a pilot script.

Hiero's Journey (Columbia, 1975). A futuristic fantasy film written in a poetic style. Full screenplay. "It's the name of a character. It takes place on another planet in another time, and everything is different. But it *seems* the same—almost. What is fun about it is that there are rules for this kind of a script. In other words, it's whatever I want to create that makes sense in a different place, within the laws of the universe. The fascinating thing is, water, as we know it, runs in a certain direction. Well, it might not on a different planet. Rain might not be the same. You could be killed by a giant abalone, a univalve. Why not?"[322] "A change of management sent this one into the scrap heap." (Alt. title: *Earthrise*.)

Ho Chi Minh (1989). Untitled "epic screenplay" announced. "I first visited Hanoi in late 1987 to research the possibilities of doing a film about Uncle Ho in the tradition of *Gandhi*. I knew it would be an uphill struggle and that forces beyond my comprehension would do everything they could to abort and defeat the effort. I have collected some incredible material… but somehow I seem to lack the strength to tackle this film. Either that or I'm waiting for divine intervention." He also reported that, while in Hanoi, he was asked by the Foreign Minister, "When do you think the Americans will recognize us?" to which he replied, "Forget the Americans. When the business opportunities are correct, they [the government] will be here. But they will never he here out of conscience. They will only come out of money and out of business."[323]

The Inheritors (Avco-Embassy, 1969). Based on Harold Robbins's novel, for Joe Levine. Never produced.

Islands in the Stream (Paramount, 1977). Adapted from the novel by Ernest Hemingway. Director Franklin Schaffner used a subsequent script by Denne Bart Petitclerc.

"Juvenile Delinquent" 1956. Polish on existing teleplay that may have been produced under a different title. No further information.

Khaki Mafia, The (1971). To be directed by Jules Dassin, an original script about corruption among the U.S. Army in Vietnam. Financing fell through after the research trip to Southeast Asia but before the writing began.

Last Man at Wagon Hound (1956). Screenplay and polish assignment for film to star Clark Gable for United Artists release (via Ruse-Field, Inc.) to be directed by Raoul Walsh.

The Long Goodbye (UA, 1974). Adapted Raymond Chandler's novel for director Robert Altman, who rejected it in favor of one by Leigh Brackett. "I think my script is far better than the one he shot," Silliphant said, allowing that he still likes Bob Altman.[324] Altman favored Brackett's glossy adaptation of Raymond Chandler's 1953 novel over Silliphant's more faithful one. In 1944 Brackett had, with William Faulkner and Jules Furthman, adapted Chandler's *The Big Sleep* (1946) for Howard Hawks. The Altman/Brackett Marlowe is a man rooted in the 1950s but living in the 1970s, baffled by modern realities. The Chandler/Silliphant Marlowe is intensely loyal and operates on a code of chivalry that, despite the reprobates he deals with, pulls him through. A discussion of Silliphant's process and a comparison may be found in *Raymond Chandler on Screen: His Novels Into Film* by Stephen Pendo (Metuchen, N.J.: The Scarecrow Press, 1976).

The Looking Glass (1980 and 1983). Partnered with producer Lin Bolen and written (first at six hours, then cut by Bolen to two hours) for ABC chief Brandon Stoddard about the "new frontier of sex."[325] "I wrote it. Turned it in. I happened to be in Hawaii when Brandon called. 'Damn you,' he said. 'I read *The Looking Glass* and threw it across the office.' 'That bad?' I asked. 'No,' he said, 'That good, but there's no way we can ever put this script on TV.' And he didn't. The network said, 'We need another word for *sex*. Something less genital, more compassionate.'"

The Masters (1979-1980). Developed for Bruce Lee and other martial arts masters, Silliphant described this as a cross between *Rocky* and *Bad Day at Black Rock* in which martial artists would be fully developed characters.

The Med-Ex (ABC, 1972). Shot but unaired pilot. Idealistic young medics return from Vietnam and, rather than go to medical school to get rich, they work instead in the remote Pacific northwest as paramedics. Silliphant said he was using the series to attack what is wrong with medicine. "It was pretty powerful stuff and, yes, I did take out after the good-ole-boy bullshit of the AMA and tried to make the point that the human touch is often more effective than surgery—not always, but certainly sometimes. Hospitals have bad vibes, the karmas stink. The networks would call this an 'action medical show.' Little does ABC know what I have in the back of my mind."[326] Alternate title: *The New Healers*.

The Menorah Men. "Based on a novel by Lionel Davidson. I went to Israel with the director, Elliot Silverstein, to complete our research and to polish my script. This was an independently financed project out of London, but never got its financing together." Also titled *The Sojourners*. Script dated February 24, 1972. Fifty-seven pages.

No Cross, No Crown (CBS Playhouse, 1968). CBS gave a green light to this project about how the Vietnam war had divided America into two polar societies. A young boy doesn't want to fight in Vietnam. The character is not a draft-dodger and won't head to Canada, but he objects to the war. Said Silliphant (still basking in his Oscar win for *In the Heat of the Night*), "The artist cannot dissociate with his times."[327] Later, he canceled the project and returned his $25,000 writing fee, saying that he was not afraid of controversy but felt that the project would be judged by the audience who favored the war. "I truly felt I could not continue with this project because it would never be judged as a piece of writing, but only as a political tract by a writer who clearly felt that America had fielded an invasion of a foreign people for neo-colonialist purposes. We [America] were even planning to build a zapper electrical fence across Vietnam at the seventeenth parallel. Jesus Christ, what fucking right did the United States of America have to even be *talking* about such an installation?" According to a Gallup poll at the time, fifty-eight percent of Americans supported U.S. involvement in Vietnam, yet when Silliphant attended the Berlin Film Festival in 1968 he found that the European public held him accountable, as an American, for America's bombing of North Vietnam.[328]

The Order. Treatment, January 15, 1974.

The Party's Over (1970). Un-shot script for political satire to be made with Cy Howard. "It was intended to star Sidney Poitier, Gig Young, Sally Kellerman, etc., etc. and was ordered by Marty Baum when he was heading ABC Pictures. Marty locked Cy and me into Cy's house for one week to do the script. Cy and I decided we'd try something new—he'd write the dramatic scenes and I'd write the funny stuff. It was a blast—WE thought—and we finished it in six days working twenty hours a day, editing each other's stuff, so that Cy ended up having written the funny stuff while I ended up writing the dramatic scenes. Marty Baum HATED the script. Or maybe it was Sidney who hated it. It doesn't really matter, because they unlocked Cy's door and I went home, never to hear another word about the project. I'm positive it never went into production."[329]

Philippine Diary (CBS). Four-hour saga of American families caught in the Philippines by the Japanese invasion in 1941. The script's anti-war, anti-stereotype sentiments worked against the network's desire for action. "True, it broke the stereotypes of Japanese soldiers with American babies jouncing on the tips of bayonets and tried to say that everyone in a war, friend or foe, is entrapped."

Pizzaro (1989). "A still-pending original I wrote three years ago with the Japanese writer-director Jûzô Itami." (Itami died in 1997.)

Poochy Noble. Late 1970s. Treatment for a film. Undated.

R&R Murders (Rest & Rec Murders, 1978). Written at the invitation of Reg Grundy Productions in New South Wales and set in the red light and legal arenas of Sydney, Australia.

Race, The (alt. title *Voice Over*). Sixty-one-page screenplay. First draft March 8, 1977.

Rivers (Warner Bros., 1984). Project developed between Pingree and Dick Clark Cinema Productions. No further information.

The Sailor Who Fell From Grace With the Sea (Brodkin-Silliphant Productions, 1976). Adaptation of Yukio Mishima's novel *Go No Eiko*, ultimately written and directed by Lewis John Carlino and produced by Martin Poll and David White.

The Sands of Time (CBS). Four-hour mini-series from Sidney Sheldon's novel. "I never did know what happened here except vague rumors that my script was 'too strong for TV.' True, I did have six soldiers rape a nun who then managed to shoot and kill three of them before she was machine-gunned."

Sister Street. First revised screenplay June 27, 1986. No further information.

Squaw Fever (1956). Raoul Walsh's personal production based on the *Saturday Evening Post* series "Squaw Fever" and "Fiddlefoot."

Snowbound (1975). Disaster film involving a blizzard. Got to script stage, then melted.

Sunset Boulevard (CBS, 1965). Signed by Paramount for $100,000 to develop Billy Wilder's classic film into a primetime serial (first title was *The Scene*) akin to *Peyton Place* that was drawing huge numbers for ABC and Twentieth Century-Fox in 1964, but the network lost interest when *Peyton Place* started to slide in 1965. "Pity, because I did some of my best work for this pilot script. We were virtually on the air, had begun casting. To give you some idea of the power of some of the scenes (it's a story of young people trying to make it in Hollywood), I'll tell you about one incident. I had written one of the key parts for a young actress who's supposed to have the talent of Bette Davis, but who's skinny, flat-chested, and scraggly-haired. I scouted all the acting classes in town until I found the girl I was looking for. She was simply the finest young actress I'd ever seen. I brought her in to read for the Paramount casting director and for some CBS types, all wearing suits. I talked to her outside the office for half an hour before the audition. This is the scene, I told her— you've been sent to the studio by its New York office. They consider you back in New York to be a find. The Hollywood crowd has taken one look at you and decided you're a dog. The casting director is now calling you in, giving you a check for a thousand dollars as an anodyne for the 'mistake' New York has made—because, frankly, young lady, the picture they sent you out here for has been canceled and we have nothing else for you, sorry—And here's a pass for Disneyland and don't worry, we'll pickup your bill at the Chateau Marmont—and here's some per diem and good luck, goodbye. Now, I told her, I want you to tie into that sonofabitch. Tell him how much you hate the fucking Hollywood system, rip open your blouse, show him your flat chest, ask him if these pitiful tits are his measure of talent—sock it to him. Where are the lines, she asked me. In your heart, I told her. In your tears. I can't ever write the words to match what I know you feel. Just go in there and *do* it—and know that I want you in this part. You've got it, as far as I'm concerned. I've found the right girl. But you have to go in there and convince *them*—because they have the money and I don't.

"She went in, and believe me—even I quailed before the fury of her assault. My nerves jangled in resonance to her anguish, all her frustrations, all her shattered dreams—at the hands of people like these. Well, unfortunately, she went over the edge—she lost it—she started weeping inconsolably and then went running out of the office. The Suits and the casting guy from Paramount sat, stunned, not knowing whether to look at their fingernails or at their shoes. The secretary of the casting director burst into the office. How dare you do that to the girl? she said. You should be ashamed. Then, weeping, she ran out. I took after the girl and caught up with her in the parking lot. I'm sorry, I told her. I should have written the dialogue for you, but I can't write that well, that truly. You went too far. I know, she said. I'm sorry I failed you. Well, I said, let's see—maybe they'll sort it out and see that what happened in there could be dynamite on film. But, of course, they never saw it that way—and, in any event, CBS decided not to go ahead with the shoot." When the plug was pulled on *Sunset Boulevard*, Silliphant hit back in the trades by damning "development deals" as hurting creative ability. "Who the hell are the TV people to do this?" he said, no doubt thinking of the actress who got carried away.[330]

The Surrogate (1975). About American sex clinics, but from a woman's point of view. Silliphant admitted to having done some research on his own. The project was developed with Dr. Aaron Stern, the psychiatrist whose credentials had originally been used by the Motion Picture Association of America to legitimize their movie rating system.[331] A mutual friend—an industry insider whom Silliphant wouldn't name—suggested the partnership. "For a period of two or three months, three times a week, I would visit with Dr. Stern while he strode back and forth dictating into a tape machine... I felt more and more ill-at-ease in the presence of Dr. Stern, so I simply removed myself and never went back, and, in the process, alienated my important and powerful industry friend. But that's life on the couch for you—and who in hell cares?"

Three Seals. In the early 1970s Charles W. "Chuck" Fries, the Screen Gems VP with whom Silliphant and Bert Leonard had worked on *Route 66*, was asked by President Richard Nixon to come to Washington, DC. "They were looking for a series to be developed to depict drug use in a negative fashion," Fries said. "*Three Seals* was a combination of the Treasury Department, an Alcohol Abuse Department and a third one that escapes me. Stirling and I worked together on developing the presentation and I made the contacts with Washington to get the cooperation of the various agencies in Washington. One of the interesting things was that, when we went to Washington to meet with Nixon, all of the characters that ended up in the Watergate affair [were three] like John Mitchell, H. R. Haldemann, John Ehrlichman and John Dean, all of whom participated in the seminar with those of us that attended from the Creative Community in Hollywood in New York. Unfortunately, when we showed up at CBS to pitch the project and had the cooperation of the Treasury Department and the others, Bob Wood, President of the CBS Television network at the time, stood up and said he can't believe it, we just bought a series with David Janssen called *O'Hara, U.S. Treasury.* I explained to him that Government Departments did not give exclusive rights to any producer, that their cooperation was conditioned on active development and production, and if *O'Hara* went forward at CBS, they would get that cooperation, but probably not exclusively. We moved around town to two other networks but we found no takers."[332]

Untitled original. February 20, 1986. Characters and outline. "A film in the genre of *48 HRS* and the French movie *Diva*, that is, a film of suspense and of action, yet, more importantly, a film about a unique and crackling relationship between two very special human beings: an investigator from the south side of Chicago and a rebellious heiress, as together they set out to find the missing younger sister of the heiress." Twenty-three pages.

Vietnam, Inc. Treatment written July 7, 1972.

Voice on the Wind (Paramount, 1965). Original Silliphant story, which he and Steve Alexander (producer of *The Slender Thread*) would produce and which would costar Elizabeth Ashley and Sidney Poitier. No doubt abandoned after Ashley was separated from what became the Anne Bancroft role in *Thread*.

We Fly Anything (1956). Series pilot written for producers Frank Cooper and Irving Pincus.

The Weather Wars (Carl Foreman, 1978). Rewrite of a 133-page main character and outline treatment for a group jeopardy picture that takes place during a global meteorological catastrophe now known as global warming. Written for producer Carl Foreman. "He was wonderful to work with. But Carl passed away and the script was never produced."

When in Rome (1980). Original romantic comedy written for Warner Bros. that never made the production schedule.

When Worlds Collide (Universal-Zanuck/Brown, 1977). "Not sure about this title, but it was a gigantic project I wrote in the mid-Seventies for Zanuck/Brown. Still a marvelous script but much too costly to make."

Winchell and Runyon. Full screen treatment about the New York newspapermen written for Warner Bros. Never developed.

Windward Passage. (Date not available). Stirling Silliphant-Bruce Bilson Production. 147 page treatment for seafaring adventure.

Zero Option (1987). 113-page screenplay for thriller.

The Zimbardo Experiment (ABC-TV). 90-minute *ABC Theatre* teleplay by Mark Silliphant based on the 1971 Stanford Prison experiment conducted by Philip Zimbardo in which twenty-four white, middle-class students pretended to be prisoners and guards and, before long, each set adapted all too well to their enforced roles.

Silliphant's personal files contain numerous additional projects for which intriguing titles, notes, snippets, or full treatments and screenplays exist, including: *A Way of Life, Ansel McCutcheon, Barnstormers, Bookin', Camp Survival, The Empty Copper Sea, Escapade, Herzog* (adaptation of Saul Bellow novel), *Kickback, The Long Lavender Look, Louisiana Story* (not the Flaherty docu-drama), *The Man In-Between, Mayday, Of My Bones Are Coral Made, The Osmonds, The President's Man, The Rattlewatch, Reunion, Saigon, The Sequestering, The Seventh Secret, Sojourners, Solitaire (a.k.a. Five Minutes of Silence), Spartan Project, The Spy Who Loved Me* (James Bond movie pitch), *Summer Reel, Take Three, Tri Makai/Trident, Tuff Enuff, Windward Passage.*

Selected Bibliography

Ball, John, *In the Heat of the Night*. New York: Bantam Books, 1967.

Brooks, Tim and Earle Marsh, *The Complete Directory to Prime Time Network and Cable TV Shows, 1946-Present, Sixth Ed*. New York: Ballantine Books, 1995

Froug, William, *The Screenwriter Looks At the Screenwriter*. New York: MacMillan & Company, 1972.

Goldman, William, *Adventures in the Screen Trade*. New York: Warner Books, 1983.

Harris, Mark, *Pictures at a Revolution*. New York: The Penguin Press, 2008.

Hirschhorn, Clive, *The Universal Story*. London, England: Octopus Books, 1983.

Hopkins, Jerry, *Bangkok Babylon: The Real-Life Exploits of Bangkok's Legendary Expatriates are often Stranger than Fiction*. Singapore: Periplus Editions (HK) Ltd., 2005.

Jewison, Norman, *This Terrible Business Has Been Good To Me*. Toronto, Ontario, Canada: Key Porter Books, Ltd., 2004.

Kermode, Mark, *Fire in the Sky, Hell Under Water*. Produced by Andrew Abbott and Russell Leven. London, England: Nobles Gate for Channel 4, 2003.

McGilligan, Patrick, *Robert Altman: Jumping Off the Cliff.* New York: St. Martin's Press, 1989.

McGilligan, Patrick, *Clint: The Life and Legend.* London, England: HarperCollins, 1999.

Mirisch, Walter, *We Thought We Were Making Movies, Not History.* Madison, Wisconsin: The University of Wisconsin Press, 2008.

Nogueira, Nui, "Wendell Mayes: The Jobs Poured Over Me," *Backstory 3*, Patrick McGilligan, ed. Berkeley, California: The University of California Press, 1997.

Orlean, Susan. *Rin Tin Tin: The Life and the Legend.* New York: Simon & Schuster, 2012.

Poitier, Sidney, *The Measure of a Man: A Spiritual Autobiography.* San Francisco, California: HarperCollins, 2000.

Smith, Dave, *Disney A to Z.* New York: Hyperion Press, 1996.

Wiley, Mason & Damien Bona, *Inside Oscar: The Unofficial History of the Academy Awards.* New York: Ballantine Books, 1993.

Copyrights and Credits

This page is an extension of the Copyright page.

Stirling Silliphant Papers, 1950-1985. (Collections 134 and 1079). Performing Arts Library Special Collections, Young Research Library, University of California at Los Angeles. The appearance in this work of previously unpublished non-interview material by Stirling Silliphant constitutes their first publication, and copyright is hereby claimed: ©2013 The Estate of Stirling Silliphant.

"OSCAR®," "OSCARS®," "ACADEMY AWARD®," "ACADEMY AWARDS®," "OSCAR NIGHT®," "A.M.P.A.S.®" and the federally registered "Oscar" design mark are registered and copyrighted by the Academy of Motion Picture Arts and Sciences.

Cliff Robertson interview courtesy of the Archive of American Television, interviewed by Stephen J. Abramson on March 1, 2005. EMMY® is the trademark property of the Academy of Television Arts and Sciences/National Academy of Television Arts and Sciences. Visit http://www.emmytvlegends. org for more information.

Excerpts from "Up Close and Personal with Stirling Silliphant" by John Corcoran, *Kick* Magazine, July-November, 1980; Hollywood, California: CFW Enterprises. ©John Corcoran. Used by permission.

Excerpts from *If I Was a Highway* and "Letters at 3AM: Stirling at Road's End" by Michael Ventura ©Michael Ventura. Used by permission.

Silliphant's IMDb credits used by permission of Internet Movie Database: http://pro.imdb.com/name/nm0798103/.

Those interested in learning more about Bruce Lee should consult the website created by his daughter, Shannon, who runs the Bruce Lee Foundation:
http://www.bruceleefoundation.com/index.cfm/page/Timeline/pid/10379

Every effort has been made to trace the provenance of photographs used in this book. The publisher will remove them or correct omissions upon presentation of certified ownership by a different party than that which is credited.

FINALLY, a note to journalists who interview celebrities: send your work to the people you cover. Only because a handful of interviewers had the courtesy to mail copies of their articles and TV interviews to Stirling Silliphant are they represented in this book. Now that the Internet has made history ephemeral, don't count on Google to save your stuff. When you interview someone, send a copy afterward. And be sure to label it.

Endnotes

1. WGA rates for 1985 were $29,320 for a screenplay for a high-budget film and $42,000 for treatment and screenplay. Silliphant usually managed to wangle a treatment first.

2. Conversation with the author.

3. *Time*, August 9, 1963. The other four fingers were Paul Henning (*The Beverly Hillbillies*), Nat Hiken (*Car 54, Where Are You?*), Rod Serling (*The Twilight Zone*), and Reginald Rose (*The Defenders*). *Time* reported that Silliphant's "manages to hold his salary down to $145,000" for tax reasons. The producer's name was not given.

4. *Cool Hand Luke*: Donn Pearce (from his novel) and Frank R. Pierson; *The Graduate*: Buck Henry; *In Cold Blood*: Richard Brooks; *Ulysses*: Joseph Strick and Fred Haines.

5. See Mark Harris's meticulous *Pictures at a Revolution* (New York: The Penguin Press, 2008), to which acknowledgment is hereby given.

6. Scholars will note that Will H. Hays, Valenti's distant predecessor, introduced "The Formula" in 1924 that was refined into what became known as The Production Code of Self-Regulation in 1930.

7. An inside joke making the rounds at the time had a producer rejecting a script by telling the writer, "Your characters are too complex for a budget this big."

8. Unless otherwise cited, Silliphant's quotes are drawn from the faxed correspondence with the author for *Backstory 3* (Berkeley, California: University of California Press, 1997) and subsequent conversations.

9. Per the Academy's official transcript: "I really have no speech. The Writers Guild doesn't permit us to do any speculative writing. I'm deeply grateful and very touched. Thank you, Rod, Norman, Walter, Sidney, everyone. Thank you."

10. Interviewed by Bill Collins, "Bill Collins Showbiz," August 19, 1979, Seven Network, NSW (Australia).

11. Interviewed by Reed Farrell, c. 1977. Archive video, not further identified, from Silliphant Estate.

12. Allan Silliphant interview, February 14, 2013.

13. By 1940 he had changed the spelling of his name to *Stirling* to honor his father's brother, Stirling. He also cringed at the middle name *Dale*.

14. In interviews, Silliphant insisted that he was born on Pingree Street ("I wasn't actually born *on* the street, you understand, but in a *house* on Pingree"), but his birth certificate lists High Street, which is a Metamora address.

15. Stirling Silliphant, "What is a Nice Movie Writer Like You Doing Out Here in the Middle of This Nasty Ocean, Anyway?" *The Pennant*, September, 1973.

16. He was on the air when the Long Beach earthquake struck on March 10, 1933.

17. Allan Silliphant, ibid.

18. John Corcoran, "Up Close and Personal with Stirling Silliphant," *Kick* magazine, July, 1980 (Hollywood, California: CFW Enterprises).

19. The story is cited in his prepared biography as "The Enchanted Lantern" but is corrected in his hand to "Little Whisperers." (UCLA).

20. To reduce confusion from now on, the father Lemuel Lee Silliphant will continue to be called *Lee*; his second son will be called *Leigh*; Stirling will be called *Stirling* or *Silliphant*. Stirling Garff Silliphant will generally be called *Stirling Garff*, and, later, Stirling Linh Silliphant will be called *Stirling Linh*. None is a Junior.

21. Stirling Garff Silliphant interview, February 14, 2013.

22. Zanuck and Skouras would trade places in 1962 when Zanuck was summoned by desperate stockholders to save the rapidly sinking studio in the wake of Skouras's failed *Cleopatra* and Zanuck's triumphant *The Longest Day*.

23. Stirling Garff Silliphant, op cit.

24. Stirling Linh interview with the author, May 25, 2013.

25. Silliphant interview (unsigned) *Sacramento Bee*, May 29, 1983. He told the story in somewhat more profane terms to William Froug, *The Screenwriter Looks at the Screenwriter* (New York: The MacMillan Company, 1972). Obviously Bogart did not anticipate today's youth market that deems anybody over 30 an antique.

26. Producer David Brown, who was in the studio's story department at the time, enjoyed recalling how Zanuck summoned all his creative people to a meeting and announced, "We are no longer interested in stories with *depth*. We are only interested in stories with *width*." (Conversation with Author)

27. Much of Silliphant's personal paperwork, including bound copies of his scripts, was destroyed in a home electrical fire in 1969 in a home where he lived in Appian Way in Los Angeles. This water-stained book survived.

28. Bulletin of Screen Achievement, Academy of Motion Picture Arts and Sciences, December 10, 1956. Hand corrections specify that screenplay came first, then the novel.

29. Released May 21, 1958, by Paramount Pictures.

30. Disneyland opened to the public on July 18, 1955. Dave Smith, *Disney A to Z: The Official Encyclopedia* (New York: Hyperion Books, 1996).

31. Source: www.originalmmc.com fan website for *The Mickey Mouse Club*.

32. It was also the title of a 1949 Alfred Hitchcock film set in Australia, which is located geographically under the Tropic of Capricorn.

33. *Time* magazine, August 9, 1963.

34. *Suspicion* was a one-season, hour-long series produced for NBC by MCA/Revue and Hitchcock's Shamley Productions. Hitchcock was executive producer but did not appear, and directed only the premiere episode, "Four O'clock," airing September 30, 1957.

35. ("Nothing more.") While Hitchcock was alive, Silliphant's interviews stressed the director's involvement, presumably out of respect for the filmmaker's reputation. This interview occurred after Hitchcock died in 1980 when Silliphant owed no fealty to the legend.

36. From John Kier Cross's short story. In a twist on *Cyrano de Bergerac*, a woman falls in love with a brilliant ventriloquist only to discover that he's the dummy and his dummy is the man who has been sending her love letters.

37. Silliphant was mistaken about the episode's flagship status. "Voice in the Night" aired March 24, 1958 and concerned shipwreck survivors who wash ashore on an island where a deadly fungus threatens them. The cast included James Coburn, who would later figure prominently in Silliphant's life and in the legendary *The Silent Flute*.

38. By actual count, he wrote thirty-one half-hour *Naked City* episodes and six 60-minute episodes.

39. "Take Off Your Hat When a Funeral Passes," airdate September 27, 1961. The teleplay is credited to Howard Rodman and Anthony Spinner.

40. Larry Siegel and Mort Drucker, *MAD Magazine* No. 60, January, 1961.

41. At one point, Silliphant purchased a set of encyclopedias about mental illnesses and, when he was stuck for a plot, he would flip through them to find somebody to base a script on.

42. Dassin would be named and blacklisted in 1952.

43. The dog's name was *Rin Tin Tin* but hyphens were added for TV.

44. CBC mainstay Elwy Yost interview, posted on YouTube. Undated, but probably 1983 at the time of the publication of *Steel Tiger*.

45. Contracts in Silliphant family collection.

46. New York: Dell Publishing Company, Inc., 1959.

47. A similar theme is found in the hour-long *Naked City* episode "Prime of Life" (February 13, 1963) in which Paul Burke watches an execution in all its detail

(except for the actual electrocution). Beside him in the witness box, incidentally, is Gene Hackman in an early role.

48. Susan Orlean, *Rin Tin Tin: The Life and the Legend.* New York: Simon & Schuster, 2012.

49. One of which was *Village of the Damned* (q.v.).

50. *Film Daily*, December 23, 1965.

51. Yost, op cit.

52. Silliphant and Dassin tried to work together years later on a project called *The Khaki Mafia.*

53. Cecil Smith, *Los Angeles Times*, February 2, 1962.

54. Concurrent with writing *Route 66*, Silliphant was also writing episodes for *Checkmate, Mr. Lucky, G.E. Theatre,* and *Naked City.*

55. "Ed" from Ednamarie, then Mrs. Silliphant, and "ling" from Stirling.

56. Silliphant may have first tried to buy *On the Road* from Jack Kerouac, who refused.

57. Maharis had appeared in several *Naked City* episodes, including a nascent pilot for *Route 66,* "Four Sweet Corners."

58. An assumption is that Buz, Tod, and Linc are always able to find jobs in every town they visit. This was not questioned in the booming American economy of the early 1960s.

59. William Froug, *The Screenwriter Looks at the Screenwriter.* New York: MacMillan and Company, 1972.

60. Few viewers may have noticed, however; that same day, NASA astronaut Alan B. Shepard made his sub-orbital flight atop Friendship 7, inaugurating America's manned space program and pre-empting most TV programming.

61. Interview with Author, February 10, 2013. Tiana refers to the classic joke about the starlet who was so stupid that she slept with the screenwriter to get the part. (Added writer Richard Powell, "If you change the screenwriter to a director, the joke doesn't work, but the starlet does.")

62. Froug, op cit.

63. The *Route 66* season finale for 1961, not Silliphant's 1981 series pilot.

64. The episode is believed to be "Sheba" (January 6, 1961) and one of the rumored reasons was a contract dispute with Maharis.

65. Contracts in Silliphant family collection.

66. Blog post, www.davidmorrell.net

67. Michael Ventura, "A Swastika in the Snow" from *If I Was a Highway.* Lubbock, Texas: Texas Tech University Press, 2011.

68. This episode was also the basis for a 1992 musical called *The Finders* by Peter Morley and David Walters.

69. Los Angeles *Times*, August 14, 1964.

70. Dayle had entered the Jesuit-run Santa Clara University but changed her mind

while still a novitiate. She married twice, both times to Jewish men.

71. Silliphant's widow, Tiana, said that his skepticism of Dayle's commitment came from her demand for a credit card on which she charged numerous un-nunlike expenses. He enjoyed telling how he visited her one day and she put on her habit so quickly that she accidentally stabbed her scalp with a hatpin. When he saw her white cornette spotted with red, he thought, thinking of stigmata, "She really *did* give herself to God!"

72. In November 1962, Maharis pulled out, citing hepatitis, and was replaced by Glenn Corbett until the series ended in 1964. The Maharis episodes ran through March of 1963.

73. Thomas J. Dodd (D-CT) had a distinguished career prosecuting the Nuremberg Trials before serving in the House from 1953 to 1957 and the Senate from 1959 to 1971. He and Senator Estes Kefauver (D-TN) held hearings in 1954, 1961, and 1964 into TV violence that produced a reactionary clamp-down. Dodd was censured by the Senate in 1967 for campaign finance irregularities. His son, Christopher, was also a Senator (D-CT) from 1981 to 2011, after which he was, perhaps ironically, hired as CEO of the Motion Picture Association of America, which controls film content, while insisting it doesn't, through its rating system.

74. Froug, op cit.

75. Including the author who, in preparing the *Backstory* interview, borrowed several and returned the favor by buying pro copies for the family when tapes turned up in used video bins.

76. www.classictvhistory.wordpress.com plus correspondence with Author. The chain-of-title itself could make a detective story.

77. The author met briefly with Leonard toward the end of 1998 to negotiate a feature film deal for *Route 66*, ennobled partly by the wishes of the late Stirling Silliphant and his widow, and interest from a legitimate production company. After several phone calls, Bert and I met on Monday, December 7 at a post-production facility in Santa Monica, California where he said he was colorizing *Rin-Tin-Tin* episodes. I found the then-76-year-old Leonard alert and affable but unyielding in insisting on writing and directing the film himself, a decision I knew no studio would accept. We parted amicably. I tried reaching him a few times after that, just in case he had changed his mercurial mind, but never got a return call.

78. Stephen Bowie, The Classic TV History Blog, June 12, 2012; www.classictvhistory.wordpress.com.

79. "A Chat with Kirk Hallam," January 17, 2008, by Ron Warnick, www.route66-news.com.

80. Shout! Factory press release, November 7, 2011, www.tvshowsondvd.com/news

81. "More details about Route 66: DVD release August 4, 2007" by Ron Warnick, posted on www.route66news.com, August 4, 2007.

82. And they were an estimable procession that included Robert Altman, James Goldstone, William A. Graham, Tom Gries, Jeffrey Hayden, Arthur Hiller,

Philip Leacock, Robert Ellis Miller, George Sherman, Elliott Silverstein, Sam Peckinpah, and David Lowell Rich.

83. There is controversy among collectors that the available versions of this episode have been shortened from the original running time. The copy viewed for this book ran 52:30.

84. In the end, he gives the $100,000 bribe to the convent anyway, "as a wedding present" for Bonnie. No mention is made that the money is tainted.

85. According to Altman's biographer, Patrick McGilligan, Altman and Wynn did some rewriting on location when they weren't drunk. Even though the results were effective, Bert Leonard vowed never to hire Altman again (*Robert Altman: Jumping Off the Cliff.* New York: St. Martin's Press, 1989).

86. Deal memo, Silliphant family papers.

87. A British army officer, citing other blond birth epidemics, points to a map and says, "In the Communist world there were two time-outs similar to the one at Midwich. One at Irkutsk, here, and the borders of Outer Mongolia. A grim affair. The men killed the children and their mothers."

88. Earlier sources reported that the outspoken Ashley dropped out of the project in a contract dispute.

89. Sidney Poitier, *The Measure of a Man: A Spiritual Autobiography* (San Francisco, California: HarperCollins, 2000).

90. *Daily Variety*, December 22, 1965.

91. Signed deal memo dated November 17, 1965 and received September 16, 1966, Silliphant family archive.

92. Among their credits: *The Magnificent Seven, West Side Story, The Great Escape, The Apartment, The Russians Are Coming, The Pink Panther*, and many other successes.

93. Source: Walter Mirish, *We Thought We Were Making Movies, Not History* (WI: University of Wisconsin Press, 2008). Jewison says $1.5 million in his autobiography. Today it would easily cost $100 million.

94. Jewison's signing was announced August 15, 1966 (*Hollywood Reporter*).

95. Norman Jewison, *This Terrible Business Has Been Good to Me* (Toronto, Canada: Key Porter Books, 2004)

96. Walter Mirisch Collection, Academy of Motion Picture Arts and Sciences.

97. Author's Note: Silliphant's human rights credentials were impeccable. Here he was writing in the characters' biased voices.

98. January 7, 1966, treatment, AMPAS.

99. Poitier interview with Author, November 16, 2012.

100. Trevor Hogg, "Daring Ideas: Haskell Wexler Talks About In the Heat of the Night & Medium Cool," www.FlickeringMyth.com, September 12, 2012.

101. Carol Munday and Robert N. Zagone, *Fade Out: The Erosion of Black Images in the Media*; Nguzo Saba Films, WNET-TV, New York, 1984.

102. ibid.

103. Jewison, *op cit.*

104. Interview in William Froug, *The Screenwriter Looks At the Screenwriter.*

105. At one point Wood becomes a suspect, allowing Gillespie to tell Tibbs, who insists the cop is innocent, another oft-quoted line of dialogue: "What do you mean I'm holding the wrong man? I got the motive, which is money, and the body, which is dead."

106. At 15:26.

107. Mirisch, op cit. There is no record of the play being produced.

108. December 22, 1965.

109. Jewison, op cit. Also *Hollywood Reporter*, August 12, 1966.

110. Mirisch, op cit

111. "Annual Report of the Committee on Un-American Activities for the Year 1952" (Washington, DC: Committee on Un-American Activities, U.S. House of Representatives, 1952).

112. *Daily Variety*, November 8, 1966.

113. *Daily Variety*, November 14, 1966

114. Sidney Poitier, *This Life* (NY: Alfred A. Knopf, 1980). He would have an equally intense acting lesson on his next film, *Guess Who's Coming to Dinner*, opposite Spencer Tracy and Katharine Hepburn.

115. The line occurs at the bottom of page 24 on Silliphant's July 1, 1966, Revised First Draft.

116. Wexler interview with the author.

117. Marilyn and Alan Bergman wrote the lyrics without credit.

118. Poitier interview, ibid.

119. In 1999, Jewison was voted the Irving G. Thalberg Award by the Academy's Board of Governors.

120. Interviewed by Bill Collins, "Bill Collins Showbiz," August 19, 1979, Seven Network, NSW (Australia).

121. *Daily Variety*, January 23, 1969.

122. It was presented to him by a contrite Academy the year before he died.

123. A partial list includes *Marathon Man, All the President's Men, Butch Cassidy and the Sundance Kid, Misery*, and *The Princess Bride*.

124. Goldman says he started each chapter on a new page to pad the book's length. It was made into a film starring Rod Steiger, George Segal, and Lee Remmick in 1968.

125. William Goldman, *Adventures in the Screen Trade*, New York: Warner Books, 1983.

126. Cliff Robertson interview courtesy of the Archive of American Television, interviewed by Stephen J. Abramson on March 1, 2005. (http://emmytvlegends.

org/interviews/people/cliff-robertson)

127. Goldman, op cit.

128. Abramson, op cit

129. Punctuate this: That that is is that that is not is not is that it it is. (Answer: That that is, is. That that is not, is not. Is that it? It is.)

130. ...which Robertson was unable to collect in person because he was in the Philippines shooting *Too Late the Hero* with Michael Caine and couldn't travel to Los Angeles.

131. Boston filmmaking crews report that some footage was shot.

132. "The Reed Farrell Show," courtesy Silliphant archive.

133. Dayle, his daughter with Ednamarie, born 1955.

134. Ethel Silliphant never remarried.

135. Stirling Garff Rasmussen interview, February 14, 2013.

136. Interviewed by Bill Collins, "Bill Collins Showbiz," August 19, 1979. Seven Network, NSW (Australia).

137. *Newsweek*, January 31, 1972. Silliphant was saying that he originated *A Walk in the Spring Rain* rather than being hired by someone else to write their project.

138. Somerset, Tennessee is ripe for scandal when the town's dignified black undertaker Lord Byron ("L.B.") Jones (Roscoe Lee Browne) hires an old-line white lawyer (Lee J. Cobb) to handle an uncontested divorce from Lola Falana, who is having an affair with a white policeman (Anthony Zerbe). Problems erupt when Falana unexpectedly fights the divorce and the white community pressures the usually docile Jones to back off. At last standing up for his dignity as a black man, Jones announces "to hell with the white man"—a decision that costs him his life.

139. For a complete report see the author's *Final Cuts: The Last Films of 50 Great Directors*.

140. Jan Herman, *A Talent for Trouble: The Life of Hollywood's Most Acclaimed Director*. New York: Da Capo Press, 1997.

141. Robert later wrote the motion pictures *The Creeping Terror* (1964), *The Beach Girls and the Monster* (1965),and the cult classic *The Incredibly Strange Creatures Who Stopped Living and Became Mixed-Up Zombies!!?* (1964). He died in 1999.

142. Washington *Afro-American*, March 18, 1969.

143. San Jose *Mercury News*, December 4, 1969.

144. Los Angeles *Times*, December 18, 1969.

145. San Jose *Mercury News*, December 4, 1969

146. Brief, In re Johnson (1995) 35 Cal.App.4th 160, 41 Cal.Rptr.2d 449.

147. California Department of Corrections and Rehabilitation.

148. Lee's other private students included James Coburn, James Garner, Lee Marvin, Roman Polanski, Joe Hyams, and Steve McQueen.

149. Linda Lee and Tom Bleecker, "Bruce Lee Goes Hollywood," *Black Belt* magazine, Burbank, California: Rainbow Publications, September, 1989.

150. Silliphant estimated the date of their meeting as mid-1968. He would later achieve second cue green belt in Shotokan karate.

151. John Corcoran, "Up Close and Personal with Stirling Silliphant." *Kick* Magazine, July-September, 1980. Hollywood, California: CFW Enterprises.

152. "Bruce Lee: The Mandarin Superstar," *The Pierre Berton Show*, Screen Gems Canada, September 12, 1971.

153. Armchair psychiatrists can ponder whether the name *Lee*, common to both Bruce and Silliphant's father, had a connection with this epiphany.

154. Lee to Silliphant, Christmas, 1967; Silliphant to Lee, letter dated (incorrectly) January 3, 1968 (sic). Silliphant collection, UCLA.

155. Philip Marlowe (James Garner) agrees to locate the missing brother (Roger Newman) of a movie starlet (Sharon Farrell) and stumbles into a blackmail plot, gangland-style ice-pick murders, and shady psychiatrists.

156. Ironically, the scene involved the sort of exhibition karate—breaking boards and such—that Lee disdained.

157. *Los Angeles Times*, December 5, 1971.

158. Broadcast September 16, 1971.

159. He often joked, "If anyone wanted to get Longstreet, all they'd have to do is stand across the street with a high-powered rifle and, as the dummy comes out with the dog, blow his head off."

160. Berton, op cit.

161. Berton, op cit.

162. Warner Bros. has maintained that they were, by sheer coincidence, developing the same idea with writers Ed Spielman and Howard Friedlander when Lee pitched it. Lee considered the loss of *Kung Fu* one of his greatest personal disappointments.

163. Berton, op cit.

164. An undated clipping from *Martial Arts Magazine* in Silliphant's UCLA Collection 134 (Box 21, File 1) reports that Hong Kong GH company found an unfinished manuscript for *The Silent Flute* and asked Chinese director Ng See-Yuen, then a staff filmmaker at Shaw studios, to finish it. There were no other details. See-Yuen made *Bruce Lee: The Man, The Myth* (1976).

165. Copied in the Silliphant collection, UCLA.

166. *New York Times*, March 28, 1971.

167. Silliphant to Corcoran, op cit.

168. In 1968, Silliphant and McQueen devised an idea called *Project Leng* for which they hired Mark Silliphant at $150 a week to find a published novel that would match their title. Nothing came of it. Silliphant also figures in Pingree Productions (q.v.).

169. Receipts owed to Warner Bros. that the Indian government insisted they spend in the country rather than remove and risk collapsing the economy.

170. *Martial Arts Magazine*, Summer, 1978. UCLA Archives, no further identification.

171. Letter, Coburn to Singh, January 13, 1971. Silliphant collection, UCLA.

172. Silliphant papers, UCLA.

173. *Game* magazine, August, 1976. The official Bruce Lee website attributes his death to the pain meds.

174. Corcoran, op cit.

175. In 1969 Mark Silliphant and Bruce Lee were asked to assign their rights in the project to Silliphant. (Letter from Barry Hirsch's office, September 16, 1969). Silliphant collection, UCLA.

176. Conversation with producer Paul Maslansky, February 4, 2012.

177. In 1953, Moore cofounded Panavision with Robert Gottschalk to develop lenses and cameras that revolutionized wide-screen photography and camera portability. He was given the scientific and engineering achievement award in 1959 from the motion picture Academy.

178. Corcoran correspondence with Author.

179. Coburn's production company.

180. Bruce Lee, *The Silent Flute*, October 19, 1970.

181. Walter had previously worked with such directors as Robert Wise, Billy Wilder, and Jack Cardiff.

182. "Bruce Lee Treatment Fighting Its Way to Theatres," *The Wrap*, April 15, 2010

183. February 4, 2013 conversation.

184. Interview with Author, March 28, 1993. Tiana's birth date on her marriage license is August 11, 1951.

185. She has also called herself Tiana Dulong, Tiana Alexandra, Tiana Silliphant, Tiana Alexandra-Silliphant, Tiana Mayo, and Catherine Mayo.

186. Madame Nhu (Tran Le Xuan) was married to Ngo Dinh Nhu, brother of the unmarried President Ngo Dihn Diem. Although not the official First Lady of South Vietnam, this did not stop her from keeping a high and demanding public profile. The Diems were first installed by, then assassinated by, the CIA.

187. *From Hollywood to Hanoi*, op cit.

188. Interview with Author, March 28, 1993.

189. Interview with Author, March 28, 1993.

190. Interview with Author, March 28, 1993.

191. Interviewed on "Let's Talk Movies," Channel 9, Manila, January 1983.

192. Interview with Author, March 28, 1993.

193. Tiana e-mail to Author, May 30, 2013.

194. Interviewed on "The Reed Farrell Show," courtesy Silliphant estate.

195. Hank Grant, *Hollywood Reporter*, February 2, 1974.

196. Billing not contractual.

197. Tiana e-mails to author, February 8, 2013 and May 21, 2013.

198. Tiana e-mail to author, May 18, 2013.

199. Kopaloff interview, May 10, 2013.

200. The pilot and first three episodes of *Kung Fu* aired between February of 1973 and January of 1973 before becoming a weekly series.

201. E-mail correspondence with Tiana, February 8, 2013.

202. One of only five made in 1976, which is when he ordered it, it took 'til 1981 to arrive. Silliphant letter to West Coast Bank, January 15, 1984. (UCLA)

203. Tiana, ibid.

204. Silliphant letter to Author, October 23, 1992.

205. The genre was resuscitated in the 1990s once computer generated effects were perfected.

206. *The Swarm* was about African killer bees hitting the U.S., and *When Time Ran Out* (produced under the modest title *The Day the World Ended*) was about a volcano blowing up on a resort island.

207. Interviewed in *Fire in the Sky, Hell Under Water*. Produced by Andrew Abbott and Russell Leven. London, England: Nobles Gate for Channel 4, 2003.

208. *Hollywood Reporter*, March 26, 1969, and *Daily Variety*, June 23, 1969.

209. Army Archerd, *Daily Variety*, June 1, 1972.

210. *Weekly Variety*, August 8, 1971.

211. *Hollywood Reporter*, November 18, 1971.

212. Mayes interviewed by Rui Nogueira, *Backstory 3*, Patrick McGilligan, ed. (Berkeley, California: The University of California Press, 1997).

213. Over the years the Writers Guild of America has codified its credit system. Writers are listed in order of work on the project and are separated by the word *and*, while writing teams are joined by an ampersand (&). Arbitration over percentage of authorship, however, remains muddy, if not downright loopy.

214. Author's conversation with Tiana on March 24, 2013 and e-mail of May 21, 2013.

215. Undated clippings in Silliphant papers, UCLA.

216. Army Archerd, *Daily Variety*, July 8, 1973.

217. As this is being written, those numbers have become minimally $200 million for a major film and $30 million for advertising.

218. By way of disclosure, if not credibility, the author was one of the regional publicists for *The Towering Inferno* and gleaned certain knowledge in the course of his duties. The budget estimate is Allen's.

219. Privately, Silliphant told the author that he only read one of the novels and couldn't remember which one.

220. This may be Silliphant's "Rosebud." Was it Ednamarie? Skouras? Irwin?

221. While Silliphant was writing *The Towering Inferno* on the Fox lot in Century City, producer Ilya Salkind, who was there finishing *The Four Musketeers,* was trying to persuade him to write *Superman: The Movie* that he was about to produce.

222. Author's conversation with Scott Newman (October 1974), Paul's son, who appeared in the film as a young firefighter and was befriended by McQueen.

223. Another twist is that McQueen spoke with a bilateral lisp ("th") and those who wrote for him quickly learned to avoid "S" words in his dialogue.

224. ADI (Area of Dominant Influence): the physical territory reached by a broadcaster's signal.

225. Forbes interview with Author, May 24, 2013.

226. Larry Collins and Dominique Lapierre.

227. *Fire in the Sky, Hell Under Water,* op cit.

228. Kopaloff interview, May 10, 2013.

229. Notable exceptions include Ethel Waters, Lena Horne, Hattie McDaniel, and Paul Robeson. One still remembers McDaniel's scripted Oscar acceptance speech for *Gone with the Wind* in which she said she hoped she would always be a credit to her race.

230. $7.1 million rentals on a $1.140 million negative cost.

231. Joel Freeman interview, February 17, 2013.

232. It didn't hurt that the Motion Picture Association of America rated the film "R," allowing the studio to use the tag line, "If you wanna to see Shaft, ask yo Mamma." Shortly afterwards, the MPAA cracked down on producers who exploited ratings.

233. Carol Munday and Robert N. Zagone, *Fade Out*; Nguzo Saba Films, WNET-TV, New York, 1984.

234. Tidyman would win the Academy Award in 1972 for the screenplay adaptation of Robin Moore's book, *The French Connection.*

235. *Shaft* financial records, Silliphant family collection.

236. *New York Times*, May 30, 1971.

237. *Hollywood Reporter*, December 3, 1971.

238. Munday and Zagone, op cit.

239. Tiana interview with Author, March 9, 2013.

240. Tidyman Synopsis and letter exchange between Arnold D. Burk, esq. and David M. Sklar, esq., August 3, 1972. Silliphant papers, UCLA.

241. A recent example is The Africa Channel that imports English-language specials, soap operas, documentaries, and other programming produced in various African countries and runs them on cable.

242. In a 1980 conversation with the author, Wambaugh called the LAPD "assholes" and blamed the television series *Dragnet* for imbuing them with a sense of self-

righteousness to the point of arrogance.

243. But not enough, as the 1991 beating of Rodney King, and the riots following the 1993 exoneration of his assaulting officers, confirmed. They spent the first decade of the Twenty-First Century under a court-ordered Consent Decree litigated by the ACLU of Southern California

244. Froug, *op cit.*

245. Michael Schiffer's screenplay for Dennis Hopper's 1988 film, *Colors*, was set in this milieu and brought the LA gang problem vividly to national attention.

246. Joyce Haber, Los Angeles *Times*, December 5, 1971. Towne, Oscar-winner for *Chinatown*, is Hollywood's most celebrated script doctor.

247. *Dirty Harry* was written by Harry Julian Fink & R.M. Fink, Jo Heims, Dean Riesner, and John Milius; *Magnum Force* by Milius and Michael Cimino, all of whom, briefly or long-term, were Eastwood collaborators.

248. Patrick McGilligan, *Clint: The Life and Legend*. London, England: HarperCollins, 1999.

249. At the time of this interview (1992), Silliphant made no mention that he had intended Harry's partner to be an Asian woman: Tiana. (See Chapter 10.)

250. In *The Hollywood Reporter* (March 4, 1976) Silliphant explained that Riesner was brought onto the project by Eastwood and producer Robert Daley after he (Silliphant) had departed for other commitments, not out of anyone's dissatisfaction with the script.

251. Neither of Silliphant's sons named Stirling is a junior. The younger Stirling took the middle name Linh but it does not appear on his birth certificate.

252. ibid.

253. A "four-wall" deal occurs when a distributor rents the theatre from an exhibitor for a flat fee and keeps 100 percent of the gate. The risk thereby falls on the distributor, not the exhibitor.

254. *Los Angeles Times*, August 12, 1970.

255. Sources include David Sunfellow, *New Heaven New Earth Pulse,* Sedona, Arizona (http://nhne-pulse.org/the-dark-side-of-carlos-castaneda/) and an unsigned article "Patricia Partin, Blue Scout Chronology" citing various Court documents.

256. Showtime mini-series, 1992.

257. Silliphant quoted the budget as $4.6 million, "probably one of the costliest pilots ever made for TV." (SS correspondence with Author, October 23, 1992).

258. Gary Conway and David C. Engelbach.

259. "Let's Talk Movies," Channel 9, Manila, January, 1983.

260. "The Mike Douglas Show," Group W Productions, March, 1975.

261. Which Tom Hanks, Ron Howard, Brian Grazier and nine other producers did in 1998 with *From the Earth to the Moon* on HBO. Eleven writers were hired for the thirteen-episode series. Similarly, Canadian filmmaker Michael Lennick created an exemplary thirteen-episode TV documentary called *Rocket Science* (2002) that covers the same territory with compelling—not to mention

actual—realism.

262. Conversation with Frank Konigsberg, March 5, 2013.

263. Perhaps also because *The Longest Day* was in black & white so intercutting footage would have been awkward.

264. Taped remarks, premiere of *From Hollywood to Hanoi* sponsored by American Standard.

265. Letter, Silliphant to Kopaloff, June 4, 1981.

266. Kopaloff interview, May 10, 2013.

267. Stirling Linh interview with the author May 25, 2013.

268. John Corcoran, "Up Close and Personal with Stirling Silliphant," *Kick* magazine, August, 1980.

269. Memo to self, January 25, 1984, Silliphant papers, UCLA.

270. December 19, 1983, letter from Co-operate Bank PLC and Bachmann & Company, Ltd., in the Channel Islands, Silliphant papers, UCLA.

271. *The Sunday Show*, July 4, 1983.

272. Charles Champlin, "Silliphant: Critic at Large: Clearing the Decks for Fiction." *Los Angeles Times*, July 20, 1985.

273. Silliphant papers, UCLA.

274. *The Pennant* magazine, September, 1973: "What is a Nice Movie Writer Like You Doing Out Here in the Middle of This Nasty Ocean, Anyway?" by Stirling Silliphant.

275. Like countless other skippers, he lived the maxim, "Your two happiest days with a boat are the day you buy it and the day you sell it."

276. This note applies to *Bronze Bell*.

277. MACV's responsibilities varied over the years but included training South Vietnamese troops.

278. October 13, 1992, letter to Author.

279. "Let's Talk Movies," Channel 9, Manila, January, 1983.

280. Quoted by Jerry Hopkins, *Bangkok Babylon*, Singapore: Periplus Editions (HK), Ltd, 2005.

281. Daniel Cerone, "Expatriate Games," Los Angeles *Times*, March 6, 1994.

282. Letter, June 9, 1992, courtesy of Charles Matthau.

283. Matthau interview May 11, 2013.

284. Budget from IMDb.com; fee from e-mail, May 18, 2013, Tiana Silliphant.

285. Federal Reserve Bank of New York.

286. Silliphant letter to Author, March 13, 1994.

287. Cerone, op cit.

288. Stirling Linh interview with Author, May 25, 2013.

289. In the ensuing years, Hampton and Tiana would become linked in entertain-

ment news coverage; she would become associate producer of *A Dangerous Method* (2011), the film version of his 2003 play *The Talking Cure*), of which she was dedicatee. Their relationship is not the subject of this book.

290. He might mean *contracture*, a chronic tightening of the muscles.

291. Undated home video footage provided by the Silliphant estate.

292. Stirling Linh interview with Author, May 25, 2013.

293. Interviewed on "The Reed Farrell Show," courtesy Silliphant estate.

294. Silliphant letter to Author, September 11, 1995.

295. Silliphant letter to Tom Brown, September 16, 1995.

296. Morrell conversation with the author, July 19, 2013.

297. Stirling Linh interview with the author, May 25, 2013.

298. Ibid.

299. San Francisco *Sunday Examiner*, April 7, 1967.

300. William Froug, *op cit.*

301. Stirling Linh interview with Author May 25, 2013 referring to Robert Ludlum's *The Bourne Identity* series.

302. Fries e-mail to Author, April 4, 2013.

303. Twenty years prior to this interview, however, Silliphant told Froug (op cit), "The only time I truly feel good is when I hit my last act…not the conceptualization period."

304. "Bill Collins Showbiz," August 19, 1979. Seven Network, NSW (Australia).

305. From "Kiss the Maiden, All Forlorn" (*Route 66*).

306. Michael Ventura, "Letters at 3 AM: Stirling at Road's End" from *If I Was a Highway* (Lubbock, Texas: Texas Tech University Press, 2011).

307. *Women's Wear Daily*, December 18, 1974.

308. *Daily Variety*, April 2, 1985.

309. *Los Angeles Times*, May 29, 1979.

310. *New York Times*, January 2, 1966.

311. Charles Fries e-mail to Author, April 4, 2013.

312. Silliphant sued Levine for $150,000.

313. *The Great Escape II* was made for TV in 1988 with neither Mirisch nor Silliphant involved.

314. *Hollywood Reporter*, October 26, 1964.

315. *Hollywood Reporter*, June 8, 1990.

316. Author's October 23, 1992, correspondence with SS.

317. Silliphant papers, UCLA.

318. *Daily Variety*, April 2, 1985.

319. *Hollywood Reporter*, undated clipping in archive

320. *Daily Variety*, April 12, 1989.

321. Tiana, e-mail, May 6, 2013.

322. Reed Farrell interview, 1977.

323. NHK television interview, 1994.

324. *Game* magazine, August 1976

325. Lin Bolen letter, July 4, 1983. Silliphant papers, UCLA.

326. *Newsweek*, January 31, 1972.

327. *Hollywood Reporter*, April 12, 1968.

328. *Daily Variety*, September 18, 1968.

329. Silliphant letter to Author, August 2, 1994.

330. *Daily Variety*, December 8, 1965

331. *Los Angeles Herald-Examiner*, April 6, 1975.

332. Charles Fries e-mail to Author, April 4, 2013.

Index

Numbers in **bold** indicate photographs